Praise for the first e
How To Write and Sell Sim
for Fun and Pr

"If a recognized authority said to you, 'You can write a nonfiction book on a topic even if you possess only what I call "thin credentials," would you believe you actually can?

"Believe. That's because the authority is Bob Bly. Bob Bly has the unique ability to show us what we may have thought is creatively impossible is not only possible but logical.

"If ever you've had—and suppressed—the urge to write a book or an article or an ad or a mailing or an online presentation, grab this book and devour it. It just might be the catalyst that changes your life."

—Herschell Gordon Lewis, author of
Internet Marketing: Tips, Tricks and Tactics

"This book contains the most detailed, concise, and useful information I've ever found on earning a six-figure income as a writer. I anticipate that the in-depth, how-to secrets in this book will be worth well over $100,000 to me in the next nine months alone."

—Joshua T. Boswell, freelance copywriter

"Writers should stop wasting time and start reading and applying Bob Bly's newest book, *How to Write and Sell Simple Information for Fun and Profit*. Bob Bly's right on the target, as usual. This book will save every new writer a ton of time getting in print and paid. Bly got to the top by writing accurate, easy-to-use, how-to books. This one's a dandy!"

—Gordon Burgett, author of *How to Get Your Book*
Published Free in Minutes and Marketed in Days

"As I write this, I'm only on page 39 . . . and it's clear this book is classic Bob. From the full picture he gives of today's evolved info-publishing opportunities to the half-dozen new product ideas he's given me already, this thing is jammed with valuable insights. Not to mention, Bob gives rock-solid instructions on how to make it all happen. Great stuff!"

—John Forde, six-figure copywriter and founding editor,
CopywritersRoundTable.com

"What do you get when you mix incomparable information with an incomparable writing style? You get Bob Bly's latest book. Bob lays out a path to success. All you have to do is follow it!"

—Marilyn Pincus, author of *GET THE JOB! Interview Strategies That Work*

"Bob Bly gives the step-by-step details which every aspiring writer needs. Read these pages, apply them to your writing, and you will have fun and profit."

—W. Terry Whalin, publisher and author of *Jumpstart Your Publishing Dreams*

"This is a valuable resource for not only the newbie writer but for the most experienced writer as well. Bob goes beyond theory and supplies the practical 'how to' of making money."

—MaryEllen Tribby, founder/CEO, WorkingMomsOnly.com

How to Write and Sell Simple Information for Fun and Profit

Your Guide to Writing and Publishing Books, E-Books, Articles, Special Reports, Audios, Videos, Membership Sites, and Other How-To Content

REVISED AND UPDATED SECOND EDITION

BOB BLY

with Fred Gleeck

Fresno, California

How to Write and Sell Simple Information for Fun and Profit
Second Edition

Copyright © 2021 by Robert W. Bly. All rights reserved.

Cover illustration: studiostoks/Shutterstock.com

Published by Linden Publishing
2006 South Mary
Fresno, California 93721
559-233-6633 / 800-345-4447

To order another copy of this book, please call
1-800-345-4447

ISBN 978-1-61035-990-0

Printed on acid-free paper.

135798642

Library of Congress Cataloging-in-Publication Data on file.

To the great copywriter Clayton Makepeace—colleague, teacher, friend—
in loving memory

Acknowledgments

Thanks to Stephen Mettee and Kent Sorsky at Quill Driver Books for having faith in me and in the updated second edition book. And thanks to my family for enduring the neglect that preparing the manuscript necessitated. Additional thanks go to the how-to writers and information marketers who so graciously allowed me to reprint their methods, ideas, and samples of their work in this book.

Special thanks go to Fred Gleeck, friend, teacher, and mentor in the art and science of selling information products *online*. Fred got me started in internet marketing in 2004, and he continues to educate, counsel, and help me today. Fred, you are a rare gem and I value our relationship more than you know.

"Now more than ever, writing is the one skill you need to succeed in life—and in your career. Words can move mountains. Make strong human connections. Spread a powerful idea. Change minds. Create hope. Leave a legacy. And if you don't know how to use them well, you risk being disconnected and misunderstood."

—Donald Miller

Table of Contents

Preface to the Second Edition

Unless you're a hermit living in a cave, you can't help notice the lightning-fast pace at which nonfiction writing, publishing, formats, and the selling of information have radically changed since the first edition of *How to Write and Sell Simple Information for Fun and Profit* (published in 2010).

Some of the changes are disadvantageous to many traditionally published writers, especially aging Boomers who prefer old-school writing and media:

- Print outlets such as magazines are waning. Issues are smaller and published less frequently. Many print editions are being shuttered and transitioning to digital only. And some of these electronic newsletters and magazines pay writers a fraction of the previous rates for print articles.

- Newspaper readership and circulation is also on the decline. Newsrooms are laying off reporters by the hundreds.

- Back in the day, many freelancers made their livings writing magazine articles. In Chapter 6, we'll explore why the magazine market for freelance articles is not what it was—and discuss alternate media where you can still write your articles for fun and profit.

- The book industry is in flux. Advances and royalties are shrinking. Fewer copies of each book are sold, and many have a shorter shelf life. And the process of selling your book to publishers has become more difficult. Chapter 7 gives you details on these changes as well as strategies to overcome them and keep writing books that sell and make you money.

- With the rise of the internet, amateurs are flooding the market with works they write on speculation and for free. The amateurs don't care about being paid. They just want to see their writing in print or online with their byline.

- When a large number of people are happy to do for free what you want to get paid for, it devalues your work and drastically reduces the fees you can earn from your writing. This reduces fees publishers pay to authors and results in fewer purchases from working writers who write for money.

Some of these changes are advantageous to how-to, self-help, reference, and instructional writers, especially younger writers who were raised in and embrace the digital electronic world:

- Self-publishing has skyrocketed over the past decade or so, making it easier for authors to get their books on Amazon while bypassing traditional book publishers.

- You can get your work published in a fraction of the time it took back in the days when print was the only publishing option.

- Digital media channels enable you to quickly and easily publish and market your writing with a fraction of the investment it took in the pre-digital age.

- Large and loyal online audiences, communities, subscribers, and fan-bases who eagerly await and buy your new writings can now get to you and your works online and buy your material in 75 seconds.

- The proliferation of print and digital publishing channels can help you increase your profit margins on everything you write by selling and reselling your writing in multiple media.

- Transitioning your writing from paperbound and print to e-books and other digital formats—once difficult and costly—is now easier and more affordable.

In this Second Edition, we address these and other major changes in nonfiction writing. Even though many markets have adopted low-pay or no-pay models, I'll show you how you can make a handsome profit writing nonfiction in many different markets, including mainstream media that pay a fair dollar for a fair day's work. Getting paid decently and in many cases lavishly is also in reach for writers who self-publish and proactively market their writings online.

So, let's get started!

Introduction

Do you have a burning desire to educate; to explain; to communicate; to exchange information and ideas; to share your knowledge, learning, and experience with others—and to put down what you know on paper, the screen, audio, or video?

If so, *how-to writing* may very well be the ideal freelance writing, publishing, and information packaging niche for you. And in this book, I'm going to show you how to profit handsomely by teaching others what you know through your writings.

Do you worry that the internet has adversely affected the market for books and other how-to materials, simply because Google now allows users to find any fact with a quick online search? Quite the opposite is true.

The web puts a dizzying amount of information, today called "content," at our fingertips. But that's all much of it is—raw data, facts, and straightforward information. As how-to writers, we must go far beyond presenting mere facts. Our mission is to show our readers, step-by-step, how to do something they want to do, or attain something they want to attain, or transform from the person they are now into the person they want to be; e.g., how to get out of debt, find a mate, advance in one's career, lose weight, get fit, survive bankruptcy, overcome infertility, train one's dog, become rich, retire early, give your kids a college education, or achieve other important goals, dreams, and ambitions.

And, even in a world dominated by the web's ocean of data—much of it instantly available with a few clicks—the wisdom, knowledge, and guidance people are seeking is in short supply. As librarian Richard Yates once observed, "We are drowning in information but starved for knowledge." As a result, the public's appetite for clear, reliable, authoritative, and actionable how-to material is insatiable, and—despite the internet user's mantra that "information should be free"—readers eagerly open their wallets to obtain it.

For instance, a recent Google search turned up nearly 25.3 billion web pages containing the words "how to." Americans spend $2 trillion a year buying content, including almost $10 billion a year on how-to books, seminars, and other self-improvement information. In fact, some of the best-selling books of all time are how-to and self-help titles. Dale Carnegie's *How to Win Friends and Influence People*, in print since 1936, has sold 15 million copies. Since its publication in 1970, Richard Bolles' *What Color Is Your Parachute?* has spent 288 weeks on the *New York Times* best-seller list and has sold more than 10 million copies. L. Ron Hubbard's *Dianetics*, first published in 1950, has sold over 22 million copies. And Robert Ringers' self-help book *Winning Through Intimidation* has sold well over 2 million copies.

To succeed as a how-to, do-it-yourself, or self-help author, you don't have to be the next Shakespeare or even the next Stephen King. "Anybody can write," says writing teacher Barry Sheinkopf. "All you have to do is want to enough." And nonfiction book author John Jerome said: "Writing nonfiction is not perishingly difficult."

Nor do you have to be the leading guru in your field to make money as a how-to writer in that topic. If you have a curious mind, enjoy learning new things, and can express your thoughts in a clear, straightforward, and organized fashion, the opportunities for you to write and publish how-to content are nearly limitless—and often quite lucrative as well.

In *How to Write and Sell Simple Information for Fun and Profit: Second Edition*, you'll discover how to:

- Find your writing niche or specialty
- Come up with ideas for saleable how-to books, articles, reports, seminars, and online courses
- Research and write effective, practical how-to instructional materials

- Build your reputation and establish a loyal following in your chosen field

- Work at home (an important advantage during pandemics!), choose your own hours, write what interests you, and be your own boss

- Earn $100,000+ a year with your how-to writing through a variety of channels, including magazines and newspapers, traditional book publishing, self-publishing, video, audio, the internet, and many more.

Whether you simply want to see your name in print in your favorite magazine, change people's lives with your unique insights and advice, pass on your hard-won wisdom to the next generation, become a published author, be a guest on TV and radio shows, or build a million-dollar how-to information empire, *How to Write and Sell Simple Information for Fun and Profit: Second Edition* can point the way for you.

"When you sell a man a how-to book, you aren't just selling him ink and paper," wrote the late how-to author Jerry Buchanan. "You are selling him a whole new life." Or as writer Joanna Wiebe puts it: "You're selling your prospects a better version of themselves."

Whether you are a writer looking for a topic to write about or a subject-matter expert seeking to share your knowledge with others, *How to Write and Sell Simple Information for Fun and Profit: Second Edition* can help you enjoy a whole new life as a successful how-to writer and information packager.

I envy you the journey ahead of you, and look forward to helping you navigate the route on your way to writing success and how-to riches.

In the meantime, you can reach me at:

Robert W. Bly
31 Cheyenne Drive
Montville, NJ 07045
Phone: 973-263-0562
Fax: 973-263-0613
Email: rwbly@bly.com
Web: www.bly.com

1

Welcome to the World of How-To Writing

Popular culture sometimes makes fun of how-to writers as the hacks of the literary world. In a 1980s TV sitcom, Bob Newhart played a New England innkeeper who was also a how-to writer, which the show lampooned as lacking glamour and excitement.

He was a nice but dull guy who wrote books on do-it-yourself home projects. One of his titles was *Grouting without Pouting*, and he did most of his book signings in the local hardware store. When he autographed his book for a store customer, the man asked, "Can I get one that isn't scribbled in?"

Instead of mesmerizing millions with the next *Harry Potter* or creating heartbreaking works of staggering genius, we how-to writers often deal with seemingly mundane topics: how to build a water garden; how to improve your credit rating; how to invest in real estate; how to make money on Instagram or YouTube; how to research your family history; how to barbecue ribs; how to maintain a swimming pool.

Because it is, on the surface, so straightforward and factual, one can argue that how-to writing is the easiest writing specialty to break into. And in some ways, it is; how-to writing provides a quicker, surer entry into publication than most other writing categories for several reasons.

Although still competitive, it is less so than journalistic and literary pursuits. After all, vast hordes dream of writing the Great American Novel, so getting a novel published by a major publishing house can be a challenge.

If you're writing a memoir, your chances of finding a publisher—unless you are a celebrity, have a dramatic story that made national headlines, or have a million social media followers—are slim at best. Children's books are similarly competitive.

In LA, people from all walks of life—from the gardener clipping your hedges to the attendant parking your car—are working on a screenplay. But the group of writers who dream of writing the *Great American Guide to Growing a Greener Lawn* is a bit smaller, making the market for how-to nonfiction less difficult to crack.

Yet the money can be considerable. The late Jerry Baker, known as "America's Master Gardener," made a fortune as a how-to writer with books and booklets teaching Americans how to grow a greener lawn, beautiful flowers, lush shrubs, and healthful vegetables.

Here's another factor: To sell a novel or narrative nonfiction work requires a high level of writing skill. But the requirements are somewhat different for how-to nonfiction, where the main virtues are not style but accuracy, practicality, clarity, instruction, and organization. Can you explain something or teach a skill in a clear, organized, and entertaining fashion? If you can, then you can succeed as a how-to writer.

Are your writing credentials thin? It's true that publishers of how-to nonfiction are more interested in your expertise than your literary flair. But being an expert doesn't mean knowing more than anybody else in the world about your subject. You don't have to study for half a century or get a PhD to be qualified to write how-to nonfiction. As best-selling author Samm Sinclair Baker said, "Whatever your lifestyle, you have some special knowledge from living experience that you can impart to others for their profit and your own."

You do not need to be the leading practitioner, scholar, or expert in your field to write a book about it. My business partner, author and speaker Fred Gleeck, explains that you only need know more about your subject than 90 percent of the people out there. "Don't worry about the other 10 percent; they're not your market anyway," says Fred.

Someone once observed, "Experts don't necessarily know more than others; it's just that their information is better organized." You don't have to be a great scientist to write a science book for the general public. But you do to need to organize your content in a sensible, logical, easy-to-follow presentation. And when you write or speak about it, your prose must be clear, engaging, and even entertaining.

What if you are not an expert in any subject?

First of all, I doubt that's really true. Every person has unique skills, training, and experiences. You certainly are an "expert" in your own life and many of the things that make up your life.

For instance, in the early 1980s, I quit my management job in the corporate world to become a freelance writer. I was soon earning six figures a year. So one thing I was an expert in (or at least had experience with and knowledge of) was how to make a lot of money as a freelance writer. I put this experience into a how-to book, *Secrets of a Freelance Writer: How to Make $100,000 a Year*, now in its third edition with Henry Holt & Co.

If you truly feel you have no expertise, go out and acquire some. Take courses. Work in a specific trade or industry you want to write about. When my colleague L. Perry Wilbur wanted to write a book on the mail order business, he started selling products by mail to gain firsthand experience and knowledge of the industry. Another writer I know was hired by an ad agency to write materials for a welding account. He promptly signed up for night classes in welding and became a certified welder.

Opportunities to learn through both reading and active participation are plentiful in most fields. A few years ago, I received a mailing about investing in silver. It interested me, and I thought it might make a good magazine article. What did I do? I called the metals company and bought a few thousand ounces of silver! Now, if I pitch the story to a magazine editor, I can truthfully say in my query letter that I have made a six-figure profit trading precious metals.

Publishers and readers prefer authors who appear to have credentials in the subject they are writing about, but, often, neither the publishers nor the readers investigate authors' credentials to any significant degree. Therefore, you can write a nonfiction book on a topic even if you possess only what I call "thin credentials." Thin credentials are qualifications that sound more impressive than they actually are. If you are going to specialize in a particular field or subject, I advise you to obtain some credentials, thin or otherwise, to establish credibility.

Years ago, I had an opportunity to earn a handsome fee writing about information technology (IT), except the client wanted to know my credentials. My degree is in engineering, not computer science. However, anticipating that computers would be a subject I'd someday want to write about, I searched for the easiest computer certification one could earn. It turned out to be a Certified Novell Administrator (CNA), which required me to take only one course and an exam to earn the certification. When the client asked me whether I had any experience in IT, and I replied that I was a trained CNA, I was hired on the spot.

What does a how-to writer do?

A how-to writer is a teacher in print, video, audio, or online. However, instead of teaching in a classroom, the how-to writer does most of his teaching in written format. The school teacher transmits knowledge in a small-group setting (the classroom) over a prolonged period (the school year), giving students personalized instruction. The how-to writer typically reaches a broader audience, on a less individualized level, using various media, although some how-to instructors offer small-group interaction in online classes, coaching, and mastermind groups.

Having experience in your topic is not mandatory, but it does give the writer an edge. It is no accident that some of the most successful writers of nonfiction books for young readers, such as Seymour Simon and Vicky Cobb, both in science, were science teachers before they became authors.

There is a huge market for materials that instruct, inform, or inspire, and the potential for a six-figure or occasionally even seven-figure annual income for authors who can provide that instruction and inspiration is large and proven. Earnings for the typical freelance writer in the U.S. are more modest, averaging a respectable but not spectacular $63,488 a year.

Oscar Wilde said, "There is nothing as depressing as a small but adequate income," and there are two primary reasons the majority of writers do not get rich from their writing.

The first is *failure to specialize*. As you no doubt already know and will be made even more acutely aware of in this book, the age of the generalist is vanishing. In every endeavor, from writing to medicine, specialists are more in demand and higher paid than generalists. In health care, for instance, oncologists and cardiac surgeons earn far more than general practitioners.

The second factor that holds writers back from enjoying a high income and the good life that goes with it is that they *limit themselves* to the traditional freelance writer's media: magazine articles and nonfiction books.

In today's electronic age, print represents only a small portion of the spectrum of communication media available to writers. The writers who make the most money often write in many media, not just books and magazine articles. "Any form of writing can change the world," states Mary Pipher in *Writing to Change the World*. "Your goal is to find the form that allows you to use every one of your talents in the service of what you consider to be your most important goals. You want to search for what you alone can say and then how you can say it most effectively."

How-to writing goes far beyond books and articles to multiple formats, media, and distribution channels. Some writers stick to just one medium: They write articles for consumer magazines, or they write a blog. Others write for multiple media, and by doing so they reach a broader audience while selling more of their writing for more money.

Here are just some of the formats in which you can write, publish, distribute, and sell your how-to writings:

Apps	Dictionaries	Radio shows
Articles	Directories	Seminars
Audio	E-books	Software
Blogs	E-newsletters	Special reports
Books	Flash cards	Speeches
Booklets	Games	Syndicated columns
Calendars	Guidebooks	Teleseminars
Cartoons	Instruction sheets	Training classes
Classes	Leaflets	Tutoring
Coaching	Magazine articles	TV shows
College courses	Membership sites	Video
Columns	Newsletters	Webinars
Consulting	Newspaper articles	White papers
Courses	Podcasts	Workbooks
Databases	Posters	Workshops

When I started my career as a how-to writer and copywriter in the late 1970s, writing essentially meant producing articles and books, and maybe some slide shows or filmstrips.

Thanks to the advent of personal computing, the internet, and social networking, how-to writers have a dizzying array of formats available to them. Today, if I have something to say to my readers, I can write an email and distribute it to my 30,000 online subscribers at the click of a mouse; post it on my blog where literally millions of internet users can access it in an instant; or say it on Twitter or Facebook.

Of course, no one pays for my blog, or my Tweets, or my e-newsletter, which you can subscribe to online for free at www.bly.com/reports. Today's how-to writers publish a mixture of paid and free content. You can make money with both. You can use the free content to sell the paid, and recycle much of the free stuff into products people buy. In this book, I'll reveal how it's done.

The state of how-to writing in the digital age

Has the internet helped or hurt the how-to writing profession? Odd as it may seem, it has actually done both.

For writers who make their living with traditional freelance writing—magazine articles and books—the web has made it tougher in many ways. Thanks to the ready accessibility of timely information on the web, newspapers and magazines are on the decline. With fewer advertisers, they publish fewer pages and, as a result, fewer articles. With a few exceptions, writing articles for magazines pays modestly.

Magazines are shrinking their page counts and many are shutting down their print editions and existing only online. In 2020, *O* magazine discontinued its print edition. Other magazines that have shuttered their print publications and are digital-only include *Teen Vogue, Redbook, Glamour, Bride Magazine, Maxim, Self, Jet,* and *Playboy,* just to name a few.

What's more, the web has spawned a new generation of writers—some professional, others amateur—who happily write articles for websites and e-newsletters for little or no pay. While consumers must pay for print magazines, they can read these thousands of articles online at no cost.

Nonfiction books still sell, although some categories have been diminished by the internet, most notably reference books. In the preinternet era, reference books were the primary repository of information. Today, you can find the content you need online, where much of it is available for free.

Reference books were always fun straightforward to write. But far fewer of them are needed today.

On the plus side, the internet gives the nonfiction writer quick and easy access to valuable data and research that can be difficult or impossible to find offline. The web is an online library that never closes! Often, you need to know odd facts and figures when writing, and with the internet, you can get them right away.

Many how-to writers choose to self-publish, and the internet makes self-publishing far less risky and more affordable than before. In the old days, self-publishing a book meant laying out $10,000 to design, typeset, and print 3,000 copies of a book you didn't know whether you could sell. You even had to store all those copies in your garage or basement. With an e-book, your manufacturing, printing, storage, and fulfillment costs are zero. And thanks to print on demand, you can even publish paperbound copies of your book, even as few as half a dozen copies, with a minimal investment.

9 ways to add value to information

With free information so easily available on the internet, it is simply not enough to compile or regurgitate facts from other sources, since everyone has immediate online access to those same sources. So what can the writer do to create content others will pay for?

Author Jeff Davidson has identified seven ways authors, speakers, and other how-to information writers and packagers can add value to content: *immediacy, personalization, interpretation, trust, accessibility, embodiment,* and *patronage.* I have added two more: *findability* and *new ideas.* By using these nine value-added techniques, you can get readers to pay handsomely for your formatted and packaged content, even though searchers can find lots of free information on the same topics online:

1. *Immediacy.* Sooner or later, a particular set of information may be available for free on the internet; however, readers will often pay to get specialized content delivered to their inbox the moment it is released. Example: online trading services that tell you when to buy or sell specific stocks or option contracts to maximize profits on your trades. When you subscribe to the service, you receive an email whenever there is an action to take on one of the stocks in the service's portfolio.

2. *Personalization.* In my book *Secrets of a Freelance Writer*, I tell writers everything they need to know to earn six figures as a freelance copywriter. Yet I have had aspiring writers pay me $2,500 each to attend private weekend workshops or get one-on-one coaching on how to start and run a successful freelance copywriting business, the very same subject I cover exhaustively in a $15 book, and which I have done successfully for four decades. They are willing to pay more for the live workshops, because they want to receive advice customized to their specific situations. Such personalized information services—seminars, workshops, training, consulting, and coaching—can command prices 10 to 100 times higher (or more) than the same content presented in a book or report.

3. *Interpretation.* A newsletter on employment law highlighted a recent case in which two employees won a judgment against their employer when a supervisor belittled them at work. You could have read about this event in a number of newspapers and websites. But the newsletter not only reported the event, it also gave tips on how businesses could prevent a similar lawsuit from happening to them. Unlike Sergeant Friday of the old *Dragnet* TV series, your readers often don't want "just the facts." They want you to interpret what the facts mean, how they are affected by them, and how they can use them to their advantage.

4. *Trust.* In May 2009, my wife was diagnosed with ovarian cancer. There is a ton of information on the internet about ovarian cancer, and my wife, being research oriented, spent endless hours online finding it. But she also made an appointment with one of the nation's top oncologists. We trusted the oncologist more than the other sources, because she is an M.D. and widely acknowledged to be a recognized authority in the treatment of gynecological cancers.

    My point? The surest way to create demand for your content and to get others to pay a premium price for your writings is to establish yourself as a guru in your niche, industry, or field. Why? Because people trust experts and want to do business with them.

5. *Accessibility.* If you search hard and long enough, you could, after many hours of work, find a lot of my articles on the internet for free.

But my online information marketing company, CTC Publishing, sells a dozen collections of my published articles; each is 50 pages and they cost $29 a pop. People gladly pay for them. Why? Because putting them in a convenient PDF they can download from my website makes the content more accessible.

6. *Embodiment.* Authors who have posted their books online have sold thousands of copies of the *physical* book, even if similar content may be read on the web free of charge. Some people just like to have a paperbound book. As the late author Howard Shenson noted, "Information buyers will pay to buy essentially the same information in multiple formats. So depending on your book contract, you might be able to repurpose some of the information in other formats, including paid speaking, videos, and audios."

7. *Patronage.* In olden days, royalty and the wealthy upper class became patrons of the arts, supporting musicians and painters whose works they wished to hear or see. An analogous situation exists today. Writers and information marketers give away free content to readers while also offering information products they can buy.

   The main reason readers buy the paid information products is that they want to learn a subject in greater depth than it is covered in the free content. But another reason readers are willing to pay money is patronage, or what Robert Cialdini in his book *Influence* calls "reciprocity." When you publish and give away a large amount of free content to your readers, they will—provided they like your stuff—feel obliged to buy your book or other information products. People are basically honest, and they don't usually want to take without giving something back in return.

   I know this for a fact. I have received many emails from readers of my free e-newsletter telling me the content is so good, and that they are so grateful that it is free, that they went to my site and purchased a product so they would not be "ripping me off." Most people don't enjoy being mooches; give stuff away for free, and many of your readers will cross your palm with silver in return.

8. *Findability.* An "aggregator" is someone who makes content from multiple sources on a single topic available all in one place. Examples

are Amazon.com for books and Netflix for movies. Here's another example: Oakstone Publishing prepares summaries of technical articles on radiology and makes thousands of them available (for a fee) to radiologists at its website. Or see my e-newsletter *Corona Business Strategies Digest* at www.corona-business-strategies.com, which aggregates condensations of articles on how business can survive and thrive during the COVID-19 pandemic.

Aggregation is not the usual model for individual freelance writers or information marketers, but a few have had great success with this model, most notably Matthew Lesko. His best-selling books, centering on how to get free money from the government, are essentially compilations of information and contacts on grants and other free giveaways available from Uncle Sam. All of this information is available for free on the web. But readers gladly pay for the books, because Matthew Lesko saves them the time and effort of looking for these resources on their own.

9. *New Ideas.* Bill Bonner, founder and CEO of Agora Publishing, America's largest newsletter publisher, says the readers of his company's newsletters on financial, travel, political, and health topics are looking mainly for "new ideas they haven't heard elsewhere."

One of my e-books, *Make $100 an Hour Giving Your Opinion*, suggests to the reader that an easy way to earn some extra cash in your spare time is to contact market research companies and participate in focus groups, for which the companies pay $100 to $250 per session. The e-book explains how these focus groups work, how to contact them, and then gives a directory of research firms by state.

A pastor emailed me to accuse me of fraud. "All of the market research firms you list can be found on the internet with Google search," he complained. I explained that what my buyers are paying for (and I have heard back from many satisfied purchasers of this book) is not only (a) my saving them time and labor by compiling the directory for them, but much more important than that my giving them (b) the *idea* of market research studies as a spare-time, money-making opportunity, which is something they had not thought of before. If I gave them the idea and they make $150 from just one study, isn't it reasonable and fair for me to ask $29 for my work? Since we get virtually no refund requests on this e-book, apparently my readers think so.

10 in-demand topics for how-to writers

There are certain how-to topics that are more in demand and easier to sell than others. These include:

1. *Saving or making money.* Consumers are always interested in saving or making money. Products that can help them save money or make money are easy to sell, because you can tell the prospects, "The small investment you make in this product is a drop in the bucket compared with the money it can make or save you." Any product that quickly pays for itself has a huge advantage in the information marketplace. Examples include a $15 do-it-yourself guide to installing solar panels, which can reduce your electric bill by hundreds of dollars, or a handbook on saving money when buying a used car.

2. *Saving time.* In our modern sped-up society, almost everyone has too much to do and not enough time to do it. Readers want to be more efficient, have more free time, increase their personal productivity, manage their time well, be organized, and achieve more. Stephanie Winston wrote a best-selling book, *The Organized Executive*, that shows businesspeople how to get more done in less time by organizing their work space and schedules better. Another example is my book on increasing personal productivity, *101 Ways to Make Every Second Count*, published by Career Press.

3. *Sex and relationships.* People want more love, companionship, friendship, romance, physical intimacy—as well as more sexual intercourse. You've heard the expression "sex sells" applied to the advertising world, where Madison Avenue knows that nothing sells beer like a girl in a bikini. Well, sex sells in the how-to world too, which is why Dr. Ruth is rich and famous. LGBTQ books have become extremely popular within the last couple of years, and many have an emphasis on sexuality and relationships.

4. *Investing and trading.* There is a huge demand for guidance on investing in the stock market, retirement planning, paying for college, avoiding foreclosure, buying real estate, trading options, owning

precious metals, and many other financial topics. Investing and personal finance are great areas for how-to writers, because your advice has the potential to give readers a huge payoff.

5. *Collecting.* The late Gary Halbert advised all information marketers to focus on selling to what he called the "starving crowd"—a market of people hungry for as much information as they can get on their topic. Collectors are one of the hungriest markets for information products out there. Top copywriter Parris Lampropoulus also says collectibles sell well.

  Whether it's baseball cards or Barbie dolls, stamps or coins, African art or antiques, serious collectors are enthusiastic about what they collect, and they will eagerly spend boatloads of money on anything related to their collecting addiction. For instance, I collect comic books, and I had success with a nonfiction book I wrote for comic book fans called *Comic Book Hero* (Carol Publishing), a book of superhero trivia with nostalgic appeal to comic book collectors and readers.

6. *Hobbies.* Collecting is a hobby, and there are many noncollecting hobbies that people devote inordinate amounts of time and money pursuing—from golf and gardening to karate and karaoke. Americans spend nearly $44 billion annually on their hobbies and crafts. According to the Hobby Industry Association, nearly eight out of ten households surveyed report that at least one member engaged in a craft or hobby. If you have a hobby you love, think about how you can turn out a line of profitable books and information products helping others enjoy it.

7. *Marketing.* With the explosive growth of the internet as a marketing channel for information products, a booming niche has become the topic of marketing, particularly internet marketing. I would discourage you from getting into this niche, as it is now overcrowded. However, I'd make an exception if you are a specialized master at marketing to a particular industry (e.g., marketing for chiropractors) or through a particular medium or strategy (e.g., marketing with Facebook groups).

8. *Small business advice.* There is a huge market for advice on how to start and run a successful small business, and marketing is just one subtopic within the business success category. Others include: accounting, bookkeeping, management, leadership, supervision, customer service, operations, finance, business opportunities, franchising, computer skills, and sales. Michael Masterson, publisher of *Early to Rise*, built a multimillion-dollar information empire publishing how-to advice for business owners and aspiring entrepreneurs.

9. *Self-help.* In the opening to the 2005–2009 TV sitcom *My Name Is Earl*, Jason Lee tells viewers: "I'm just trying to be a better person." Millions of Americans are also trying to be better people, and they spend millions of dollars a year buying self-help books and tapes, and attending seminars to help them do just that. As I mentioned in the introduction, sales of self-help products in the United States were $9.9 billion in 2017. Self-help books can cover relationships, spirituality, and wealth-building. An example of the latter is T. Harv Eker's *Secrets of the Millionaire Mind*, which has sold over a million copies.

10. *Pets.* People lavish time, attention, love, and $72 billion a year on their pets. There are nearly 85 million household pets in the United States, including dogs, cats, hamsters, and others.

The above list represents the tip of the iceberg. The number of topics people want to know about is nearly limitless, and for a goodly percentage of these, they will give you money if you can deliver the information they want.

5 ways to stand out from the crowd

Here are five strategies that can help you stand out from the crowd of journeymen how-to and self-help writers and earn a handsome six-figure income writing and selling simple how-to information online and offline:

1. *Become a recognized guru.* The quickest way to add value to content is to become the trusted source for information on that topic—the recognized expert in the field. Lots of people know Creole cooking, but when the TV talk shows want to do a segment on that cuisine, they call Emeril Lagasse, because he is the recognized expert on that topic.

Readers are more inclined to buy how-to advice from people they recognize as gurus. But the more how-to material you write and publish, the more you gain a reputation as an expert in your topic. So being a prolific writer and publisher on your topic in multiple media channels can accelerate your ascent to guru status.

2. *Narrow your niche.* "Marketing" is too broad, but if you specialize in marketing for chiropractors, your information becomes more specialized and valuable, and there's less competition. It's difficult to sell general information on marketing; it's much easier to sell advice on marketing for chiropractors. The more specialized and narrow the niche, the more money you can charge for the book. For instance, Fred Gleeck's loose-leaf-bound, self-published book *Self-Storage Marketing* sells for a hundred dollars a copy.

Newsletter publishers have made this observation many times: The easier a topic is to write about, the more difficult it is to sell a newsletter on that topic. The reason for this is that the fun and easy topics—time management, leadership, public speaking—are not highly specialized, and therefore everyone thinks they know them already and can write useful material about them. Conversely, newsletters on specialized and narrow topics are easier to sell and can command higher subscription prices because reliable information on these subjects is more scarce.

3. *Write for all four learning modalities.* Don't doom yourself to a mediocre income by thinking of "writing" solely as "books and magazines." The wealthiest how-to writers today produce and publish content in many different media. Yes, Tony Robbins writes best-selling books. But he probably makes more money from his live seminars and from the audio programs sold through his infomercials.

You should narrow the subject matter you write about (e.g., raising orchids is better than gardening), but publish on that subject in as many media as you can. Why? Because different people have different media preferences. The four basic learning modalities are: *reading* (books, e-books); *listening* (audio CDs, downloadable MP3 files, podcasts); *watching* (DVDs, TV programs, online video); and *doing*, also called "experiential learning" (workshops, seminars, courses).

Most people have a primary learning modality they prefer, one or two secondary modalities they can use without too much difficulty, and one or two they don't like. For instance, my primary learning modality is reading (books, magazines, newsletters) and my secondary is listening (audio programs). I am not a visual or participatory learner.

By publishing in different media addressing all four of the major learning modalities, you can reach the broadest audience possible, which means more sales and income. On the other hand, if all you write is books, learners who don't like to read will not buy or benefit from your content.

4. *Promote.* You can't just write a book or training program and expect the world to beat a path to your door. You have to proactively, aggressively, and continually market and promote your work. Often those who are most successful are not the best writers or the most knowledgeable on their topic. Rather, they are the best at self-promotion and marketing.

5. *Keep writing.* Unlike Margaret Mitchell (*Gone with the Wind*) or Harper Lee (*To Kill a Mockingbird*), it is highly unlikely that you, as a modern-day, how-to writer, will produce one great work and coast for the rest of your career. The successful how-to writer is always writing new material and updating existing publications. You must do this because you are always learning and improving your knowledge, and your readers want your latest thinking, ideas, and methods.

How much money can you make?

If you include self-help and pop psychology in the how-to category, and I do, then the sky's the limit. Tony Robbins, Dr. Wayne Dyer, Dr. Phil, and Deepak Chopra all earn fortunes from information empires that include books, seminars, audio programs, and instructional videos; all of them are multimillionaires.

Even if you are not a celebrity, you can emulate their model, albeit on a somewhat smaller scale. There are many millionaire internet information marketers, including Jeff Paul, Jeff Walker, Matt Furey, Mark Ford, Marlon Sanders, Armand Morin, Alex Mendossian, Terry Dean, and Joe Vitale, to name just a few. A few of these are best-selling authors, but most self-publish their how-to advice as e-books and other information products.

In part, your income will be determined by how you see yourself. If you think of yourself as a traditional freelance writer and spend the bulk of your time sending query letters and writing articles for magazines, you can expect annual earnings averaging about $65,000 a year. Likewise, if you just write nonfiction books for traditional publishers, you may get a $25,000 advance for a book that takes you three to six months to write. How many books can you write in a year? I'd estimate that the average author of mid-list or backlist nonfiction books is lucky to earn around $50,000 a year from advances and royalties.

I met a how-to writer whose specialty is ghostwriting nonfiction books on a flat-fee basis for professional speakers. He charges $24,000 per book and, if he pushes himself and works all the time, he can produce three or four books a year. At that pace, he works like a dog, barely earns a six-figure income, and builds no equity—he doesn't own the content he creates for his clients, and he doesn't share in the royalties. But, he is smart: He also writes his own books for major publishers under his byline, for which he gets royalties. And he earns a hefty $5,000 for a one-hour talk as a successful professional speaker.

In this book, you'll learn how to become a multifaceted how-to writer who disseminates information in many formats, including paperbound books, e-books, special reports, workshops, magazine articles, newsletters, blogs, and more. Some of your works will be published by traditional publishers—book and magazine publishers—while some of it will be self-published.

By following the plan laid out in this book, you can earn a comfortable six-figure annual income from your nonfiction writing. And you can do it when and where you want, while writing what interests and pleases you. Plus, you can work at home—no boss, no commute, no suit and tie, no alarm clock.

One writer I met at a seminar years ago told me he earned $100,000 a year writing about wine. Rachael Ray earns considerably more with her TV show and best-selling cookbooks. Running my writing business exactly the way I show you throughout the book, I have earned an annual income ranging from $300,000 to $700,000 for many years. And I have been earning six figures as a freelance writer consistently for close to four decades. You may earn even more . . . and if you follow my plan, I think you can realistically get to the $100,000 to $200,000 a year income level within 12 to 24 months.

Of course, that's just an estimate of what I think is possible. How much you make as a how-to writer—and how quickly you earn it—depends mainly on you, your talent, and the effort you make.

The 3 most common how-to writing questions

Q: How can I write something and get it published, when today every topic under the sun has already been exhaustively covered?

A: First, it's not true: New ideas, inventions, methods, problems, solutions, and technology arise all the time.

Second, consumers with a strong interest in a topic (e.g., coin collecting, trading futures) will buy multiple books on the topic. This is in sharp contrast to, say, household appliances: If I buy one washing machine, I won't need another for years.

Third, if 90 percent of your content is stuff the reader has heard before, it convinces him that you know what you're talking about. And if 10 percent is new to him, just getting one fresh idea or tip from your book can pay back the price of your book 100 times over or more.

Q: With the total amount of human knowledge doubling every 13 months, and that pace is forecast by IBM to accelerate to doubling every 12 hours with the build-out of the Internet of Things (IoT), how can I possibly keep up with the topics I write about?

A: First, write mostly in one niche or subject matter area.

Second, within that niche, focus on a small slice of your broader topic and concentrate on that segment.

Third, become a lifelong student or active participant in the topic you choose. Sometimes your writing may contain original ideas, analysis, and tips. Other times it's the clarity of your presentation that stands out.

Q: There is already so much content available to the consumer, how would he or she have the time to read, listen to, or watch mine?

A: Many of your readers are "information junkies" who crave non-fiction of an instructional or useful nature. Information junkies are addicted to acquiring more and more content on their favorite topic. So they will seek you out.

2

Choosing Your How-To Writing Niche

In the 1980s, when I started writing books, writers frequently wrote books on multiple topics, often in unrelated fields. Isaac Asimov, who wrote 465 published books, claimed he could write with equal ease on any topic, and he proceeded to demonstrate this by writing books on history, science, humor, Shakespeare, and the Bible.

I'm no Isaac Asimov, and today, if anyone knows me, they think of me as a marketing guy. But I've written published books on everything from *Star Trek* and satire, to sex and science fiction, to real estate and email marketing.

But those days are almost gone. Today's successful how-to authors establish a platform—a reputation as a subject matter expert and a built-in audience in a particular topic or niche—and focus their writing in just one or two areas. The more you build your platform in your niche, the more money you will make. Therefore, the first and most important decision you must make as a how-to writer is choosing the right niche. Choose carefully and wisely, because it's a decision you will live with for a long time.

Advantages of specialization versus being a generalist

There are still writers today who are generalists, flitting from topic to topic, project to project, and writing about anything. While a few of them break away from the pack and achieve an unusually high degree of success and status, most journeymen writers toil in relative obscurity and eke out a modest living.

Yet freelance writing as a generalist comes with other perks. Chief among these is the joy of going where your curiosity takes you, exploring new fields, and writing about what interests you at the moment. Also, as a nonspecialist, you approach new topics as a beginner, just as many of your readers are doing. Since you are learning the topic along with your readers, you will write clearly and simply so that even the beginner can understand. And you will likely ask and answer many of the same questions that are on their minds, adding value to your book or report.

The problem facing generalists is that they are confronted with the explosion of information, particularly its rapid rate of creation and growth. There is so much knowledge and information available today that no one can hope to master anything but the smallest fraction of it. Simply speaking, we just can't keep up!

When you are a generalist, the situation grows even more hopeless because there are hundreds of topics to study. But when you are a specialist, you can focus your limited time and concentration on just one or two topics. You won't know *everything* about your chosen topic, but at least becoming fairly knowledgeable is within your grasp.

Another key reason to specialize in a particular niche is money. Publishers are more likely to give a book contract to a writer who is a specialist in the topic of the book. Many magazines prefer specialists, too. For years, *Scientific American* was written largely by professional scientists, and *Stocks and Commodities* publishes articles contributed mainly by portfolio managers, analysts, brokers, and traders.

When customers are buying information online, the closer your product is matched to the specific needs of these readers, the easier it will be to sell and the more you can charge. *When you target a niche market, you have a small universe of potential readers, but they will pay surprising amounts of money for specialized information in their area of interest.* My colleague Don Hauptman says that with specialized information products, we tend to overestimate the number of people who will buy from us, but underestimate what they are willing to pay for specialized information.

"Always target a niche market," advises internet information marketing expert Stephen Pierce. "If you want to get rich, target a niche. If you want to go broke, market to all the folks. Identifying a problem in that niche market is priority #1. Creating a desired solution for that problem is priority #2. Delivering that solution for a profit to your niche market is priority #3."

What is a niche?

What is a niche? Speaker Wally Bock defines a niche as the intersection of an industry with a skill or knowledge area.

Say you were a bank teller. Your industry is the banking industry. What do tellers do all day? Service customers. So your niche could be customer service in the banking industry. The title of your special report or audio album could be "The Bank Teller's Guide to Success: Customer Service Strategies for Success in the Banking Industry."

There are tons of gardening writers and gardening websites. But I ran across a fellow with an unusual niche: carnivorous plants! He got his start selling Venus fly traps by mail. Jerry Baker, America's master gardener, covered all of gardening but also had a niche in lawn care. The late Ralph Snodsmith, the gardening author and radio commentator, specialized in houseplants. (At one home and garden show in New Jersey that my wife and I attended, I met Ralph at a table he had for selling his books.)

Countless authors write about marketing and small business topics. Perry Marshall's niche is marketing with Google advertising. Gary Gerber, who writes for several trade journals, specializes in practice management and marketing for eye doctors—largely because he is one. Fred Gleeck writes about marketing for the self-storage industry.

A good rule of thumb is that the narrower and more specialized your niche, the more in demand you will be and the more you can charge for your writing, speaking, and other communication products and services.

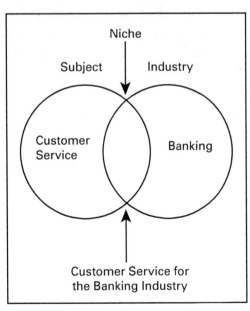

Fig. 2.1. A niche is the intersection of an industry and a skill.

You can charge more for specialized information than for general topics. When self-publishing your how-to information, consider the effect of the format on perceived value. As a rule of thumb:

- Trade paperback books have a slightly higher perceived value than mass market paperbacks.

- Hardcover books with dust jackets have a higher perceived value than trade paperbacks.

- Hardcover books with faux leather covers have a higher perceived value than that of regular hardcover books with dust jackets, because they are seen as reference volumes, much like the rows of expensive leather-bound books you see in law offices.

- Books printed on 8½ by 11-inch sheets, three-hole punched, and put into a loose-leaf binder have a higher perceived value than hardcover books. That's because the perceived value of a traditional book is determined by other bookstore books, most of which are priced from $10 to $30, while the value of nonbook formats is determined by the content. This loose-leaf format is excellent for information products in niche markets.

- You can greatly increase the perceived value of a loose-leaf book by packaging it with a few disks containing audio, video, software, or document files. *People will pay much more for multimedia programs.*

- You can charge even more when you include quarterly updates, which come three-hole punched for easy insertion into the binder, keeping your manual up to date. After a year you can continue to offer updates on a paid subscription basis.

- Give the reader your email address or phone number and let them know that as the owner of the binder (these were once known as loose-leaf services), they are entitled to ask questions about the material in the binder. That adds even more value.

Since specialized information targeted to a narrow niche can command high prices, it's best to package such information in one of the high-perceived-value formats. Because hardcover books are expensive to produce, especially per copy in short runs, I recommend the three-ring binder format.

You can offer the same pages as a PDF, but PDFs have a lower perceived value than a hard copy binder, especially one containing disks or other media. Also, although consumers will read very large PDFs on their screens, many do not like printing hard copies. Hard copies consume a lot of paper and ink, must be punched and placed in a loose-leaf binder the customer has to obtain separately, and very large files often jam up some printers.

Choosing your niche

"But I'm not a specialist," you may be saying about now. "So what niche can I choose?"

For some how-to writers, the niche is immediately obvious. Karen, a dietician, logically wanted to write about nutrition, diet, exercise, and health. Ray, an auto mechanic, wanted to write do-it-yourself guides for servicing one's own car.

But many of us aren't pulled so strongly in any one direction. And our varied backgrounds—a liberal arts major, perhaps, followed by a string of jobs in different industries—don't readily suggest a niche for us. What then?

The answer is to take a personal inventory—to figure out what you know, have training or qualifications for, and are interested in teaching others.

The question then often arises: Should I choose a niche that I love, or should I choose a niche based on demand? The answer is to choose one of the niches you are most enthusiastic about, and of those niches, to select one in a large, growing, or active market. In his book *A Year in the Writing Trade*, John Jerome explains why writers should choose a niche they care about:

> *I believe that things that are truly engrossing to work on will end up better written than those aimed at grabbing a market. The writer will be clearer, more painstaking, more thorough in the writing of them. The subjects that are powerful to work on are also the ones that are going to pull the richest material up out of the unconscious. Then all that remains is the work of finding out, with the conscious mind, why things are so rich, so powerful.*

But how do you find a niche if you're not sure what your topic will be? Perform a self-audit. Here are the ten questions you should ask yourself. As you think of the answers, write them down:

- What do I like?
- What am I interested in?
- What am I good at?
- What do I have an aptitude for?
- What is my education?
- What do I know?
- What is my experience?
- What have I accomplished?
- Which of the above areas affords the least competition?
- Which of the above areas pays high rates?

A quick note about online research: Are people searching the topic on Google? What keywords are they using? You can find out using the Google Keyword Tool, which you get access to when you open a Google Ads account. Just open your account and click Keyword Planner on the screen. A few of the many other keyword research tools are listed in the sidebar below:

Some keyword research tools

- Alexa.com
- Google Keyword Tool
- Jaaxy.com
- Keywordsnatcher.com
- moz.com/explorer
- SEMrush.com
- WordTracker.com

When answering the 10 questions above, list as many subjects under each point as you possibly can. You can list them in a spreadsheet or (my preference) on index cards, one per card. Once you have completed your lists, look them over, and set aside the cards for any items that look like possible niches.

Next, pick the five most interesting potential niches. Put the cards in order of preference.

Now look at the list. Chances are that one or two of these subjects are things people routinely pay to learn about. Pick one and you've found your niche. As Aristotle said, "Where your passions intersect with the needs of the public, therein lies your vocation."

What if none of the five items on your list is sufficiently appealing to you as a niche? Pick the next best five items from your index cards and repeat the process until you discover a niche you are enthusiastic about.

How many niches?

"How many different niches can I have?" is a question I am asked all the time. Some writers specialize in one area only, such as Carl Sagan did on astronomy. Others have multiple niches: Arthur C. Clarke wrote about astronomy as well as oceanography (he was an avid scuba diver).

The late Dan Poynter, author of *The Self-Publishing Manual*, believed three niches are the most you should attempt to handle. His three niches were parachuting, self-publishing, and being an expert witness. All three niches were based on his life experiences. Dan was an avid skydiver, so he knew parachuting. When he looked around for good parachuting books, he couldn't find any, so he began writing and publishing them himself. This experience made him knowledgeable in self-publishing—another niche— and as the author of parachuting books, he was called by attorneys as an expert witness in cases involving skydiving accidents. From there, he began to publish books and reports on being an expert witness.

I tend to agree with Dan. *If you participate in too many niches, you spread yourself thin and cannot give each the attention it deserves.* Three is the recommended limit. And remember, you are competing against other writers and information marketers. If they are 100-percent dedicated to the niche, and you are not, they have the advantage.

The exception to the three-niche maximum is having an area of knowledge or skill set that is easily transferable to multiple industries. Going back to our bank teller, he can start with customer service in the banking industry, because he knows customer service best and has direct experience in that industry.

But the principles of good customer service are pretty much the same from industry to industry. So our bank teller could develop customer service programs for many other industries, each opening up a new market; e.g., customer service for the brokerage industry; customer service for insurance agents; customer service for the mortgage industry. The common thread is customer service in face-to-face situations in financial services.

My colleague Fred Gleeck operates in this manner. His basic niche is showing small business owners how to get more customers, which he does for ten different industries, including caterers, videographers, professional speakers, voice-over actors, independent consultants, and owners of self-storage facilities.

The smaller the niche, the more you can charge for your how-to information. Similarly, the fewer competitors you have, the more you can charge. For instance, Fred sells books on getting customers for around $20 in niches such as professional speaking and consulting, which have lots of buyers and many writers. He publishes a manual on obtaining customers in the self-storage industry, but this one is packaged in a loose-leaf binder and sells for $100. There are relatively few self-storage owners in the United States and there is a scarcity of industry-specific how-to business information aimed at them. So, Fred may sell fewer copies of this book, but he can charge more for it.

Niche size

OK. Next then, how do you select the audience for whom you're writing the how-to material? How do you make that selection? The main consideration is that you have to have a large enough audience to have a market for selling your information. Maybe you have a pan flute band and want to create an information product on "How to start a pan flute band." But how many pan flute players are there? Of those, how many want to start a band?

The late Jerry Buchanan, founder of the Tower's Club, had a rule of thumb that your niche must ideally have 100,000 people in it to be profitable. He arrived at the number as follows: Jerry figured that the minimum number of copies of a book a publisher wants to sell is 5,000 (this was all before the internet). He also figured that it is a realistic goal to sell to 5 percent of your total market. To sell 5,000 books at a 5 percent closing rate required an audience of 100,000.

Table 2.2. Estimated Monthly Search Volume

Search Term	Google	Yahoo!	Bing
foreclosure listing	90,500	45,250	24,435
free foreclosure listings	74,000	37,740	17,020
free foreclosure listing	27,100	14,092	6,504
foreclosure listings	450,000	220,500	112,500
free list foreclosure	22,200	11,544	5,106
foreclosure list	90,500	45,250	23,530

Jerry's other rule of thumb for determining whether a niche had enough potential customers to support him as an information marketer or writer was: Does the industry have an association or trade journal dedicated to it? If so, you can then reach the members easily and affordably. The existence of a magazine or association also proves the people in this group are willing to spend money for information on the topic.

I agree with Jerry's assessment, but I would also add that today some markets can be reachable mainly online. For instance, if large numbers of internet users search the term "Persian cats" on Google, that would indicate a ready market for information on Persian cats. Table 2.2 above provides sample search results for terms related to real estate foreclosures. You can determine the volume of online searches that a keyword or phrase gets by using the keyword research tools in the sidebar shown earlier.

Is there a market for your topic on the internet?

The internet is an extremely affordable medium for marketing information products of all kinds. But are there people on the internet looking for information on your topic and willing to pay for it?

To find out, first Google the topic—for instance, if your topic is how to buy investment properties, you might Google "make money in real estate."

A ton of independent websites will come up. Some give away free information. Some are company websites for real estate agents. But you'll notice that many are selling information products on real estate investing.

Don't be put off if other people are selling information products on your topic. That's a good sign: They wouldn't be creating and selling these information products unless people were buying. If the market seems too crowded, you can narrow your niche even more; e.g., "make money flipping single-family homes."

Next, use a keyword research tool such as SEMrush.com to determine whether people are actively searching the internet for information on your topic. These tools tell you how many people are searching for a particular keyword or phrase per month on search engines. How many searches on your keyword are enough to indicate sufficient interest? A rough guide is that you want to see 100,000 to 500,000 or more searches per month. More than 100,000 means there is a healthy market of internet people searching for information related to your topic. Much more than 500,000 means the niche may be too competitive, with the keyword being too expensive to bid on for pay-per-click (PPC) advertising.

Traditional publishing versus self-publishing

Should you self-publish or publish in traditional media such as books and magazines? Many how-to writers, including me, do both. But there are certain times when the topic itself, more so than your personal preferences, better determines the answer.

A good question to ask yourself is: "Where would people tend to look for, find, and buy information on this topic?" If the answer is "in a bookstore," then a traditional publishing house might be your best choice. The reason is that mainstream publishers have sales reps who distribute books to the bookstores. As a solo author, you can't hope to duplicate a major publisher's bookstore distribution on your own. They amortize the cost of their sales force over hundreds of different titles published annually; as a small operator, you may publish only one or two books a year.

On the other hand, what if people would find a book such as yours in a specialized store or magazine? Books on scuba diving are often sold in dive shops and advertised in diving magazines. In that case, the publisher's bookstore distribution network is less valuable to you (they probably don't have a list of dive shops for their reps to call on), and self-publishing might make the most sense. Carefully research book distribution into the specialized stores that pertain to your book; in some circumstances, you may be able to reach a distribution agreement with a distributor who has good penetration into that particular retail niche. And while you may also be able to sell books directly to chains or individual stores, this is usually a time-consuming approach with low odds of success.

Micro-niching

How do you get more writing assignments, write more royalty-producing materials, and gain a reputation as a top author in your field?

One way is through micro-niching: narrowing your niche further and further and making it more and more specialized. In our bank teller example earlier, our writer/speaker's niche was customer service for the banking industry. An example of micro-niching would be customer service in commercial banks, or thrifts, or credit unions.

For many years, as a freelance copywriter, I specialized in writing direct mail, versus other copywriters who wrote TV commercials and magazine ads. As more and more copywriters began getting into direct mail, I micro-niched by further specializing in direct mail packages to sell subscriptions to investment newsletters. Then, as more and more copywriters began to compete for those assignments to write financial packages, I narrowed the niche more by specializing in writing direct mail packages for option trading services.

You get the idea. I know one copywriter who specializes in writing text for chat buttons appearing on websites. That's about as "micro" as a niche can get!

One way to reduce competition in your niche is to choose a subject that is somewhat technical. You find dozens of books and information products on goal-setting because it is a fairly generic topic and not specialized: Anyone can understand it and write about it. But if you teach using Python for full-stack website development, that's a little more technical. Fewer writers and information marketers know how to use Python, let alone program website functionality, and they are not inclined to learn, so the field is more open.

Adjacent niches

Micro-niching is a strategy to improve your writing career and income by becoming even more specialized within your topic than you are right now.

Another strategy used by some how-to writers is to write in "adjacent niches." These are topics that have something in common with your main niche or topic but are not exactly the same. As an example, I read a book on software system design by a systems analyst. He had an entire chapter about architecture—not software architecture, but buildings. Why? There is a parallel between designing a building and designing a system, and by teaching his readers something of traditional architecture he felt he could help them become better software architects.

Let's say you want to write information on how to take care of hamsters. A micro-niche strategy would be to write something on how to take care of Russian dwarf hamsters. An adjacent-niche strategy would be to write something on how to take care of guinea pigs, ferrets, or rabbits.

Mark Ford, a best-selling writer and information marketer, uses this strategy. He began by writing primarily about starting and growing successful companies. As he built his many companies, he became wealthy and began investing in real estate. So he published a course on real estate investing. Because the success of many of his companies was a result of strong marketing, at which Mark excels, he coauthored a book on multichannel marketing.

Going wider instead of deeper

Yet another strategy for creating more writing opportunities is reverse niching: Instead of going narrower and narrower, you get wider and wider.

My colleague Perry Marshall wanted to write about internet marketing. He decided to make his niche pay-per-click (PPC) advertising, largely because it had little competition. The reason for the lack of competition, Perry told me, is that the subject is slightly technical, so many people shy away from it.

To make a long story short, Perry is now a multimillionaire how-to writer and the recognized expert on Google ads. Of course, online advertising is not all that Perry knows. To sell his original Google ad guide, he had to learn many facets of information marketing.

And guess what? Perry now has coaching programs and other information products on the broader topic of how to succeed in internet marketing. He started with his micro-niche and established his reputation there. Once he became known as the Google ad expert, people easily accepted him as a guy who is extremely knowledgeable in all things related to internet marketing.

But Perry hasn't stopped there. In his writings and talks, he has widened his scope even further, going from just internet business success to business success principles in general. However, Perry is not the best-selling business success author of all time. Brian Tracy, Tom Peters, and a dozen other authors dominate the business book best-seller lists. But, Perry has a huge following online—his list has well over 150,000 subscribers—people who trust him and his advice on business success. So Perry can sell reports, teleseminars, and other content on the broad topics of business success very profitably to his fan base.

Having a "fan base"—a group of people who follow you and eagerly await new writing from you—is an important part of your success strategy as a how-to writer. And your fan base does not have to be huge for you to earn a handsome living from your how-to writing: If you have 10,000 online subscribers who spend on average just $100 buying your books and other information products a year, your annual gross income would be $1 million.

3

Research and Knowledge Acquisition

To be a successful writer, you must have something to write about, and this is where some writers in almost every genre, both nonfiction and fiction, fall short.

Many writers have limited education and experience, and they live mainly inside their own thoughts. Unfortunately, unless you are Sanjay Gupta or Warren Buffett, your thoughts are of little interest to the reading public. So works that are streams of consciousness, particularly your own consciousness, have little or no market value. Yet reflections on inner thoughts and feelings are precisely what many writers focus on, to their detriment.

The how-to writer must have something concrete to write about. This chapter shows you how to acquire that subject matter content for your writing.

Mark Ford says that good writing is a great idea clearly expressed and backed up with lots of proof. It is nearly impossible to come up with a great idea or back it up with proof if you don't know anything about your topic. I agree with Mark about the need for a great idea and clear writing, but to that I would add "great content."

Your information has to be accurate, useful, and educational: Readers should learn something they did not know before reading your book. If they already know what is in your book, but aren't doing or using it, your writing should motivate them to put your methods and ideas into practice.

The hierarchy of content: information, knowledge, and wisdom

"Content" is the facts and ideas in your writing—the knowledge, strategies, and wisdom it conveys.

And content has a hierarchy. The lowest level of this hierarchy is information. Information consists of facts; e.g., on the Kelvin scale, the temperature of absolute zero is zero degrees K; it takes eight minutes for light from our sun to travel through space and reach Earth's surface.

Reference books largely contain information. At one time, reference books were very popular and sold well, and nonfiction writers could make a good living writing and selling reference books. Some still do; look at Matthew Lesko and his incredibly profitable books on how to get free money (grants and loans mostly) from the federal government.

But for the most part, you can't make a good living writing content that is merely informational. The culprit is the internet. For instance, Isaac Asimov wrote a great reference book on world history, *Asimov's Chronology of the World*. Before the internet, if you wanted historical information, owning a book like Asimov's would save you a trip to the library. And it's fun to read.

But now, any topic you'd care to look up in Asimov's book you could find faster, with more up-to-date and detailed information, by doing a Google search. Therefore, reference books are becoming archaic and obsolete. They may not vanish, but the demand for them has lessened significantly.

At the next level of content, above information, is knowledge. Knowledge is a deeper understanding of the facts. Information is that zero degrees Kelvin is absolute zero. Knowledge is understanding what absolute zero is (cessation of all molecular motion) and its importance (eliminating electrical resistance to allow superconductivity).

The highest level of the how-to writing content hierarchy is wisdom. Wisdom helps the reader determine a course of action or make a choice. It is based on years of accumulated experience, analyzed so that rules and guidance may be extracted from it.

The content hierarchy—information, knowledge, wisdom—should not be obvious in your writing. Content is not organized according to the hierarchy. Good how-to writing contains a mix of all three: information, knowledge, and wisdom. Just as the ingredients in a sauce or stew are well mixed to create a great dish, the three content elements are mixed in how-to nonfiction to create content that is clear, compelling, and complete.

"Content matters," writes copywriter Joe Robson in *Copywriter Digest Newsletter*. "What does your write-up say? What value can the readers get out of it? Are you substituting big words because you have nothing else to say?"

The 4-step how-to writing process

Why do we need to research information and accumulate knowledge so that we acquire wisdom? Because we need to dispense all three—information, knowledge, and wisdom—liberally in our writings. One of the main causes of poor writing I see in students is that they do not have enough information about, or mastery of, the topic they are writing about.

Research and accumulation of knowledge is the critical first step in the how-to nonfiction writing process. This process has four steps:

1. *Research and knowledge accumulation.* The late Paul Sarnoff, a successful author and investment newsletter editor, said: "If you are an expert in something, you will never go hungry."

   Before you can write, you need to have something to write about. This means acquiring extensive knowledge and a deep understanding, through a combination of research and experience, of a subject people will pay to learn about. In Paul's case, it was gold and gold mining stocks.

   When you read a piece of weak writing, the likely cause is that the author either did not understand the subject, or that he did not have enough information about the subject to write a content-rich composition of the desired length.

   In this chapter, we will review the different methods by which you, as a how-to author, can acquire the practical knowledge of your subject required to write useful instruction and advice about it.

2. *Organize your content.* What's the best way to present your subject? Is it a process with definite sequential steps that must be performed in a specific order? If it is a linear process, your outline can be a series of numbered steps describing what you do first, next, and so on. For an article or book on vitamins, you could use alphabetical order. And for a document on the animals of Africa, one option is size. Another might be the region of Africa where the animals are from.

3. *Teach your subject to the reader.* Use illustrations, stories, examples, case studies, photos, diagrams, tables, analogies, metaphors, comparisons, activities—whatever it takes to make your subject clear to the reader. Give plenty of examples, worksheets, resources, and model documents that the reader can copy so he does not have to reinvent the wheel.

In fact, teaching a class is a pretty good way of assembling the content you need to write a book, manual, home study course, or other information product. Good teachers organize the class syllabus into modules; these modules are the analog of chapters in a book. In addition, students often bring in interesting materials related to the discussion, and some of these, with permission, can be used in your book.

If you teach a class, you may want to make an audio or video recording of it and transcribe the sessions. This transcript will capture a lot of your content and your explanations of it, in roughly the order you would present them in a how-to book or series of articles.

Transcribing recordings is, however, a time-consuming, tiresome, and somewhat boring task. I have a virtual assistant who does the transcribing for me. Or, you can use professional transcription services (see sidebar).

4. *Polish your prose.* Teaching a class requires research and organization, but not writing. So even if you transcribe your class lessons, you will need to edit them into clear, coherent prose.

Here's where your writing skill comes into play. When style is not dictated by the client, publisher, or format, write in a natural, conversational style, like one friend talking to another, or like a patient teacher looking over the reader's shoulder. Use small words, short sentences, and short paragraphs. Avoid jargon. Write in plain simple English. Use frequent heads and subheads to break the writing up into short sections. Use bullets and numbered lists to make the text easier to scan and read.

Okay. Writing in general and how-to writing in particular is a four-step process: (1) research and acquire knowledge, (2) organize your information, (3) present it in such a way as to effectively teach the reader, and (4) polish the writing so it is clear, crisp, and concise.

In this process, knowledge acquisition is the first step. But how do you, as a how-to writer, acquire the knowledge you are going to transfer to your readers?

Transcription services

Writer's Cramp, Inc.
63 Dakota Drive, Hamilton, NJ 08619
(608) 588=8043
www.wtrscramp.com

Verbalink
11150 W. Olympic Blvd. Suite 950, Los Angeles, CA 90064
(877) 983-7225
www.verbalink.io

Internet Transcribers
P.O. Box 544, Lexington, AL 35648
Rhea Perry
www.internettranscribers.com
info@asapbusinesssolutions.net

Rev
222 Kearny St, 8th Floor, San Francisco, CA 94108
And:
1717 W. 6th St. Suite 310, Austin, TX 78703
(888) 369-0701
www.rev.com
support@rev.com

Gathering material

The knowledge you must acquire to be a successful how-to writer is of two kinds: general and specific. Specific knowledge is information directly related to the writing task at hand. For instance, a writer working on a gardening book will check reference books and search the web for information on plants and flowers.

The second type of knowledge is general knowledge. It has often been said of writers and writing: Everything is grist for the mill. As a nonfiction writer, the more you know about everything, the better. When writing, you draw on your general knowledge to make comparisons, give examples, make analogies, support your points, and prove your arguments.

How do you acquire the general and specific knowledge needed to be a good how-to writer? The different techniques of knowledge acquisition for the freelance nonfiction writer are listed below:

- *Do.* Acquiring real-world experience in the thing you are writing about, whether it's flipping houses or trading futures, gives you greater understanding of the topic and greater credibility with your reader. Conversely, not being an active participant in the topic you are writing about makes you a journalist, and not an expert. And, as the late how-to author and publisher Dan Poynter said, "We need fewer books by journalists and more books by subject matter experts."

    Your participation can be as a regular practitioner or as a writer trying something out strictly for research purposes. An example of a how-to writer being a regular participant in his topic would be the late Omar Sharif and his long-running bridge column. An example of a nonfiction writer trying the activity for the sake of writing authentically about it would be George Plimpton getting into the ring and sparing with Archie Moore for a round in order to write convincingly about boxing.

    Each of the three choices—being a journalist who is strictly an observer, trying the activity for yourself, or being a regular participant—can be a viable position for the how-to writer. However, I recommend involvement in the activity you are writing about at least occasionally, and preferably on a fairly regular basis. The more you do the thing you write about, the greater your accumulation of knowledge that you can pass on to your readers—and the greater your credibility with them.

    Also, think about the reader. Is it fair to your readers to give them advice on something you don't know much about yourself? An investment author once explained to his readers why he boasted a bit about his financial success and accumulated wealth in his writing, asking: "Why would you want to take financial advice from someone who makes less money than you do?"

- *Watch.* When asked why he wrote about the movie business instead of actually writing movies, former entertainment reporter Andy Neff replied: "It's more fun to watch." While learning by doing is powerful, you can often pick up a lot by watching the best at a particular craft or task perform it. That's why golfers like to buy how-to golf videos—so they can see someone do it right, and then imitate the swing the way the golfer on the tape does it. Former heavyweight champion Mike Tyson watched countless hours of fights on film. Writers can learn a lot about their subject through careful observation and note-taking.

- *Listen.* There is always more to learn about your topic. That's why I advise all how-to writers and information marketers to become avid listeners to audio CD or MP3 digital learning programs.

  Driving in the car in silence or while listening to music is a waste of time. But by listening to audio courses while you drive, you can turn your car into a classroom on wheels. If you hear something so valuable in the audio program that you want to use it in your own writing, pull over and write it down.

  I also advise all writers to always, without fail, carry either a smartphone or a pad and pen in their pocket or purse. I always wear button-down shirts (and never polo or T-shirts) because I need a shirt pocket to hold my phone or pad and pencil. You never know when you will have an idea or hear or see something that you can use in your writing. However, you waste these opportunities if you don't record the information, because you will likely forget it.

- *Read.* Of the hundreds of professional writers I know or have met personally over the years, only one I can think of is not an avid reader. Reading prodigiously is how you acquire a constant stream of new general knowledge. I am a voracious reader of books, e-books, reports, websites, newspapers, magazines, e-newsletters, and any other written information I can get my hands on—both offline and online.

  Tip: Whenever your local library is having a book sale, go and buy books that either have value as general reference or cover your specific niche topic. You can usually add gems to your personal library for fifty cents each. And you can usually get at least one thing you can use in your own writing from every book you buy. Where else are ideas on sale for half-a-buck each?

- *Face-to-face interview.* A major research tool for the how-to writer is interviewing subject matter experts (SMEs). The request for an interview can be made by email or telephone. The SME is more likely to agree to the interview if you put a time limit on it; e.g.: "This will only take 12 minutes of your time." During the interview, you should offer to stop after the 12 minutes are up; if the SME is having a good time or is just a nice person, he or she may give you more time. But always respect their busy schedules.

There are pros and cons of in-person versus telephone versus email interviews. I virtually never do live interviews because they take too much time. I simply do not have the time to travel. In addition, SMEs express themselves most concisely in email; somewhat concisely in phone interviews; and least concisely in live interviews. I can get as much information from an SME in a half-hour over the phone as in an hour in person.

Some writers tape and transcribe all interviews. I prefer to take notes. Because I am an extremely fast typist, the notes capture all pertinent information. And real-time note-taking eliminates the time-consuming task of transcribing the interview later on.

Occasionally, I do have a project where getting exact quotations from the interview subjects is important. In these situations, I conduct the interview over a conference line where it is automatically recorded, such as www.freeconferencecall.com. I then send the link to the MP3 recording to a transcription service that transcribes it for me.

When doing in-person interviews, call the morning of the interview to confirm the SME is in and can see you. There are few bigger time-wasters than to drive an hour or two to an interview only to discover that the SME is out sick with the flu.

Make sure the SME can deliver the content you need before investing time in an interview. Once, while listening to the radio, I heard an odd commercial: A guy was selling billy goats to people for keeping their grass short. Sensing this would make a good feature for a newspaper where I freelanced, I called and asked if he could see me about the billy goats. Come right now, was his reply.

I got in the car and drove 75 minutes. When I got there, the place was an outdoor power equipment dealer. Why were they selling goats? I, of course, wanted to see the billy goats. He took me to a showroom where he proudly displayed his line of shiny, metal, and new Billy Goat–brand lawn mowers. In addition to the embarrassment, I wasted half a Saturday. I *should* have said while making the appointment, "These are *live* billy goats, right?"

- *Phone interview.* Face-to-face interviews are best when there is something to see—a laboratory, a petting zoo, an ecosphere, a classic car collection—in addition to someone to talk to. But when there is nothing to see, I prefer doing my interviews by phone. It saves time and is more efficient. Also, I type faster on my desktop PC than I do on my laptop or a tablet. If you are interviewing someone overseas, you can save money by using Zoom or Skype.

- *Email interview.* When doing remote interviews, I ask subjects whether they prefer to have me email them questions they can answer via email or have me interview them over the phone. Whichever the subject prefers, I do. The nice thing about email interviews is that you often receive more detail and greater accuracy in the answers than in a phone interview; for instance, a typed reply shows you the correct spellings of names and technical terms.

  Also, often when the plan is for me to interview an SME, and I send him questions prior to the interview via email, the SME often sends me back an email with the answers written out, despite my not asking him to do so.

Online research services

Nurit Mittlefehldt
16251 Brookford Dr., Houston, TX 77059
(832) 725-5028
nurit77@att.net

Tyler Honts
tyler.honts@aol.com

Gregory C. Byrne
gcbat65@gmail.com
(218) 409-4337
www.internetresearch836797739.wordpress.com

Magdalena Szczeglik
(832) 429-5514
www.goldenresearchservices.com

Maxine Foster-Hockett
maxinelfh3@gmail.com

- *Google search.* How-to writers must learn to use Google and other search engines. You can do your own internet research or, as I do, outsource it to freelancers. Expect to pay an internet researcher $20 to $35 an hour or more.

  When doing your own internet research, print out the pages with information you find. You need these hard copies as proof that your information is accurately sourced, and since websites change, update, and delete content frequently, you need the hard copy as proof of what you found.

  Also, add a footnote to your manuscript containing the URL where you found the material online. That way, if you are ever challenged about your content or its source, you have double backup: the hard copy in your file and a link to the same material online.

- *Library search.* Despite the power of Google, library searches still have value. You come across books and publications that you would otherwise miss online. Browsing the stacks can lead your research in other directions and to new sources. I also find great information in the books I buy at the aforementioned library sales and in used bookstores.

- *Blogging.* Blogging is a form of research for writers. When you write short posts on topics you plan to use in information products, your blog readers will comment on these posts. Their comments can give you additional information on the topic, as well as feedback on how readers are reacting to your ideas.

- *Social networking.* Social networks like LinkedIn, Twitter, and Facebook can help you connect with SMEs and others possessing information of potential value to you for your how-to writing. I often post research questions on my Facebook wall, and the comments from my Facebook friends are another form of gathering useful content.

- *Research assistant.* If you value your productivity, you should consider outsourcing all or part of your research. In particular, I use freelance internet researchers as well as my virtual assistants to search the web for straightforward information such as facts, dates, statistics, charts, and graphs. Most of this is routine work and is just as easily done by an administrative assistant or a freelancer as by you. By outsourcing your routine internet research, you free up your time for more important writing tasks.

What you know can make you richer

Each month, I am besieged by nice, well-meaning folk who desperately desire to be writers, consultants, coaches, speakers, and information marketers. Many of these people actually have quite a bit of talent for writing, consulting, coaching, speaking, and authoring information products.

Yet most will not succeed for a single common reason: They have nothing to teach, write, or speak *about*. I see this all the time:

- Marketing consultants who have never held a corporate marketing job or worked at an ad agency or created a single winning marketing campaign.

- Numerous sales trainers who were mediocre sales reps, many of whom have never sold anything at all.

- Business opportunity marketers who have never actually done the businesses that they write and talk about.

- Financial newsletter editors who haven't made a dime in the market in years.

To succeed as a writer, speaker, consultant, or coach, you need just two things: (a) the ability to write, speak, consult, or coach and (b) something to write, speak, consult, or coach about. To be fair, you also need to know how to (c) market, promote, and sell yourself to get leads and clients. Lots of people have the (a), and the (c) can be learned, but too many lack the (b)—a subject to write about.

The best way to gain this knowledge is as a participant in or practitioner of the skill or specialized field you want to write about. Some wannabe gurus decide they will master a field by reading about it and studying it, but they neglect to actually participate in it.

That's a mistake. Book learning is important, but there are limits to how far book learning alone can take you, and it is no substitute for real-world experience.

For instance, years ago, I signed up at a local adult education program to take a course in mail order. At the time, I had a small mail order business, and I had been in direct marketing for decades . . . but I am always reading and taking classes to see what extra knowledge I can pick up. When the class started, it was obvious the instructor—a business teacher at a local community college—was reading from a textbook and had absolutely zero experience in and knowledge of mail order.

The class members bombarded her with questions that she could not answer. Since I had identified myself when the teacher took attendance, I was tapped into answering them and pretty much teaching the rest of the class—not what I wanted.

I once read an article by professional speaker Mike Aun in which he talked about the fact that in addition to being a speaker, he ran a successful insurance agency. He asserted that no one should be solely a full-time professional speaker; having a real business gave him the knowledge and content he needed to deliver in his talks.

I agree with Aun. When I give a seminar on copywriting, I am frequently asked whether I just give seminars or do I still write copy. I am proud to reply that I am an active participant in every area (copywriting, internet marketing, book publishing, freelance writing) that I teach others through my how-to writing and speaking.

I don't see how I could do otherwise. Active participation keeps your skills sharp and your knowledge level current. It also gives you a living laboratory in which to test out your ideas to make sure your advice works in the real world. And, it establishes your credibility with the audience or reader.

I once heard a speaker tell a group of aspiring speakers to read books on their topics an hour a day every day for a full year. "If you do, you will be an expert on your topic and qualified to teach it to others," the speaker said. To which I reply: no, you won't. You will have a theoretical knowledge of your topic. But you will lack the confidence and depth of knowledge that having actual experience in a process, skill, or activity gives you.

The other danger of learning only by reading instead of doing is that a lot of how-to writers don't know their subjects that well, and they frequently give wrong advice. But if you have no experience and don't test out an idea or method, you have no way of knowing that what you are reading is wrong, and you will likely pass misinformation on to others, doing your readers and listeners a disservice.

Get other people to write your book for you online

If you find SMEs who prefer to answer interview questions via email rather than over the phone, consider yourself fortunate, because their answers are, in a sense, rough drafts of sections of your book.

Ask one or two questions at a time instead of many in one email, if the SME is agreeable. When you only ask one question per email, the SME's answers are typically longer and more detailed. Print and file each email reply from your SMEs as back-up documentation for your source material.

Use the text copy-and-paste feature to clip the answers out of the email directly into your document file. Edit as needed and attribute the information to the source. If something is unclear or you want more information, reply to the email asking for clarification or elaboration. Those answers too can be copied out of the email and pasted directly into the document.

The advantage of email interviews is twofold. First, it saves you time, because the interview subject is effectively doing the writing (at least the first draft) for you. Second, SMEs tend to be more specific when writing email replies than in phone or face-to-face interviews. Reticence disappears and they happily type away, giving you useful answers.

The disadvantage of email interviews is also twofold. First, some interview subjects do not have the time or are not willing to be interviewed by email, so the technique isn't always applicable. Second, the email interview, while interactive, is less so than a traditional interview. Plus, you can't hear the tone of voice behind the answers or observe body language, so you may miss emotional aspects or get incomplete information.

Tip: You can use multiple interview techniques on a single SME. I do, and my process is as follows: First, I email a list of 10 to 12 questions in advance of the phone interview, so the subject can prepare. Then I call and conduct the interview over the phone. Once the interview is finished, I review my notes, and invariably a few more questions arise. These I email to the subject, who usually prefers to answer with quick back-and-forth emails.

Interviewing subject matter experts

How can you get subject matter experts to share their expertise with you, especially when you are not compensating them in any way? It is surprisingly easier than you might think.

If you are writing a magazine or major website article, tell the SME the name of the publication or site. Many experts seek publicity, and they will talk to online reporters, bloggers, magazines and newspapers in the hopes of getting free PR.

If you are self-publishing the material, many SMEs will still talk with you. A percentage of people love to talk and share what they know, and it is this group that will be your best interview subjects—far better than someone who, though a knowledgeable expert, is aloof and uncooperative.

How do you find experts in your field? If you are an active participant in your niche, you are already aware of who the gurus are. They are the people who give keynote speeches at the conventions, write the books, and contribute the articles and columns to the trade publications.

Thanks to the internet, it is easier to reach out to these gurus than ever. In many instances, their bios and blurbs contain their website address and sometimes their email address. If not, most can be found quickly with a Google search of their name. Get in touch, reference where you heard about them (e.g., you read their most recent column), and ask whether they would mind answering a few questions.

> **Tip:** Use the 2X rule to determine how much research you must do. The 2X rule says you should gather approximately twice as much research material as you think you will need to write the piece.
>
> **Reason:** Having gathered 2X as much information as you need, you can be selective and use only the research that best supports and illustrates your points. When you collect the bare minimum research to get by, the piece you write invariably sounds thin and puffy.

Launching writing projects on your blog

Robert Scoble published his book on blogging, *The Red Couch*, on his blog as he was writing it. The advantage to this is you get feedback in the comments after each post, which you can use to do rewrites and edits.

Your blog is a good place to test out new ideas for books, articles, and reports. Post a brief version of the idea. If it generates a flurry of comments and conversation, you may have a winner. In addition, the comments may give you additional information and insight into the topic that aids you in your writing.

I am not an attorney, but I suspect that using comments on blogs in other writings is a gray area. That's ironic, considering bloggers routinely quote writings from other sources without asking for permission. Still, print has more permanence than the web. So if you want to incorporate blogging content into a hard copy publication, you may want to check with an attorney.

Writers with an outsider's perspective

To be fair, not everyone agrees that the more the writer knows, the better, although dissenters on this opinion are in the definite minority. One such dissenter is Nicole, a freelance writer who makes the argument that the less she knows about the topic when she begins an article, the better. "I've been writing feature articles for a local magazine for four years, and in my experience, the better articles have been the ones I knew the least about going into it," says Nicole.

How can knowing less about a topic rather than more be an advantage to a writer? "The less I know, the more curious I am, and the more questions I have," says Nicole. "Also, I think I write more objectively when I am learning something new, rather than having opinion or bias from the start."

As a how-to writer, you can generally get away with having less knowledge of a topic only when you are writing to an audience of neophytes who also know little to nothing about the topic.

"I'm a go-between from the expert to the general public," says Nicole. "The less I know about the topic, the more I know what questions they [the public] are likely to want answered. When you have experience, it's easy to forget what someone may not know about a subject. I do the research and interpret the information for my readers."

Use free content in the public domain

Any published material that is no longer protected by copyright law for one reason or another is in the public domain. For written works, that would generally mean anything published before 1923. The long answer is a little more complicated.

The US Copyright Office's publication on doing copyright searches states: "The U.S. copyright in any work published or copyrighted prior to January 1, 1923, has expired by operation of law, and the work has permanently fallen into the public domain in the United States."

For various reasons, another long body of works entered the public domain in 1963. Generally this happened because they were not eligible for copyright protection originally or the owner failed to renew the copyright in the last year of its original protection.

Works created before January 1978, but not published with a copyright notice or registered, are permanently in the public domain. Works created on or after January 1978 are automatically given copyright protection—generally the life of the author plus 70 years or 95 to 120 years, whichever is shorter.

Public domain in contrast to works whose use is restricted by copyright

Most original works of art—literature, paintings, film, photographs—are protected under copyright laws for a specific period of time. When the copyright expires, the work enters public domain.

It may be in public domain for many reasons other than a lapsed copyright. The work may have been published before there was a copyright law or its protection has expired. Maybe the copyright was lost or never applied for. Sometimes authors or artists dedicate their work to the public domain so that everyone has free access to it. It may even be that the work was never entitled to copyright protection, as are many government publications.

Attorney Stephen Fishman in his book *The Public Domain: How to Find & Use Writings, Music, Art & More*, states: "Copyright experts estimate that 85% of all works of authorship first published in the United States between 1922 and 1963 are in the public domain." He says there are at least 85,000 works in the public domain.

There are even works published today that might contain items that are in the public domain, such as the facts and ideas in a work. U.S. government works and many blank forms are denied copyright protection completely and are, therefore, in the public domain. This is because these government publications are all paid for with taxpayer dollars, and so everyone in America who pays taxes should be entitled to use them in any way we please.

When work enters the public domain it is available for anyone to use as they see fit. An example of this would be *Grimm's Fairy Tales*. Disney was able to take the original stories, edit them, and turn them into film because they were in the public domain. Does that give you any ideas?

Copyright laws are specific to the country in which the intellectual property was produced, so if you want to use something from Great Britain, for instance, you'll have to research their copyright laws and be sure the piece you want to use is no longer protected. At www.gov.uk/intellectual -property-an-overview you can find information on intellectual property use in Great Britain.

And it may be more difficult to search records in countries other than the United States. For example, the above-mentioned intellectual property website in the UK states: "You should remember that as copyright is an automatic right, there are no registers that can be checked to locate the creator or right holder in a work. There are, though, organizations representing copyright owners who may be able to assist you in tracking them down."

But if a country is a treaty party of the U.S. (a "treaty party" is a country or intergovernmental organization other than the United States that is a party to an international agreement), works created by nationals of that country are eligible for copyright protection in the United States, according it (the work) protection by the US Copyright Laws now in effect. In any case, all works are subject to the laws of the country in which they were created.

You can learn more about the copyright laws of other countries by going to the UNESCO website (www.unesco.org) and then searching international copyright laws, or at the WIPO (World Intellectual Property Organization) site: www.wipo.int/portal/index.html.en.

For our purposes as information packagers, the main use for public domain content is creating an information product to sell. Three ways to do this are:

1. Find a public domain work and republish it as is.

2. Find a public domain work and publish an illustrated, annotated, expanded, or otherwise enhanced edition.

3. Compile multiple shorter public domain works into one "new" work.

If you want to make money marketing information products on the internet, but you're not a writer and you don't know where to start, public domain content can help you start and run a successful information marketing business online.

Selling public domain content

Suppose you've discovered a niche market that you know the public is interested in and you want to get information out to them. Or suppose you have a service and you want to promote it by creating an e-zine. Public domain information may be the easiest way to fill the niche.

Starting from scratch, researching the information and then writing it may take endless hours. You could spend half that time finding the content in the public domain, making it suitable for your purpose, and putting it on your website. If you can't write, it can be much less expensive to find something in the public domain and use it instead of hiring someone like me to write it for you.

You can use existing works to resell, to promote your own product or service, to add value to what you're selling, or to capture addresses for further marketing. The possibilities are endless.

New works are created every day from existing public domain content. Stage and screen plays are adapted from stories we know and love. Edgar Allan Poe was grist for many wonderful horror movies.

When a work enters the public domain, reproductions are possible. Royalties no longer have to be paid. We then have low-cost editions, making the work more accessible to everyone. Best of all, when you find a great public domain work that nobody else knows about, you can create a valuable info product out of it without writing a word yourself. Some other things you might do are:

- Use portions of different books to create a new themed book of your own. It can be much easier to use existing works than to start from scratch. You can update archaic language and facts and annotate and add to the existing material.

  My republishing of *Scientific Advertising* by Claude Hopkins is a good example of this. The original by Claude Hopkins is offered intact, but I added reprints of ads that illustrate Hopkins's principles, as well as annotations explaining how to implement his ideas. These illustrations and annotations surround the complete text of the original book. I also added a "lost" document of 47 creeds Hopkins wrote, which was also in public domain.

- Use public domain content to create bonus reports for inclusion with your product or as an incentive to purchase. My e-book *How to Become Successfully Self-Employed* has a report in the appendix created from a public domain book from 1908 purchased in a used bookstore for $5.

- Use public domain content to create an e-course and market it on your website. You can begin by using the table of contents to develop your e-course. There are many courses in the public domain that just need a little updating. From there you might turn it into a video to sell online. For instance, the famous Audio Forum foreign language cassette course, promoted in ads with the headline "Speak Spanish Like a Diplomat," was made from public domain audio recordings. Millions of dollars' worth of these tapes were sold.

- Use public domain poems and photos to create posters. There are a wealth of photos and illustrations available in the public domain that you can match up with sayings or poems to create posters to sell on your site.

Copyright laws were enacted to encourage artists to create unique works and to protect them when they did. The really wonderful thing about public domain content is that it promotes artistic freedom.

When a work is copyright protected, the author can restrict how it is used. Suppose you want to produce a play, but you want to modernize it somewhat. If it is copyright protected, you'll have to get the author's permission to make any changes. This limits your own artistic expression. Once it enters public domain, you're free to interpret it any way you like.

Once material enters public domain it is available to us all to view and to read. No one creates in a vacuum. Access to these works can inspire you to create works of your own, or may be sold by you "as is" to others.

Don't forget PLR content

Public Label Rights (PLR) is content that, similar to public domain works, can be used by you in your information products, but with two important differences.

First, PLR content is in the public domain *not* because it has an expired copyright. Rather, PLR content is created specifically for you and other information marketers to reuse in our own writings and information products.

Second, while PLR is deliberately not copyrighted, the PLR sellers do charge a license fee for the right to use their PLR content. The fees are usually extremely affordable, making PLR an economic source of ready-to-use content for your own information products.

You can buy and download PLR content online at numerous sites; here are a few resources for finding and downloading PLR content online:

- www.plrproducts.com
- www.master-resale-rights.com/private-label-rights
- www.idplr.com/38-e-books

Use other authors' works with permission

You can use content from other authors' copyrighted works in your own writings. The author's copyright, when in force, covers the exact wording of the text as it is written.

You may use short excerpts without permission. Though these guidelines are not absolute, excerpts should be 50 words or fewer from an article, and no more than 300 words from a book.

These guidelines fall into what is commonly called "fair usage," which allows using another author's words in your own writings without permission or payment, but only for relatively short excerpts.

You can use longer excerpts from a copyrighted source only by getting the publisher's or author's permission in writing.

These rules apply to using content from the source document exactly as written. Copyright technically covers just the author's text—sentences and paragraphs written by her. But it does not cover ideas or information.

You are generally allowed to appropriate ideas or information from other sources, though it is customary to acknowledge the source when doing so, usually in footnotes, end notes, or within the body of the text.

No part of any poem, song, drawing, graphic, or photo from other sources may be reprinted in your work, even minimal excerpts, without written permission; see Appendix B for a model permission letter you can use.

Note: I am not an attorney and therefore this advice should be considered as a guideline only; it is not legal advice. To minimize any potential liability from using material from other sources, consult an attorney, preferably one with copyright and trademark expertise.

Your content gold mine

For the how-to writer, content is solid gold. Much of that content is locked away in your brain as experience, skill, knowledge, and memory. You carry it with you and, naturally, your recall and retrieval—unless you possess a photographic memory—is imperfect.

But in the email and computer age, a lot of your knowledge is documented in writing: in emails, memos, newsletters, blog posts, tweets, articles, books, reports, PowerPoint presentations, and any other written content you have created. Author Jeff Davidson suggests that many of these business reports could (with permission, where needed), easily be turned into useful how-to articles.

Unlike the content in your brain, your written content can be retrieved in its accurate and original condition, provided it is stored in a manner that allows you to find it quickly, and in a format (say, Microsoft Word or Google Docs) that makes it easy to use in your new writings.

If content is gold on the internet, your hard drive becomes the gold mine. Here are some tips for managing the content gold mine on your PC's hard drive to your advantage:

1. Create a sensible electronic filing system, with directories and subdirectories organized in a manner that is logical and intuitive to you, regardless of whether it is logical and intuitive to others.

2. When you create a document, type the file name in the upper-left corner of page one. That way, when you have a hard copy in hand, you always know the file name and can quickly retrieve it from your hard drive with the file search feature.

3. Save any content related to your niche that you think you might have use for some day. These include your own writings, as well as content from outside sources.

4. *Always indicate on the file the date the content was created and, if taken from an outside source, details on the source* (e.g., name of publication,

issue date, page numbers, author, title). Without these attribution details readily available, you may not be able to use the material. For hard copy files, such as articles you clip from the newspaper, write the source on the article in pen.

5. Convert materials you may want to use in the future to file formats that are easy to paste into Word documents.

6. When you acquire source documents, print and save the documents in a file cabinet, but also save the electronic versions. Why? Because you can capture images (charts, graphs, and diagrams) to use in your own writing. Of course, you need to obtain the author's permission; for this, use the permission form in the appendix.

7. When in doubt, clip and save material you might want to refer to someday for a writing project. At the same time, don't be like the famous Collier brothers, who saved every newspaper they ever bought in their Manhattan brownstone until it became a rat-infested fire hazard; some of the piled newspapers tipped over and killed one of the brothers. When you want to save something, tear it out of the magazine or newspaper, and save just the clipping, not the entire publication. Make sure the publication name, date, and pages are noted on the clipping.

8. Back up your entire hard drive to the cloud every 24 hours. I automatically set mine to back up in the middle of the night while I am sleeping.

As a how-to author, your readers are not buying your stuff for your dazzling prose style. They are buying it for the valuable problem-solving information you provide. To make your how-to writing more useful to these readers, you need solid content. Even if you are a subject matter expert yourself, your writing will be stronger when you augment your own knowledge with additional material. That's why every serious how-to writer must research and accumulate facts, knowledge, methods, strategies, and ideas to share with readers.

Subject-specific web-based research sources

General Resources

General resources are bound to cover subjects in an incomplete manner. However, they have their uses, especially when you look for a subject which is not often discussed, such as, say, Polish presence in the U.S.

catalog.loc.gov/vwebv/searchBrowse—The Library of Congress Online Catalog web page. You can search the catalog with the "basic search" function by title, author, subject, keywords, etc., or by "guided search," which is much like the advanced search feature offered by various search engines.

search.credoreference.com—"Searching 3,588,406 full text articles in 4,174 titles from publishers." You can search by topic page.

www.wikipedia.org—Wikipedia, though it provides readers with varying degrees of credibility, can be a good initial place for your research. Credible articles have references at the end, so start with these.

libguides.cos.edu/az.php—College of the Sequoias in California. 75 academic electronic databases.

library.nyu.edu/locations/bern-dibner-library—The Bern Dibner Library at the Polytechnic Institute of New York University. In the "Articles & Databases" section, you'll find numerous databases for various disciplines, such as biology, computer science, business, health science, and more.

guides.nyu.edu/az.php—New York University (NYU) libraries: Databases A-Z. Extensive list that can be narrowed done by subject, database type and publisher; organized alphabetically.

hostingfacts.com/internet-facts-stats—Hosting Facts publishes yearly statistics about the internet.

News Resources

allmedialink.com—An extensive list of national and international newspaper and media sources.

www.loc.gov/rr/news/lists.html—A page on the Library of Congress website titled "News & Periodical Resources on the Web." It presents a comprehensive list, arranged by Newspaper Websites, Current News Services, Other News & Hybrid Lists/Engines, and Periodicals. Some of the links lead you straight to a website; others—to more links.

www.onlinenewspapers.com—Directory for the world's newspapers, listed by region and country.

Finance Resources

Note: all the sites listed below are free.

finance.yahoo.com—Yahoo's excellent site for all money matters: it provides information about the stock market, funds, industries, financial news, and much more.

www.google.com/finance—Google's finance section is yet another site focused on market-related news, quotes etc.

www.wtrg.com/daily/crudeoilprice.html—WTRG's website provides daily oil prices.

www.kitco.com—KITCO is a website devoted to precious metals (gold, silver, platinum, and palladium) and provides news, quotes, and charts.

bigcharts.marketwatch.com—The BigChart site presents charts for all traded stocks, mutual funds, futures, etc.

www.sec.gov/edgar.shtml—Edgar online, the SEC's (Security & Exchange Commission) website.

moneyqanda.com/five-best-websites-for-stock-quotes—List of ("best") websites or stock quotes.

Statistics Resources

www.lib.umich.edu/clark-library/collections/government-information—The University of Michigan Library, Clark Library Government Information, which includes statistics, reports, legislation, and policy information from all levels of government.

www.bls.gov—U.S. Department of Labor, Bureau of Labor Statistics site; provides statistics about employment, consumer-related matters, earnings, occupations, and much more.

www.usa.gov/statistics—Data and statistics about the U.S.; has links to various government statistics sites.

www.census.gov—U.S. Census Bureau; presents comprehensive data. The entire data base is updated every ten years. However, reports on various subjects are published frequently (e.g. a report from May 23, 2019, on the fastest growing cities in the nation). A side note: the home page has a running population clock in the U.S. and in the world (you'll need to click on the arrow to its right).

www.cia.gov/library/publications/resources/the-world-factbook/index.html—The CIA World Factbook.

www.worldometers.info—An interesting page that runs a continuous clock on various subjects (population, economics, spending, social media, food, energy, deforestation, and more).

researchguides.library.tufts.edu/SocSciData—The Libraries of Tufts University (Medford, MA): Social Science Data and Statistics Resources. Datasets and statistics by subject.

Marketing and Commerce Resources

Market research studies are a great source of information. However, free access to results of market research studies is very limited and is usually second-hand information, typically by way of an article quoting the study. (Prices for each of these reports are usually in the hundreds to thousands of dollars range.)

www.dmnews.com—DM (Direct Marketing) News provides comprehensive coverage of direct marketing, databases, and online marketing and advertising.

thedma.org—The Direct Marketing Association is a global trade association of business and nonprofit organizations using and supporting direct marketing tools and techniques. The site includes also information about marketing compliance resources and marketing accountability.

Business Resources

www.linkedin.com/directory/companies—LinkedIn Company Directory: Top companies listed on home page; browse alphabetically.

www.yelp.com—Find companies by type of business and geographic location.

www.bbb.org—The Better Business Bureau. Find companies by type of business (or a specific company) and geographic location. Companies are graded, including those that do not have accreditation with the BBB.

www.yellowpages.com—Again, find companies by type of business and geographic location.

blog.hubspot.com/blog/tabid/6307/bid/10322/the-ultimate-list-50-local-business-directories.aspx: provides a list of 50 online local business directories.

Health and Medical Field Resources

In many instances, you can find the best sources for information about medical and health matters via queries on the scholarly search engines.

nnlm.gov—The National Network of Libraries of Medicine has a comprehensive list of questions to ask yourself while evaluating health websites. Most of the points in this list are actually good for evaluating any website, while some are specific to health-related online places.

www.nlm.nih.gov—The U.S. National Library of Medicine website has numerous databases: PubMed/MEDLINE (which includes scientific articles), ClinicalTrials.gov, TOXNET (toxicology data), and many more. The complete list of databases is at wwwcf2.nlm.nih.gov/nlm_eresources/eresources/search_database.cfm.

www.thelancet.com—The Lancet is a peer-reviewed medical journal. A considerable amount of information is available free on this site.

www.dhhs.gov—U.S. Department of Health and Human Services website.

www.webmed.com—A well respected site offering health information.

www.medscape.com—Another well-respected site, geared more toward health professionals.

www.mayoclinic.org—While the previous references present information in the form of articles, the well-known Mayo Clinic page is actually a search engine where you can find information on health matters. Additionally, you can find information on specific diseases.

www.healthy.net—Another vertical search engine. You can search "articles," "news," or "all." Additionally, it has expert columns, discussion boards, information about healthy ways to live (products, food, and recipes), and much more.

Science and Technology Resources

As with the health and medical arena, you may find some of the best sources for scientific information using scholarly search engines.

www.sciam.com—The periodical *Scientific American* online.

libguides.library.albany.edu/c.php?g=536836&p=3675232—SUNY (State University of New York) Albany's libraries website: Computer Science: A Brief Guide to Library Resources: Databases & Indexes.

www.nature.com/scitable—Scitable defines itself as "A Collaborative Learning Space for Science" and is hosted by Nature Publishing Group.

Social Sciences Resources

libraries.indiana.edu/research—Sources supplied by the libraries at Indiana University, Bloomington, for history, politics, culture, etc. Alphabetic search for various subjects.

guides.library.ucla.edu/reference—University of California, Los Angeles (UCLA) library: reference sources in the social sciences and humanities.

researchguides.library.tufts.edu/c.php?g=249153&p=5455468—The Libraries of Tufts University (Medford, MA): Social Science Data and Statistics Resources. Datasets and statistics by subject.

Entertainment Resources (Movies, TV, and More)

www.imdb.com—The Internet Movie Database website is probably the single best source for information about movies, actors, directors, TV shows, etc.

Government Resources

www.whitehouse.gov—The White House's website, usually with news, press releases, policies, etc.

www.senate.gov—The U.S. Senate website has legislations, schedules, statistics, information about the senators, and more.

www.house.gov—The U.S. House of Representatives website gives information about bills, committees, information about the representatives, and much more.

www.statelocalgov.net—The State and Local Government Internet directory provides convenient one-stop access to the websites of thousands of state, city, and county agencies. It collects information from over 11,500 websites, organized by state, topic, or local government. Although the site is updated frequently, information related to individual state or local government may not be up to date.

Legal Matters Resources

sjclawlibrary.org/research-resources—San Joaquin County Law Library's research resources. Since it is located in California, some of the sites concern local matters such as county and state. However, the site includes resources for federal laws. Click on "Catalog" and you can conduct searches by keyword, title, author, or subject.

www.lexadin.nl/wlg—The World Law Guide website claims that it supplies "More than 70,000 links to legal sites in more than 180 countries."

natlaw.com—The Kozolchyk National Law Center (NatLaw), a not-for-profit research and educational institution affiliated with the James E. Rogers College of Law at the University of Arizona in Tucson. The Center has been assisting international, as well as national governmental entities with all matters regarding free trade (including the NAFTA agreement), trade in general, and commercial law.

uscode.house.gov—Office of the Law Revision Counsel, Laws of the United States, and the U.S. Code ("The United States Code is a consolidation and codification by subject matter of the general and permanent laws of the United States").

www.priweb.com/lawdictionaries.htm—Prichard Law Webs is a commercial site of a consultant to law firms. It lists legal dictionaries on the web. Each listed site is accompanied with a short description and commentary.

www.ilrg.com—PublicLegal: over 2000 legal forms and documents from the Internet Legal Research Group (ILRG).

4

Products, Titles, and Outlines

L et's recap. In Chapter 1, we reviewed the basic tasks of the how-to writer and covered the four modes of learning (hearing, watching, reading, doing). In Chapter 2, we chose our niche or topic area. "How-to books cover just about all areas of life today," wrote L. Perry Wilbur and Jon Samsel in their book *How to Write Books That Sell*. "Just name a subject, and chances are good there is a how-to book on it." In Chapter 3, we looked at ways to research our subject.

The next three decisions the how-to writer must make are: 1) determining what media and formats to write for; 2) selecting the title of the how-to product; and 3) assessing the contents—what to cover in the product. What is the subject of the document? How narrow or broad is the coverage of the topic? How much detail and depth will it go into?

Media and format selection

Media refers to the medium in which the information product is published. The basic media are digital (PDF, streaming audio, and video), hard copy (books, magazines, newsletters), physical media (flash drives, CDs, DVDs), and interactive (software, websites). Within each medium, content can be formatted in different ways. For example, audio can be burned onto a CD or downloaded as an MP3 file. A flash drive can contain all of these, plus data, reference tables, graphs, videos, and software.

Which media and format should you choose for the how-to instructional information you write? If you are self-publishing, the sky's the limit. Even traditional publishers are being more creative these days, packaging books with CDs and objects (e.g., a book on card tricks comes with a deck of cards).

There are four factors that determine which medium and format are best for presenting how-to material: learning mode, topic, personal preference, and profit potential.

1. In Chapter 1, we talked about the four modes of learning. One reason why how-to writers today publish in multiple media is to reach the widest audience by creating how-to materials for all four learning modes. My observation is that most people have a major learning mode, one or two minor learning modes, and one or two learning modes they don't care for at all. Table 4.1 shows the four learning modes and the information products that appeal to each.

Table 4.1. Learning Modalities, Media, and Formats

Learning Modality	Media and Format
Reading	E-books, books, articles, reports, websites, tip sheets, monographs
Watching	TV, online videos, DVDs, YouTube, movies
Hearing	Podcasts, MP3s, audio CDs, teleseminars, webinars, lectures, speeches
Doing (experiential learning)	Workshops, boot camps, classes, training sessions, coaching, e-classes

2. Your *topic* might dictate the most appropriate learning mode. Some subjects are taught best in specific modes. Golf, for example, is learned primarily through doing (practice), with watching being the second choice; i.e., you can watch the pros do the swing you want to learn on video, which makes DVDs and online video a good medium for golf instruction.

3. The third factor that dictates learning mode is personal preference, both yours and your audience's. For example, a large segment of my list is writers and aspiring writers. Most writers prefer *reading* as the primary learning mode, so a lot of my information products are traditional books, e-books, and other text-based media.

4. The fourth factor that dictates choice of media and format is profit potential. Will you make more money putting on live golf classes or producing and selling a golf video? Can you charge enough for the video to make a decent profit? What channels of distribution would your video sell through?

Word length and information density considerations

Be sure to factor in word length when considering format and media options. (Word length, of course, refers to the number of words in the document; Microsoft Word makes it easy to write to a specific word length, because it shows you how many words and characters are in your document.)

When you are writing under contract for a publisher or publication, word length is specified by your contract. I produce a column for *Target Marketing* magazine every other month that must come out to 1,000 words; the editor will not accept a piece that is shorter or longer by more than 20 percent.

When you produce the information product yourself, whether it's a self-published book or a 60-minute podcast, the length is determined by the format you choose. You cannot, for example, fit a 20,000-word lecture into a one-hour online radio show; no one talks that fast. Typical word length for a variety of formats is shown in Table 4.2.

Table 4.2. Word Length of Different Information Products

Information Product	Approximate Length in Words
Paperback nonfiction book, 200 pages	80,000
E-book, 50 pages	15,000
Audio CD, 60 minutes	7,000
Video, long, 60 minutes	6,000
White paper, 10 pages	3,000
Speech, 20 minutes	2,500
Free e-newsletter	400+
Magazine article, 2 pages	1,500
Magazine column, 1 page	800

Information density refers to the number of points or ideas per page or per chapter. Are you trying to cram too much information into your how-to document? You can have a higher word density when writing instruction for people who are experienced or professional. For instance, research studies published in medical magazines are often densely written with heavy use of technical terms. These journals are written by doctors for other doctors.

When writing to newbies or others with limited knowledge and experience, the information density should be lighter. Limit the content to one central idea or skill per chapter, section, or page. Instead of overwhelming the reader with too much content, it's better to ladle it out bit by bit; readers like to understand concept A before going on to concept B.

Titles, heads, and subheads

By title we mean the title of the book; by head, we mean the title of a chapter; and subheads are the bold headers used to separate sections of a chapter.

A good title can boost sales of a book tremendously. One of Ray Bradbury's novels has the rather poetic title *Something Wicked This Way Comes*. If he had simply called it *Here Comes Something Bad*, I don't think the book would have sold as well.

The title is vitally important because it is often used in the marketing copy created to sell your book. You can come up with a wholly original title, or you can model your title after what people are already using. For example, "Quick and Easy" is a popular phrase in titles, as is "Made Easy." So if your book is about baking cakes, your title could be *Quick and Easy Cake Baking* or *Cake Baking Made Easy*.

The main purpose of the title is to grab readers' attention and make them want to get their hands on the book. Emotional titles are more compelling than titles that are just a straightforward description of the book contents. Dale Carnegie sold millions of copies of *How to Win Friends and Influence People*. Would he have sold half as many if he had titled the book *Interpersonal Skills*? What do you think?

Effective titles appeal to fundamental human desires that drive our behavior. According to marketing consultant Wendy Montes de Oca, the core drivers of human behavior include the desires for belonging or love; control and security; change; recognition; achievement; growth; pride; and the need to contribute.

While there is no set word length for titles, as a rule, shorter titles are better than longer ones, for one simple reason: the shorter the title, the bigger and bolder it can be on the front cover. If you have a title much longer than ten words, consider breaking it into two parts: a title and a subtitle. In such a two-part title, the main title is usually a grabber, while the subtitle is more descriptive of the contents. One example is a career book I wrote years ago called *Dream Jobs: A Guide to Tomorrow's Top Careers*. Exceptions? Of course.

Sometimes a longer title is needed to tell the whole story; e.g., *How to Write and Sell Simple Information for Fun and Profit*. We could have shortened it by moving "fun and profit" to a subtitle; but we didn't feel it had the same ring to it. Part of title selection is simply your subjective appraisal of how snappy and appealing the title sounds.

The chapter titles and subheads help guide the reader through the material and break the writing up into short sections. Is this a good thing? Yes. As a rule, you should use short sentences, short sections within chapters, and short chapters.

When in doubt about whether to break a very long chapter into two chapters, choose the latter, because readers like short chapters. Many readers feel obligated to keep reading until they finish the current chapter, and they don't want to wait too long to accomplish that goal.

Table 4.3. Titling Conventions

Titling Convention	Example
101_____	101 Ways to Save Time and Money
Everything You Ever Wanted to Know About _____ but Were Afraid to Ask	Everything You Ever Wanted to Know About Sex but Were Afraid to Ask
How to _____	How to Win Friends and Influence People
The _____ Hand-book	The Copywriter's Handbook
Secrets _____	Secrets of Successful Telephone Selling
_____ Made Easy	Horseback Riding Made Easy
A Guide to _____	A Guide to Marketing with Social Networks
_____ that _____	Ads that Sell
Get Paid to _____	Get Paid to Gamble
_____ for Fun and Profit	Growing Earthworms for Fun and Profit
_____ in a Box	Résumé Business in a Box
_____ Toolkit	The Landlord's Toolkit
Getting Started as a _____	Getting Started as a Professional Speaker
_____ on a Shoestring	Trading Options on a Shoestring
The 10-Step _____ Plan	The 10-Step Marketing Plan
_____ Manual	The Become-A-Millionaire Manual
Quick and Easy_____	Quick and Easy Cake Baking
_____ for Beginners	Bridge for Beginners
The ___ Most Common Questions About ___	The 17 Most Common Questions About Divorce . . . and One Good Answer to Each
_____ for_____	Careers for Writers
Quick Tips for _____	Quick Tips for Better Business Writing
____ing for _____	Writing for Interactive Media
_____ : The Complete Guide	Grouting: the Complete Guide

Organizing your content

Selecting the right organizational scheme for your writing is vital to making your how-to document easy to follow. As editor Jerry Bachetti points out: "If the reader believes the content has some importance to him, he can plow through a report even if it is dull or has lengthy sentences or big words. But if it's poorly organized, forget it. There's no way to make sense of what was written."

"Organize your material logically," writes Marcia Yudkin, "then use headings to make it super-easy for readers to know what is discussed where."

In some instances, the material itself dictates the organizational scheme. In other situations, there is no "right way" to organize the piece, and so you must decide how you want to organize the material. Here are some common organizational schemes used in how-to writing today:

- *Alphabetical order*—A book on vitamins and minerals could present topics in alphabetical order, from vitamin A to zinc.

- *Order of location*—A book on the solar system could begin with Mercury, the planet closest to the sun, and end with Pluto or Neptune, depending on whether you still classify Pluto as a planet.

- *Order of increasing difficulty*—Training manuals often start with the easiest skills, so the user can experience success early in the training program. Then they move on to increasingly more difficult tasks.

- *Chronological order*—Presents the facts in the order in which they happened. History books are written in chronological order, as are profiles, biographies, and case studies.

- *Problem/solution*—Another format useful in case histories, as well as reports and marketing materials, the problem/solution document begins with "Here's what the problem was" and ends with "Here's how we solved it and the results we achieved" (e.g., your electric bill was too high; the solution was to install solar panels on the roof).

- *Inverted pyramid*—The newspaper style of news reporting where the lead paragraph summarizes the story (telling who, what, when, where, why, and how) and the paragraphs that follow present the facts in order of *decreasing* importance. You can use this format in journal articles, reports, letters, memos, and press releases.

- *Deductive order*—Lead with a generalization, and then support it with particulars. Most newspaper editorials are written using deductive order. Scientists use this format in research papers that begin with the findings and then state the supporting evidence. An example is Charles Darwin's *On the Origin of Species*. The book states that we evolve through natural selection, and then it presents hundreds of pages to prove the point.

- *Inductive order*—Begin with specific instances, and then lead the reader to the ideas or principles these instances suggest. Inductive order works well for nonfiction articles and scientific research reports.

- *List*—Content that is organized as a list is easy to read and easy to write. Examples include *The 7 Habits of Highly Effective People* and "The 7 Early Warning Signs of High Blood Pressure," the latter an advertisement selling a book on controlling your blood pressure.

- *Question and answer*—Ask and answer a series of questions your readers are likely to have about the subject; e.g., "The 7 most common questions about search engine optimization—and one good answer to each."

Outlining with mind maps

In the previous section we looked at common organizational schemes for how-to writing. But how do you decide what to include and what to leave out? How do you organize the material you do include?

Software programs like Mindjet allow you to organize your topic using mind maps. In a mind map, you start with a central topic, and then branch out to related ideas. And you don't have to use software, either. I created the mind map shown in Figure 4.1 with nothing more than a pencil and pad.

How does it work? Write your main topic in a big circle in the center. Following along in Fig. 4.1, that would be "Nonfiction Writing."

Next, off of that circle, add circles with major subtopics in them; e.g., "Media."

From media, I instantly thought to break it into three subtopics: audio, video, and print. If I leave something out, I can always go back and add more circles. From audio, I had two sub-subtopics connected to it: podcasts and audio CDs (by the way, Fig. 4.1. is incomplete).

Fig. 4.1. A mind map for this book.

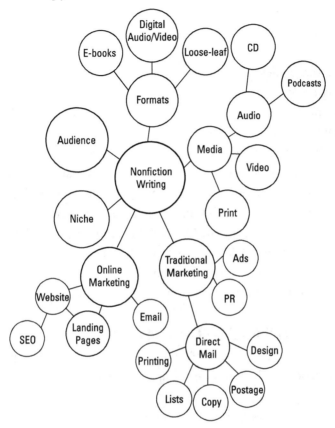

You work with the diagram, adding more and more topics and subtopics as you think of them. When you absolutely can't think of another, you're done!

The center circle is the main topic of your book. The circles radiating from the center are chapters. The circles radiating from the chapter topics are headers for the various sections of the chapter.

Mind maps are great for authors who think visually, because they are a picture of the outline. For authors like me who think in words, a straightforward and conventional outline works best, which is why the mind map in Fig. 4.1 remains incomplete. But how do you create such an outline?

Index card method

Here is an easy method of creating a book outline or table of contents. It requires no computer or software—only a pack of small index cards and a pencil.

Write topics that you should cover in the book, one topic per card. Don't worry about organizing anything or whether the subject is a topic, subtopic, or sub-subtopic. Just keep writing until you can't think of any more subjects to cover.

Next, make piles of the cards according to major categories. For a book on setting up your first aquarium, you might have one pile of cards on the different species of fish, another on setting up the aquarium, and a third on maintaining your fish tank. Additional card piles might cover topics like fish food and feeding, another on disease treatment, and yet another on breeding.

Write a broad description of each topic (e.g., breeding) on a blank card and put each of these title cards on the appropriate pile. Within each pile, organize the cards under each title card in a sensible order.

Next, put the piles into one big stack in the order in which you want to cover the major topics. When done, type what is on every card into a Word file, with the category for each pile in boldface. When you are done, you will have a rough outline for your book or report.

Check out competing table of contents

After you have used mind-mapping, index cards, or simply adapted one of the organizational schemes in this chapter, how do you know whether your outline is complete?

Go to the bookstore, library, or online. Find nonfiction books and white papers on the same topic as your information product. Look at the table of contents in each. When you see a major topic that you omitted, make a note of it in a note pad you carry with you. After you are done, compare the notes you've made against your outline. Add any topics or subtopics you missed that you think you should include. Now you can rest comfortably knowing you've done your "due diligence" on the outline.

Next up . . .

Okay. You have a detailed, accurate, comprehensive outline with topics organized in a way that makes sense. You have accumulated your research materials and identified content sources. Now it is time to sit down and write your how-to book, e-book, white paper, article, or report. We'll look at how to do that job in Chapter 5.

5

Becoming a Master How-To Writer

It's easy to be a mediocre how-to writer. And while becoming a good or even great how-to writer isn't brain surgery, it does require practice, persistence, dedication, and mastery of a few principles most writers seem unaware of.

Levels of the game

The most basic mistake made by even experienced writers who turn their hand to how-to and self-help writing is telling readers "what to do" instead of showing them "how to do it."

My friend Dr. Jeffrey Lant gives the example of a book on small business marketing that told the reader to "try advertising on matchbook covers." That's "what to do" writing.

At the next level up, said Jeffrey, you should tell the reader *how* to do advertising on matchbooks. How many words of copy can you fit? What does it cost per thousand matchbooks? Who do you call to place your ad? What products are appropriate to advertise on matchbook covers?

At the highest level is *doing it for them*. In this case, the book could have supplied templates for sample matchbook ads the reader could adapt to his own business.

The lazy writers out there think they are writing how-to, but are really writing mostly what-to-do.

Experienced how-to writers strive to write clear instructions with sufficient details to enable the reader to perform the function or complete the task. You should do the same. If you can figure out a way to get to the highest level and do some or all of the work for your readers, they will love you for it.

A good example is Brownstone Publishing, which publishes paid subscription newsletters on legal issues for laypeople in various fields (schools, building management). Its articles don't just tell subscribers what to include in contracts. They provide boilerplate clauses the reader can drop into actual contracts!

Table 5.1 shows the hierarchy of instructional writing: what to do; how to do it; doing it for them. The lower you scroll down the table, the more satisfied your readers will be.

Table 5.1. Levels of How-To Writing

Level	Where Found
Why to do it	Motivational talks
What to do	Magazine articles
How to do it	Books, e-books, seminars, workshops
Do it for them	Online tools, templates, model forms, software

The 7 most common how-to writing mistakes and how to avoid them

One way to become a good how-to writer is to learn what not to do in your writing. In my role as a small online publisher, I frequently hire ghostwriters to write e-books for me. Though these are all professional writers, the quality of the writing ranges from good to downright abysmal. Here are the seven most common mistakes the writers I hire make when writing how-to e-books for me:

Mistake #1: Laziness

Many writers are just plain lazy. They don't want to do the hard work of researching their topic, so they fake it. As a result, the readers don't get the information they want or need, and they become frustrated. For instance, here's a paragraph one of my writers submitted to me in a draft of an e-book I hired her to write:

How much does printing postcards cost? Unfortunately, there's no good answer to this question. Depending on whether you use full color, black and white, black and white on colored paper, bleeds, die-cuts, odd-shaped postcards, how many you order and any number of other variables, you can spend anywhere from 5¢ per postcard to a dollar or more.

What's wrong with her copy is that there is a good answer to this question of what postcards cost to print. It's the writer's job to find it and present it to the reader. I told the writer to visit the websites of companies specializing in postcard marketing; their pricing schedules are listed right on the sites.

Mistake #2: Visit this site/Google it

The next draft was better. Instead of saying there's no answer to the question "What do postcards cost to print?", the writer gave the URLs of three websites of companies that specialize in postcard printing and told the reader to Google "postcard printers" for more.

That's fine, except the reader has paid us for a book that is supposed to give the information, not refer him to the internet for it. If he has to look at these sites for prices and then Google to find more price information, he is in essence doing the writer's job.

It's okay to suggest websites or Googling, but only after you have presented the information the reader needs. I would have given a summary of average printing costs for various postcard sizes and paper stocks instead of making the reader look for it.

Mistake #3: Logical contradictions

A logical contradiction is a statement that logically cannot be true. Here is an example from a manuscript one of my writers handed in to me:

By having a product on the internet, you have no overhead to worry about. All you have to do is have the product available for fast download for the customer. By watching your overhead, you can increase your profit margins. Also watching your overhead can influence product pricing.

Can you spot the logical contradiction? In the first sentence, he says internet businesses have no overhead. In the third sentence, he talks about watching "your overhead." If I have no overhead, what am I watching?

Mistake #4: Rambling

Here is an excerpt from a draft that same writer wrote for me for a book on measuring web metrics:

> *Many people seem to overlook this function of metrics. Or at least they don't pay much attention to it. When people come to your website, they perform actions which can be in the form of communications. These communications can be email, forms, video, chat, or whatever mechanism is in place to allow for such communication. By understanding the function of communications in metrics, it will force each webmaster or online business owner to pay more attention to this facet of their data collecting and measuring. For example, when someone clicks on an email link, fills out a form, or clicks to view a video, each one of these steps is a form of communication that webmasters should measure. This way they will know what actions their visitors take when visiting their website.*

It takes 135 words and basically says, "Web metrics are important and should be measured." Given that the reader has shelled out $29 for an e-book on web metrics, it's safe to assume he already thinks it's important. Therefore, this paragraph adds no new information or value and just takes up space. It's rambling and has no point or purpose.

Mistake #5: Not realizing that words have meaning

It frustrates me when professional writers I hire hand in e-book copy like this:

> *Your client owes you money. He/she has not responded to your calls or emails. You must assume at this point that something is wrong. Here's what I suggest. Find out why they are not responding to your calls or emails. You need to collect on the money that they owe.*
>
> *Your client did sign off on your work, agreeing to pay you. And, the company still owes you money. Importantly, this client may have*

done work for you in the past, and you want to perform more work with them in the future. Don't lose your client by being too aggressive, nasty, or rude. You must somehow reach them in a manner that will make everyone happy.

Every sentence is weak. "You need to collect on the money that they owe." Duh! "This client may have done work for you in the past." Wrong: You performed work for them. "You must somehow reach them in a manner that will make everyone happy." That's *what* to do, which is embarrassingly obvious. What the writer needs to tell us is *how* to reach them to collect the debt without offending anyone.

Mistake #6: Writing that says nothing

It's hard to believe, but the sample below was also submitted by a professional writer. It's an article for a chemistry website I have on careers in chemistry:

In order to consider a career in chemistry, you will need to study. Start with a major in chemistry. After this, depending on the career path you've chosen, you can move on to other courses. These will depend entirely on the job you want.

Becoming a chemist isn't for everyone. However, if you are particularly fond of atoms, then this could be for you.

In the first paragraph, we are told that to have a career in chemistry, we need to study chemistry. Wow, that's a helpful tip! And then after that, the courses we take should depend on what job we want. There's an original concept!

The second paragraph reads like a joke, except the writer was serious: A career in chemistry is for people who are "fond of atoms"? How someone can write this, submit it to me with a straight face, and expect to be paid is beyond me. Of course I made him rewrite it.

Here is the lead of an article I clipped from my local penny-saver newspaper. Why am I showing it to you? It's not a how-to piece, but it caught my attention because of its clean, simple, straightforward style:

> *During a Sept. 16 meeting, the Rochelle Park Township Committee issued a strong warning to owners who neglect their properties: Clean up or face a hefty fine.*
>
> *Mayor Frank Valenzuela said that properties are being left unattended throughout the township due to foreclosures, estate sales, etc. These property owners will now have to pay maintenance charges accrued by the Department of Public Works.*
>
> *"We're serious about this," said Valenzuela. "Any property that's in limbo and not being kept up is a quality-of-life issue."*

Notice how the piece flows smoothly and pulls the reader along in the story. I especially like the colon separating the two parts of the sentence in the first paragraph, which seems to propel the reader forward. Compare this bold, confident, competent writing with the weak, rambling drafts submitted to me in the five examples above.

Mistake #7: Running out of steam

Too many authors start off with great enthusiasm and write great introductions and opening chapters, only to gradually lose steam as they write, becoming lazier with each subsequent chapter.

I often get e-book manuscripts from writers where the initial chapters average ten pages each, but by the time we get to the middle and closing chapters, some chapters are literally a page or even half a page. This is a clear indication to me that the author is getting tired or running out of steam, and he is cheating the reader by delivering increasingly inferior and superficial chapters the further he gets.

Yes, to get and hold the reader's attention, the introduction and first chapter must be great. But that doesn't mean the rest of the book can be mediocre. The trick is to start on a high level and stay there.

While it's not mandatory, it's a good idea to have chapters that are similar in length and density. Having Chapter 3 be 50 pages and Chapter 15 be three pages is a sign of author fatigue. The solution? Either beef up Chapter 15 with more content or divide Chapter 3 into two or more smaller chapters so the chapter lengths throughout the book are more equal.

Note: Of the mistakes listed here, the last sin is the least egregious, and I have been known to make it myself from time to time. Still, it is better to avoid it if you can.

Matters of voice

By "voice" in how-to writing, we mean the writer's expertise in the topic matter and status in the field in relationship to the student's knowledge and position.

"To be a powerful and effective communicator, whether in print, on the platform, on TV or radio, you need to communicate in your own special voice," said Ted Nicholas in *The Success Margin*. Nicholas defined "voice" as "nothing less than the sum total of your words, expressions, personality, and mannerisms that make you—you."

As my colleague Nick Usborne points out, there are three basic voices you can take:

1. *The first voice is the "experienced expert."* If you have been in the field a long time, have a lot of experience, and are highly educated in the subject, your voice is that of a top expert patiently teaching others his craft or topic. This is the voice I use when writing about marketing and copywriting, which I have done all of my professional life—for more than four decades. You can find it on my main website, www.bly.com, especially on the Articles page. Other examples of the experienced expert include Larry MacMillan on options trading, Suze Orman on personal finance, and James Lange on retirement and estate planning.

2. *The second voice is the knowledgeable participant.* This is the voice to use when you have not spent your life learning the field, but you do have more experience and expertise than your readers, and you are at least one or two steps ahead of them in the learning curve. You teach what you know, but are honest and admit you don't know everything, and point your readers to experts who know more in certain subtopics whenever appropriate.

3. *The third voice is the enthusiastic amateur.* Here, you freely admit that you are a peer of the reader rather than a superior, and your writings chronicle your adventures as you progress in your mastery of the craft or subject you are writing about. It has a collegial tone of "let's explore this great subject together!" You can find this tone

on my hobby site for aquarium hobbyists, www.aquariumdetective .com. John McPhee wrote several books on geology using this voice, because he was a reporter, not an expert.

Matters of tone

By tone, we mean: How does the writing sound? In good how-to writing, the tone should be conversational, easygoing, and natural. Your how-to writing should, in the words of a how-to writer in the personal computer field, sound like "a friendly, patient teacher looking over the reader's shoulder." We call this a personal or informal writing style.

Even if you are the authoritative expert, you should keep things simple and accessible. Remember, part of your job is to motivate readers into pursuing the activity, not scare them into quitting.

According to an article in the *Harvard Business Review*, here are the qualities of a personal writing style:

- Be warm.
- Use the active voice.
- Use personal pronouns.
- Use contractions.
- Write in a natural, conversational tone.
- Write in the first person and second person.
- Vary sentence length.
- Let your personality shine through.

Matters of style

What about "style"? Well, what is style? In his book *Opus 300*, Isaac Asimov notes that there are two chief aspects to any piece of writing: (1) what you say and (2) how you say it. The former is content and "the latter is style," says Asimov.

Since the primary goal of how-to writing is to communicate information, instruction, and ideas—and not tell a story, paint word pictures, or evoke strong feeling or emotion—the best style for the how-to writer is to say what you have to say in plain, simple English. "I think most writers, even the best, overwrite," said Truman Capote. "I prefer to underwrite. Simple, clear as a country creek."

A simple, unpretentious, informal, conversational style with a friendly, patient tone is ideal for how-to writing. Literary or poetic style has no place here, nor does obscurity or intellectual wordplay.

"I have an informal style, which means I tend to use short words and simple sentence structure," says Isaac Asimov. "The informal style pleases people who enjoy the sensation of feeling that the ideas are flowing from the writer's brain into their own without mental friction."

The 3 C's formula for nonfiction writing

The 3 C's formula is for all types of nonfiction writing, not just how-to. When you follow the formula, your writing will be quick, easy, and pleasurable to read, all of which are goals you should strive for. Here is the formula:

The first C is clarity. What you write must be clear. Not just to you or the client or the marketing director or the product manager, but to the prospects you hope to sell the product to.

Ralph Waldo Emerson defines clarity this way: "It is not enough to write so that you can be understood. You must write so that you cannot be misunderstood."

The typical advice given in writing classes about clarity is to use small words, short sentences, and short paragraphs, and this is sensible advice. Breaking long documents up into sensibly organized sections, each with its own heading, also helps.

But clear writing stems primarily from clear thinking, and the converse is also true. If you don't really understand what you are talking about, your writing will be weak, rambling, and obtuse. On the other hand, when you understand your subject matter, know your audience, and you have a useful and important idea you want to convey, the clarity of your writing will inevitably reflect your well-thought-out idea.

The second C is concise. The key here is that concise and brief are not synonyms. "Brief" means "short." If you want to be brief, you simply cut words until you reduce the composition to the word count desired. "Concise" means telling the complete story in the fewest possible words. It means we convey information with no rambling, no redundancy, no needless repetition, no using three words when one will do.

The third C is compelling. It is not enough that the copy is easy to read. It must be so interesting, engaging, and informative that the reader cannot put it down, or, at minimum, the reader feels compelled to at least skim the document to glean the important points.

Create systems for success for your readers

Inept how-to writers write vapid, run-on prose full of puff words. Their pages say nothing and fail to mask the fact that, for the most part, they either don't know what they are talking about or, if they do, they cannot articulate it to others.

Mediocre how-to writers at least take the time to Google the topic, read some web pages on it, and put some information into their text. Unfortunately, the information is not presented in a coherent fashion, and so it is "what" writing rather than "how" writing.

Good how-to writers not only fill their pages with valuable content, but they explain it in such a way that the readers gets valuable tips to improve his skill or results.

Great how-to writers organize the content and tips into a step-by-step system and include actionable advice that, when followed, allows the reader to begin at the beginning, progress, and achieve the objective, whether it's creating a Japanese rock garden or starting a business.

The more you can present your instructions as a system for getting something done, the more valuable your how-to writings will be to your readers. The keys to creating a good system are:

- Clear writing with a helpful, motivating attitude
- Short, bite-sized, easy-to-digest steps and sections
- Material organized according to the process the reader wants to master or the goal she wants to achieve
- Well-defined objectives and measurable milestones for each step; e.g., after step one, you will have finished X
- A goal or accomplishment the system leads you to complete.

Motivating the reader to follow your instructions

To recap: At the lowest levels of the craft, how-to writing merely conveys information. At higher levels, it teaches you a body of knowledge, a skill, a task, or a process. Even better than that, great how-to writing *motivates* the reader to learn the material.

Here is the lead of a manual on how to operate a workstation for controlling processes in plants. It is accurate but stuffy and unexciting:

> *Module 1: Overview*
> *The Operator's Workstation acts as the interface between the Operator and the processes being monitored and controlled. It allows the Operator to perform his or her duties in an efficient manner.*

We changed it to:

> *Module 1: Getting to Know Your Workstation*
> *Your job is to monitor and control processes in your plant. Your operator's workstation can help you do that job better and faster.*

I submit that the rewrite is better because it contains a benefit—a reason why the reader should make the effort to read and master the material. Remember, if your reader doesn't read and apply your how-to writing, it has done him little good. The most satisfied customers are not those who simply enjoyed the book, but those who followed the advice and got the results they desired.

Avoid content overload

Avoid what I call "content overload" or the "Google syndrome": cramming as much information as you can find on Google into the manuscript as space allows.

In the pre-internet days, the challenge for the nonfiction writer was finding enough information to fill a book, manual, or report.

In the internet era, we have the opposite problem. We are overwhelmed with the amount of information we find on our topic. The inexperienced writer feels compelled to cram everything he finds into his manuscript. The result is an unappealing mass of wordy and pointless prose.

To write nonfiction well in the internet age, the key is selectivity. In each section of your document, have points you want to make and ideas or techniques you want to teach. Include only those facts that help prove, illustrate, or support your points. Omit everything else. Expect to research and find at least twice as much research material as you can use.

Don't fall in love with your research materials. Know when not to use something and don't be afraid to throw it away. Actually, you don't have to throw it away. You can keep it in a file for the project. Just know what to include in the actual writing and what to omit.

Why you should minimize hyperlinks, cross references, and content appendices

Some authors load their e-books with hyperlinks to websites, sales pages for other e-books on related topics, or resources that discuss a topic in more detail than is covered in the book.

This is fine, but don't overdo it. Your book or manual should be clear, simple, and complete on its own. If the reader has to click a link in every sentence to read something else, she will become annoyed and dissatisfied.

Some how-to authors love to add long appendices to their how-to books, loaded with resources and references to obtain additional content on the topic. Appendices listing resources add value to the book, but resist the temptation to pad your manuscript with these. Your book should be sufficiently meaty and thorough even with these appendices taken away.

Avoid unnecessary links for topics the reader either knows or can easily find on his own. It is unnecessary, for example, to hyperlink the word "Mars" to the Wikipedia article on Mars when writing a piece about space exploration.

Too many writers are overly concerned about selling and cross-promoting their other works in whatever info product they are writing at present. Their concern clearly is to make additional sales, and not to service the reader, and it certainly comes across that way.

I am annoyed when I hire a writer to do a book for my online publishing company and the first question he asks me is whether he can include links for products he sells (his own as well as others he sells as an affiliate). That tells me he is focused on his affiliate commission checks and not on the book he is writing or the reader he is writing it for.

You can reference your other works in your current writing project, but do so sparingly and only when it adds value for the reader. If every other sentence recommends another of the author's books and gives a hyperlink to the book's order page, the reader will quite correctly conclude that what he has bought is not education but a thinly veiled sales pitch—exactly what you do *not* want to do.

How to extend the shelf life of info products

Here is a simple trick for keeping your book current: Create a companion website to the book. On the book's title page, add a box that says: "This book will never go out of date, because new information is continually posted on the companion website"—and include the URL in the box.

Another way to promise that a book or how-to product will never go out of date is to publish a free e-newsletter on that topic. Include a free subscription to the newsletter with the purchase price, and let the readers know the newsletter brings them the latest information on the topic in a timely manner.

For print information products in loose-leaf binders, you can send periodic updates—pages with new or updated information that can be inserted into the binder. Typically with a high-priced loose-leaf information product, the updates are quarterly; the first year's updates might be free, with an annual subscription after that to continue to receive all new quarterly updates.

Quick start guides

Not all, but many of my e-books describe processes. Whenever possible, I organize the contents according to the steps in the process. Each chapter or section covers a step, and they are numbered in sequence.

Readers of how-to information like to feel they have learned something valuable within the first few minutes of reading. One way to fulfill this desire is to present a short, practical tip early in the book, often as a boxed sidebar.

Another is to print a short "quick-start guide" at the beginning of the book, after the front cover and copyright page, and before the main text starts. The quick-start guide simply indicates the steps of the process in numbered order, with a two-sentence summary of each. In my marketing, I sometimes stress the quick-start guide as a value-added feature, saying the reader can learn the gist of the process in just seven minutes reading time.

Formats and pricing

When you are writing your how-to manuscript, keep in mind the format in which your manuscript will be published. Will it be a trade paperback? This is a paperback book the same size as a hardcover book. "Mass market" paperbacks, by comparison, are the smaller paperbacks sold in supermarkets and drugstores.

The format can affect the length of your manuscript, the tone, and even the content. Traditional trade paperback books are often written in a lighter, breezier style than, say, textbooks, which are denser and more technical.

Format dictates price more so than amount of content. For example, a 200-page trade paperback contains 70,000 to 80,000 words and sells for around $15 to $20. By comparison, a 60-minute spoken-word audio program contains only 7,000 words or so, but sells for $29 or more. The program gives you one-tenth the amount of information but is double the price.

Table 5.2 lists typical information product formats and their price ranges.

Table 5.2. Types of Information Products

Information Product Type	Price Range
Hardcover, professional and reference book (200–400 pages)	$40–$85
Trade paperback (200 pages)	$15–$29
E-book (200 pages)	$9.99–$12.99
PDF e-book* (50-100 pages)	$19–$59
Audio CDs	$29–$49 per CD
Audio MP3 downloads	25%–50% less than audio CDs
DVDs	$39–$79
Streaming video online	25%–50% less than DVDs
Membership site	$29–$79 per month
Webinars (60–90 minutes)	Free–$179
Book content in 3-ring binder	$49–$179
Above binder + multiple audio CDs and/or DVDs	$99–$299
Online courses	$497–$997
Big-ticket online master class	$1,000–$10,000
Mentoring programs	$1,000–$5,000
Mastermind groups	$2,500–$10,000
Coaching	$1,000–$2,500
Clinics	$1,000–$2,000
Info product licensing	$250–$5,000
Forms kits	$49–$99

* See Chapter 8.

6

Getting Started with Magazine Articles

The bread and butter for many how-to writers has traditionally been writing articles for print magazines and, to a lesser extent, newspapers, though in the digital era, this is now changing.

In part because of the rise of the internet, the print magazine industry is experiencing hard times. As advertising in magazines loses ground in popularity against online advertising, magazines lose revenue and ad pages, resulting in thinner issues with fewer pages for editorial content and smaller budgets for buying articles. In addition, an increasing number of magazines are folding their print editions and existing only as online publications. As I write this in 2020, *Playboy* announced it was shuttering its iconic print edition after nearly 70 years of publication.

Despite these challenges, there is plenty of opportunity for freelance writers to write nonfiction articles for magazines. First, as mentioned, most magazines now have on online presence, offering hundreds, if not thousands, of targets you can pitch to. Second, many magazines publish how-to articles, known in the trade as "service articles." Bridal magazines, for instance, are filled with how-to articles related to all aspects of planning a wedding. Outdoor magazines have an endless appetite for well-written how-to pieces on fishing, camping, and hunting.

There are some pros and cons for the freelance how-to writer who wants to write for the magazine marketplace. One huge advantage of magazines—both print and online—is that the publisher distributes your work to thousands of readers, giving you exposure to a wider audience than you might garner on your own.

More than 40 percent of people surveyed by Mequoda said they'd read an average of 2.66 digital magazine issues in the last 30 days. From 2015 to 2020, digital magazine revenues increased from 16 percent to 30 percent of total consumer magazine revenues.[†]

In addition, being published in a consumer magazine adds a valuable credential to your writer's bio. My bio always mentions my article in *Cosmopolitan*, which is the biggest magazine I have ever been published in—and it impresses potential publishers as well as direct buyers of my writings.

Pay is a mixed blessing. A top consumer magazine might pay $1,000 to $3,000 or more for a major feature article. However, most magazines pay in the hundreds of dollars. Small regional and local magazines often pay nominal sums or not at all. Trade publications also pay small sums or not at all.

Keep ownership of your content

Here is an important tip: When negotiating the sale of your article to the editor, specify that they are buying "first rights only." Type "first rights only" in the upper left corner of page one of the manuscript.

"First rights" means you are selling the magazine the right to be the first to publish your article. You can't publish it anywhere else until the magazine you sold it to runs it first. After that, you are free to publish or use it however you please.

"First rights only" is not a minor point. It's critical that you maintain all rights to everything you write, including articles. Why? Because the articles you write for magazines can be used again and again in so many different ways:

- Post them on your website
- Excerpt them for your blog
- Condense them for your e-zine
- Compile multiple articles into a special report

---

† www.paperlit.com/blog/the-huge-growth-of-digital-magazines/

- Expand the article into a book
- Make reprints and distribute to potential clients.

Content has value, but writing good articles takes a lot of work. Therefore, you waste time and labor by not recycling your articles for multiple uses. I view the library of articles I have written as a resource I can dip into again and again, whenever I need content for any application, from a sales letter to a website. I call it my "content gold mine."

Recently, I decided I needed to publish a new e-book on one of my core topics, copywriting. My customers had been asking for it, and I had neglected the task. So I needed to quickly put together a great e-book.

The answer was in my library of already published articles on copywriting, to which I owned all rights. The book has 17 chapters, each on a major copywriting principle. When I checked my hard drive, I found that I had written articles on every one of those principles.

Because I maintain all rights to my work, it was a simple matter and an hour or so of my time to cut and paste these articles into the appropriate chapters of my e-book. By recycling the articles in this way, I can continue to sell and profit from the material I wrote, rather than letting it languish on my hard drive.

How to identify your markets

In magazine writing, your odds of selling an article are extremely low if you don't read the magazine you want to write the article for, have never even seen it, and know virtually nothing about it. Yet many freelance writers attempt that feat almost all the time.

When I want to write and publish an article, I usually start with the magazines I already either subscribe to or read on a regular or sporadic basis. Reason: I am familiar with what they have run recently, so I avoid proposing something they just ran. Also, as a regular reader, I know whether they have columns or departments that regularly use freelance articles. I am familiar with their style and topic preferences. And I know the names of the editors.

If none of the magazines I know is right for the article I am planning, I turn to a directory called *Writer's Market*, published by Writer's Digest Books. Available in most major bookstores and published annually, *Writer's Market* lists thousands of magazines by category. Turn to the category you are interested in (e.g., travel, sports), read the descriptions of the publications (types of articles they take; whether they use freelancers; word length; pay rates), and look up the magazine's latest articles and guidelines for freelance writers on their website. Listings also include the name and contact information of the magazine editor.

Writing your query letter

Once you become familiar with the magazine, write a letter to the editor describing the article you would like to write for him or her. This is called a "query letter," because you are querying the editor to see whether he or she would like to read the article and publish it. To have an article published in a magazine, you do not as a rule write the article and send it off cold to the editor; instead, you send a query letter.

Query letters traditionally have been sent in a #10 envelope with a self-addressed, stamped envelope (SASE) enclosed. The SASE is for the editor's use in replying to your query.

But first, check the magazine's website: Today, most if not all magazines have an online submission form which you can use to electronically send your query letter directly to the editor. No postage, paper, or envelope needed!

The query letter we'll look at here got me an assignment to write a feature article for a slick consumer magazine for a four-figure fee. Another query letter of mine, which got me an assignment to write a feature article for a business magazine, is reprinted in full in the appendix.

The query letter should be personalized and addressed to the correct editor by name, and the name must be spelled correctly. The first two paragraphs should catch the editor's attention, using some device like an interesting statistic, fascinating fact, or dramatic story.

"For a Kiwanis piece on refugee children, I needed a dramatic opening showing a traumatized youth's arrival in his country of refuge," says Sandra Dark. She found a young Congolese refugee in the United Kingdom and began her article using his story to personalize the refugee issue.

The lead of the letter is written pretty much as you would write the lead for the article, and so gives the editor a good idea of your style. Here is a query I sent to a health magazine that also became the lead of my piece:

Mr. Steven Florio, Articles Editor
ABC Magazine
711 Third Avenue
New York, NY 10017

Dear Mr. Florio:

I was on the telephone with a client when I suddenly became unable to speak or take notes with a pen. When these symptoms disappeared after a minute or so, I did the stupidest thing I ever did in my life: I ignored them and went back to work.

What I had was a TIA, or Transient Ischemic Attack. A TIA, which is a temporary decrease of blood flow to the brain, is a warning sign of an impending stroke—and if more men knew about it and recognized it, thousands of needless strokes could be prevented.

I'd like to write a 1,200-word article for ABC on stroke prevention. Tentatively titled "You're Never Too Young to Be Struck by a Stroke," the article would outline the 7 warning signs of stroke as identified by the American Stroke Council. (They include slurred speech and temporary loss of the use of a limb, both of which I had.)

When you have even one of these symptoms, quick action can prevent a full-blown stroke and minimize your chances of long-term damage. I'll outline why you should go to the emergency room immediately and the actions you and your doctors should take.

Notice that I suggested a word length. Check out the magazine and see what word length typical feature articles are, and based on this and the amount of information you have to convey, suggest a length. If the editor wants fewer or more words, she will tell you. Today, a common length for magazine features is 800 to 1,500 words, which works out to one or two pages in the magazine.

Anyone could write a mediocre article on virtually any topic by doing Google research. The editor prefers that you go beyond that. If the article is based on experience, say so. Also outline the experts you are going to interview when writing the piece:

In my case, I wasn't smart enough to go to the ER. Four weeks after my TIA, at age 43, I had a full-blown stroke. Friends were shocked I had a stroke so young, but one out of four stroke victims is under 65.

I will share with your readers what Dr. Allen Grossman, my cardiologist, and Dr. Phil Desplat, my family doctor, say I could have done to prevent this, including their recommendations on diet, exercise, and blood pressure and cholesterol monitoring.

Now, give a capsule bio telling the editor who you are, what your writing or expert credentials are (e.g., you are a cardiac surgeon; you wrote a book on the topic of the article), and why you are uniquely qualified to write this article for their magazine.

By way of introduction, I am a freelance writer and the author of more than 50 books including 101 Ways to Make Every Second Count: Time Management Techniques For More Success with Less Stress (Career Press). My articles have appeared in Cosmopolitan, Science Books & Films, Amtrak Express, and New Jersey Monthly.

The close is standard. Ask the editor whether she is interested in seeing the article.

I can have this article on your desk in 3 to 4 weeks. Shall I proceed as outlined?

Sincerely,

If the editor says yes, she will send you a standard contract for writing the article. The contract will specify rights, deadline, fee, and kill fee. These terms are negotiable, but if you negotiate too hard, the editor will find another article and another writer to publish. Magazine writing is a buyer's market.

Although opinions vary, I advise you to query a particular article idea one magazine at a time. If you submitted the query to multiple magazines and more than one said "yes," you'd be in the unfortunate position of explaining to at least one editor why she can't have your article after all. If you insist on simultaneous submissions, let the editor know the query is a simultaneous submission when you send it in.

"Kill fee" means the editor is not obligated to publish the piece, even though they gave you a contract. If the editor does not like the article and feels you can't revise it to her satisfaction, she kills the project and pays a fee to you to compensate for your time and effort. The kill fee is usually small—10 to 20 percent of the full fee. But you are free to take the article elsewhere and try with another magazine and another editor.

Tips for writing killer query letters

"If you can't write a selling query letter, you can't write a selling article, or so thinks, correctly, the editor to whom you are trying to sell," says veteran author and seminar leader Gordon Burgett. He goes on to say:

> The only articles I ever sold without queries either paid nothing or were read by an audience of about seven. To survive by writing, query.
>
> When you are very famous you can call an editor, give your name, and query right then. But 75 percent of the editors still won't know that you are famous or even who you are, so that path usually bruises your ego and gets you no farther ahead.
>
> The rest of us always query when we want somebody else to pay us. That's because paying editors expect to see evidence of our writing first (in a query letter), give a go-ahead, write our names down in the "coming articles" calendar, receive the manuscript when promised, shriek quietly with delight when it arrives and makes sense, pay us on acceptance, print the piece, and do it the very same way again and again.

As far as repeat assignments, don't expect that, once you have written an editor, you will automatically be chosen to do so again, warns Gordon. Editors will quickly forget about you. So the best thing to do is to get in print, then follow up within weeks (or at most months) of a sale, with another great idea. That way you improve your chances by at least 50 percent. The third time you do this the editor will know you and be inclined to accept most of what you propose thereafter—or know better.

Do not telephone editors with query ideas. Usually, you just irk them. The best you get is, "Sounds like it might work. Send me the idea in a query letter." Duh. Save the irk and the call.

Lisa Cool, in *How to Write Irresistible Query Letters*, has a five-step checklist for writing queries similar to my own:

- *Lead.* Does the opening paragraph grab the editor's attention, is it appropriate in tone and style, and does it tell what the article will be about?

- *Summary.* Are the three key points (or more, but not many more) of the piece mentioned? Are the facts and quotes new? Did you mention the authorities to be cited or quoted? Is the message and direction of the article clear? (In other words, does the editor know what he is buying?)

- *Bio.* Do you present the key stuff about you that the editor should know? Did you answer the editor's question, "Why you?"

- *Length.* Is the query one single-spaced letter page, presented in at least 11-point type?

- *Format.* Does it follow conventional business letter requirements?

What is the best buying ratio you can expect from cold queries to editors who have never bought from you? According to Burgett, maybe 33 percent at best, but 15 percent is a very good ratio. Later, after you've sold to an editor, over 50 percent to that same editor is possible. But if you don't send queries, your article publication rate will be close to zero.

Magazine writer Carolyn Campbell gives these additional tips for writing successful query letters:

- For maximum sales potential, try to keep queries to one page. Two-page queries sell sometimes; three-page queries almost never sell.

- Remember to include as many elements of the finished article or book as possible. After you write a query, send batches of it out to as many potential markets as possible.

- When querying by mail, always include an SASE the editor can use to reply to your query.

Should you enclose clips with your query letter?

Query letters may open the door to publications, but your clips (samples of your published work) can mean the difference between that door staying open and it slamming in your face. And while reams of resources exist for professional and aspiring writers, surprisingly few books or articles offer much information on presenting your clips properly.

Here are suggestions on how to use your clips to your best advantage:

- Send your best work. Once you've narrowed it down to your best, go for the most recent, as well as those clips that show you can write the kind of story you're proposing (e.g., if you're querying about a profile, include a profile clip).

- If an editor accepts clips via email, follow submission instructions carefully, especially if she requests a certain format. If she asks for clips as attached PDFs to your email, but you send them as attached Word documents, your clips will likely be deleted unread.

- Always include the name of the publication where your article appeared and the date of publication. If these facts aren't included on the page with your clip, improvise. It's fine to simply write the name of the publication and the date neatly on the top of your clip.

- Send copies of your clips instead of the originals. If an editor does want originals, she'll specifically request "tear sheets" or "hard copies" in the writer's guidelines.

- I post my clips on a Portfolio page on my website, www.bly.com. To send a sample via email, I cut and paste the URL of the clip from my website into the body of my email query letter.

All of the above can help increase your chances of making a sale. But none of the above is required. So, if you are a complete novice, don't fret: If your article idea and query letter are strong enough, it can still sell.

Quote outside experts

Many how-to writers write magazine articles only on subjects they know well, often subjects they have written about in other articles, columns, booklets, and books.

Let's say you know your how-to topic cold. Does that mean you're exempt from research? Not at all.

Even if you are a subject matter expert, magazine editors love quotes from multiple expert sources. Most will specify that they want quotes from between two and five outside experts in addition to your own opinions and ideas. It's for this reason that writing articles for magazines is so much more time-consuming and less profitable than it need be.

Your own experience and expertise should also be prominent in the article, particularly if you yourself have done what the article teaches. For magazine articles, you cannot rely on Google research as heavily as you might for a book. Magazine editors prefer primary sources. Tip: Whatever you do, don't quote Wikipedia in your article, because its reliability and accuracy is widely suspect.

Dealing with revisions

Whenever you write for an outside client who is paying you a fee, and you are not publishing your work yourself, you can expect to be asked to make revisions. These may be minor edits or major rewrites.

Some writers have an adversarial relationship with editors and carp whenever asked to change a word of their copy. This is a sure road to failure. The editor is the customer. He has a right to get a product he knows his readers will enjoy. It is your job to rewrite the manuscript until he is satisfied.

Can an editor make unreasonable requests? Yes. It doesn't happen often. However, if you feel the revisions fall outside the scope of the original article as described in the query proposal the editor accepted, you can point that out and suggest a small additional fee to compensate you for the extra work.

If you are solely a traditional freelancer, writing articles for magazines, and your article is rejected, you can always try to sell it to another publication. Book authors can incorporate text from rejected articles into book chapters. Information marketers can use articles as sections of e-books or special reports, or post them as free content on their websites to attract search engines queries.

Writing for trade publications

Big consumer magazines can be tough for rookies to break into. If you're concentrating on trying to sell your manuscripts to *Esquire, Reader's Digest, Travel & Leisure, Sports Illustrated,* and the other consumer magazines with limited luck, you should know about a larger, less competitive, and potentially more lucrative "other world" of magazine markets: the trade journals.

Thousands of business magazines, or trade journals, are eager to hire rookie writers—as long as they can fill their pages with relevant, well-written material directed at their specialized audiences. (For a complete listing of trade journals, consult *Writer's Market.*)

What stories would a trade editor assign to a freelancer like you? A popular format is the case history, where you tell how one company solved a particular problem, including what the problem was, the solutions they considered, the method or product they chose to solve the problem, how they implemented the solution, and the results they achieved.

Another is the industry roundup, where you might do brief profiles of products or companies in a particular area (for example, in a construction magazine you might discuss the available types of building insulation). Many trade journals run articles on business skills or management topics, such as how to be a better leader or reduce stress on the job.

Pay scales for trade publications are generally lower than for consumer publications. However, the editors aren't as demanding and require fewer interviews and rewrites.

Writing for trade publications is a great way to break into magazines, get a byline, hone your skills, and build a folder of published articles. The best place to start: Look at the trade journals you get at work. Your familiarity with your industry and those publications will give you a better feel for how to speak to the magazine's readers.

I think you'll find breaking into these specialized magazines easier than breaking into the big-name, general interest publications, too. Be aware that per-article pay rates don't rival *People*'s or *National Geographic*'s, but neither does the competition among freelancers.

Since trade journals accept a larger percentage of the articles proposed by writers, you may be able to make more money writing for the trades than for consumer magazines. Trade magazine editors often rely on "outsiders" for much of what goes into the magazine, sometimes as much as 60 percent of the copy. Because the trades have smaller staffs and a strong feeling of loyalty to their readers, they often welcome new ideas from those familiar with their field.

I've had many pleasant and rewarding experiences writing for the trades. For example, an editor at a computer magazine obtained material from my seminar on technical writing. The editor asked me to turn it into a 1,200-word article on how to write user's manuals. Using the material already at hand, I wrote the piece and had it in the mail in under an hour. A week later, I received the magazine's check for $750.

Before you attempt to make your own profits in this market, it's essential to understand just what these magazines are about. Trade magazines serve the needs of a special interest market: accountants, actuaries, barbers, florists, pharmacists. The trade journal exists to help these specialists do their job better and run their business more profitably.

Trade journals exist in just about every field. Whether you're interested in aviation (*Aviation Daily*), fertilizer (*CropLife*), turkey hunting (*Turkey & Turkey Hunting*), or motorcycles (*HOG Magazine*), there's usually at least one appropriate magazine for you to approach.

Trade journals exist to keep professionals up-to-date on developments, conferences, trends, and practices in their field. Readers need the information the journals provide to help them do their jobs better. As a result, trade articles are practical and specific, and depending on the magazine, can be in-depth or technical. All provide straightforward coverage of a specific industry.

Unlike their consumer cousins, these magazines don't strive to be flashy or singularly entertaining. They look different, too, being generally less slick than the mass-market magazines. Visuals are used to communicate information, not to add glitz or lure readers.

Your first step in writing for the trades is to decide which journals interest you, and which match your background and writing capabilities. You don't need industry experience or an engineering degree to write about most subjects covered by the trades, but you will have to know how to research and interview.

Take me as an example. I have a bachelor's degree in chemical engineering. But I find that my background doesn't affect my ability to turn out clear, comprehensible trade articles on a wide variety of topics. I've published numerous articles outside my chemical engineering specialty, including pieces on semiconductors, aerospace, defense, and computer software. My wife Amy has written about such diverse subjects as meat packing, printing, health insurance, strategic planning, prefabricated metal buildings, and public relations.

Since thousands of trade journals are published, you must zero in on the publications that are appropriate markets for you.

First, make a list of subjects you're interested in writing about. Then, search next.SRDS.com online or *Writer's Market* for listings of trade journals that cover these topics. Standard Rate and Data Service (SRDS) contains the most listings, but *Writer's Market* provides a more detailed description of each journal's editorial requirements.

From that list, access or obtain digital or print copies of trade magazines that relate to the subjects you listed. In studying these issues, see what kinds of stories the editor uses and note their degree of technical difficulty.

Determine whether these pieces are written by staff writers, outside technical experts, or freelance writers. (Check article bylines against the masthead's list of staff writers or read the author bios printed with articles.) Most trade editors combine work from staff writers and from freelancers.

If every contributed article carries the byline of a chemist or an engineer and you are neither, querying the editor is probably a waste of time. Likewise, if the material seems hopelessly technical to you. On the other hand, if you have an interest in, say, computers, but terms like "asynchronous" and "ASCII" are unfamiliar to you, a dictionary of computer jargon might be all you need to write an acceptable article.

7

Your First Nonfiction Book

For decades, nonfiction books have been a primary writing format for how-to writers, and they continue to be one today. In 2018, book sales in the U.S. generated $25.82 billion in revenues, from 2.71 billion units sold. Even with the rise of online and electronic media, becoming a nonfiction book author—specifically of a paperback or hardcover book—is the quickest way to build your reputation as a guru in your industry and significantly increase your writing income.

Becoming a published book author

Let me share with you an opinion based on personal experience: Few events in a writer's life are as thrilling as the day your first book is published.

Imagine that you've completed your manuscript, had it accepted by the publisher, and publication is scheduled for this month. Your editor has promised you an advance copy, and you've been eagerly checking the mail each day.

Finally, it arrives. You tear open the envelope, and you hold in your hands a beautifully printed, 200-page hardcover or paperback book. It takes your breath away: The colorful cover shows the title and the author's name. And the author is—you!

Soon, the book shows up in bookstores and at the library. The local newspapers call to interview you. You are featured as a guest on radio shows . . . perhaps even on cable or network TV. Book reviewers write glowing reviews, which are published in your favorite magazines. Royalty checks from the publisher begin to pour in, and the publisher asks, with eagerness and enthusiasm, "When will you be sending us your next book?"

Sound impossible? Not at all. In fact, by following a series of eight simple—but essential—steps, you can sell your nonfiction book idea to a major publishing house, get a $2,500 to $15,000+ advance, and become a published author.

This chapter presents my proven formula for writing and selling nonfiction books to major New York publishing houses. Is there one single method for writing and selling nonfiction, one magic formula? No. Each author has a slightly different approach. You will use what works for you. That may be my formula, a variation of it, another author's approach, your own approach, or a combination of these.

There are a number of different options for publishing your book today. In this chapter we discuss two. The one we have been discussing and that is the focus of this chapter is "traditional publishing"—selling your book to a publishing house. This can be a major publisher such as McGraw-Hill or John Wiley & Sons, or a smaller independent publisher such as Quill Driver Books or BenBella; I have sold books to all four companies.

The big-name publishers ostensibly carry more prestige and they certainly pay larger (though usually far from lavish) advances. You usually cannot sell to them unless you have a literary agent representing you. Since they publish many books per season, marketing and PR for your book is likely to be perfunctory.

Small presses will look at books submitted directly by the author and do not require you to have a literary agent. In fact, some prefer that an agent not be involved. Their advances are usually nominal. But since they publish fewer books than the big presses, each subsequently gets more editorial, marketing, and PR attention.

The other publishing option we will discuss is self-publishing, which is now, more than ever, a viable pathway for how-to writers.

8 steps to getting your book published

My method of writing and selling nonfiction books gives you several advantages when you use it to sell your how-to book to a publishing house.

First, it saves you an enormous amount of time and effort. In my selling method, you sell the book to the publisher first, on the strength of a well-crafted proposal, and then write it only after you have a signed contract and advance payment in hand. Doesn't that make good business sense for the author?

Many authors write the entire book first, then go out and try to find a publisher. This is a mistake, in my opinion, for two reasons: a) it requires an enormous investment of time and work in an idea that may never sell, and b) for nonfiction, most publishers actually prefer to see a proposal rather than a completed manuscript (because it saves reading time), so handing in a completed book may actually reduce your chances for a sale!

The second advantage to my method is that it's proven to work. I use it on every project and, as I've said, I have sold dozens of books to publishing houses over the past 40 years. All of my proposals follow the same formula. If you want to learn how to do something, find someone who is doing it successfully, study their method, and model your own efforts after it. You'll get the results you want.

Third, my success rate is very high. Of the book ideas I have taken to "full proposal," I have sold approximately 90 percent of them. Only a handful did not sell, and I predict that eventually I will be able to sell one or two of those, based on current interest from publishers.

Fourth, my method is logical, simple, and easy-to-follow. "You break everything into a series of easy steps," said an attendee at one of my book publishing seminars recently. "That makes the whole process far less intimidating."

To many of us, the idea of writing a book may indeed seem a bit daunting. Breaking it up into a series of eight steps using my process makes it less so. You will have an easier time if you stop focusing on "writing a book" and instead focus on the immediate step of the process in front of you, whether it's researching your topic, generating ideas, creating the book's table of contents, or even writing up your bio. These smaller tasks seem less intimidating and more doable, and the completion of each one brings you one step closer to your ultimate goal.

By the way, this concept of breaking a large task into small, manageable steps is useful in virtually every type of writing. When I am writing a book, I break it up into chapters, and then further divide each chapter into subtopics. This way, instead of facing the daunting task of writing one big, 200-page book, I simply have to write 100 two-page mini-essays on the 100 subtopics in my chapter outline. That's easy!

Here, then, are the eight steps to getting your book published:

Step 1: Come Up With a Good Idea for Your Book

If you already have a good idea, move on to Step 2. If not, use the mind map technique in Chapter 3 to brainstorm ideas for information products, including reports, e-classes, teleseminars, and of course books.

Some first-time authors are intimidated by this step. They feel they lack the creativity to come up with good ideas. My experience is that all of us are capable of coming up with good ideas, including ideas for books. The hard work is not coming up with the idea; it's writing the book.

Isaac Asimov, the prolific science and science fiction author, said that he would frequently get calls from readers who had ideas for science fiction stories. Their proposal to him was that they would supply the idea, he would write the story, and they would split the profits 50–50.

"I have a better idea," Asimov always told these callers. "I'll give you an idea for a story, you write it, and when it's published, you send me 50 percent of the profit."

No one ever took him up on his offer.

Step 2: Evaluate Your Book Idea

There are many ideas and titles that sound good, but once evaluated with a critical eye must be rejected because they are not commercially viable and would not appeal to a publisher.

When I ask potential authors why they think a publisher would want to publish their book, and why a reader would want to buy and read it, a lot of them answer, "Because it's a good book" or "The subject is important."

In today's marketplace, that's not enough. *People read nonfiction today either for information or entertainment.* Your book has to entertain or inform them. A book that does neither is going to be extremely difficult to sell.

Remember, your book competes for the reader's time and money, not just with other books on the same topic, but with movies, iTunes, podcasts, magazines, video games, and TV. Unless your book delivers more entertainment or valuable content than these other media, it will be passed over by consumers in favor of those other options.

Step 3: Create the Content Outline

Once you decide on a topic for your book, I recommend that you develop a content outline. A content outline is similar to the table of contents you find in any nonfiction book in the library or bookstore, except it's more detailed and fleshed out.

Developing the content outline has several purposes. First, it helps you determine whether you can produce enough text on the subject to fill a book. Second, it is perhaps the single most powerful tool for convincing publishers that your book idea has merit. Third, it will save you an enormous amount of time when you sit down to write your book proposal and the book itself.

I always make my content outlines detailed rather than sketchy. I am convinced this is important in selling the book to a publisher. Chapter 4 shows you different ways to create and organize outlines for books, reports, and other content. These include the index card method and mind maps.

Step 4: Write Your Book Proposal

The book proposal is often the most mysterious part of the book publishing process, especially to beginners. The reason: You know what books look like, because you've seen hundreds of them. But chances are, you don't know what a book proposal looks or sounds like because you have never seen one. To review an example of a real book proposal that worked, see the appendix.

Step 5: Get an Agent

Although it's possible to sell directly to publishers, I recommend you get a literary agent. Many publishers, and virtually all of the large ones, will not even consider your book proposal unless you are represented by an agent, more about which in a minute. However, as mentioned previously, the exception is smaller publishing houses, which typically do not require you have an agent.

Step 6: Send Your Proposal to Publishers and Get an Offer

If you have an agent, the agent will send your proposal to book publishers in an attempt to get an offer. If you choose to go without an agent, you can send a short letter to publishers asking if they'd be willing to look at your book proposal. Or, you may just send the proposal along with a cover letter. It's up to you, and both ways can work.

Step 7: Negotiate Your Contract

If you have an agent, the agent negotiates the contract on your behalf, with your input and approval; if you don't have an agent, you handle the negotiations yourself. Even if you sell the book without an agent, once you have an offer, you may want to find an agent to represent you. Negotiating book contracts is complex and unfamiliar territory to first-time authors, and it is often well worth paying an agent a 15 percent commission on advance and royalties to negotiate it for you.

The main contract clauses are the advance and the royalty. An advance for a nonfiction book from a first-time author is typically low, ranging from less than $5,000 to $15,000. Royalties average 7 to 8 percent for paperbacks and 10 to 15 percent for hardcover books. Some publishers base royalties on gross revenues but most base them on net revenues.

When you buy a $10 book, you pay the seller $10, which is the gross revenue on the sale. Net revenue is the gross revenues less what the seller paid the publisher for the book. So if the bookstore got the book wholesale for 40 percent off the cover price, the net revenue is $6. Therefore you as the author make more money with royalties based on gross rather than net.

Make sure your book contract contains a clause that says if the book goes out of print, the rights revert to you, the author. In addition, the contract should also stipulate that when the book goes out of print, the author is given first right of refusal on purchasing the remainders (unsold copies) at either the best prevailing market rate or at cost plus a dollar.

Step 8: Write and Deliver the Manuscript

The publisher will typically give you four to nine months to write and deliver your manuscript. Create and stick to a writing schedule that enables you to meet that deadline.

Let's say the deadline is nine months from today. That's 36 weeks. If the book has 12 chapters, you should write a chapter every three weeks. Stick with this schedule. It's tempting to put off working on the book because the deadline seems so far away and you have other, more pressing deadlines. But before you know it, the deadline will be looming, and there is nothing worse than having a book deadline a month away with many chapters still unfinished.

I actually like to set my schedule so that I will finish one month *before* the deadline date, though it's not always possible. That gives me an extra four weeks to polish and proofread the manuscript so it is as finished as can be.

Some authors don't agonize over proofing and rewriting, and they figure the editor is going to change what they write anyway. I prefer to hand in a book manuscript that's as clean as possible, and I know my editors like it that way. Many other writers do the same. "I still feel that it's a writer's job to get everything right, from the spelling of words to the name of the capital of Albania," writes Robert Silverberg in *Asimov's Science Fiction, Thirtieth Anniversary Issue.* E. B. White rewrote *Charlotte's Web* nine times before handing in the manuscript to his editor.

Self-publishing your book

For self-publishing a hardcover or paperback book, the options are to use a short-run book printer or a print-on-demand (POD) publisher. The POD has a higher manufacturing cost per unit but requires no minimum print run; you can run off the books one at a time as they are ordered, eliminating the need to shell out thousands of dollars for a first-run printing of a book that you don't know you can sell.

Once you see that orders are coming in, you can lower the cost per unit by going to a short-run book printer, though the minimum print run is likely to be at least 500 to 1,000 copies. And you will need to arrange storage, either in your house or at a fulfillment house, which will charge a monthly warehousing fee.

Of course, your book does not have to be published as a physical book at all. You can self-publish it electronically as an e-book, either through a major e-book self-publishing platform (such as Smashwords or Amazon's Kindle Direct Publishing program) for distribution to e-book reading devices (including smartphones), or as a downloadable PDF file, which is often the best choice for how-to writers. Either way, for the self-publisher the advantages of an e-book include no printing or binding costs, no inventory to store, and no shipping or fulfillment costs.

Table 7.1. Book Publishing Options (1 = weak, 5 = strong)

Publishing Option	Prestige	Author's Advance	Speed of Publication	Cost Per Copy to Author	Distribution to Bookstores
Large publishing house	5	4	1	50% of cover price*	5
Small publishing house	4	2	2	50% of cover price*	4
Self-published (short run)	2	None	3	$1–$3	1
Self-published (POD)	2	None	4	$3–$9	1
E-book	1	None	5	Zero	Not applicable
PDF -e-book	1	None	5	Zero	Not applicable

*When purchased directly from publisher.

To self-publish is, in one sense, easier than regular publishing, because it guarantees that your book will see print (since you are paying to have it printed at a print shop!).

But in another sense, self-publishing is more difficult, because to sell the book you need skills and knowledge in many areas in addition to writing. As we've noted, these include: advertising copywriting, direct mail, small business management, inventory control, purchasing, shipping, distribution, sales, marketing, and many others.

The immediate cash flow in publishing is more favorable for traditional publishing than for self-publishing. In traditional publishing, you get an advance of thousands of dollars to put in your bank account before you write the book. And there are virtually no out-of-pocket expenses.

In self-publishing, there is no advance, and the up-front costs—book design, typesetting, printing, and advertising—can be considerable, adding up to many thousands of dollars in checks you will write to vendors.

However, if you do decide to self-publish your book, you should be aware of the fact that the newest technologies now allow you to do so for a very nominal cost—as little as a couple of hundred dollars in initial setup costs. This is all thanks to the print-on-demand publishing revolution.

Years ago, if you decided to self-publish your own book, your only option was taking the book to a short-run printer, which, as the name suggests, is a company specializing in producing small print runs of books. You could expect a print run of one thousand copies to cost $3,000 or even more. Today, thanks to POD, it is easy to print-on-demand any quantity you choose (even a single copy).

If this sounds like something you would be interested in, contact a company called IngramSpark (which is a division of the nation's largest book wholesaler, Ingram, Inc.). IngramSpark makes self-publishing POD books incredibly easy—you just upload a PDF of your book to their website, and they turn out a book that is virtually indistinguishable from a book produced by a conventional printer. Additionally, for a small additional cost, you can also have them produce an e-book edition.

The tricky part is creating a PDF that's ready for your publication. Even though you're only submitting a computer file, you must have that file prepared to be output as a book. What prints out of that file is exactly what appears in your book. IngramSpark will not typeset the text, insert page numbers, headers, footers, or indexes. If you are not familiar with these aspects of book preparation, you will have to hire someone to do it for you.

Using IngramSpark has an additional benefit that is very important. Because they are a division of Ingram and most bookstores order their books from Ingram, IngramSpark can distribute your self-published book to online and brick-and-mortar bookstores around the world. Once your book is in their computer, IngramSpark will actually print your book one copy at a time as orders come in from the bookstores. IngramSpark will then include your just-printed book along with the rest of that store's order. (You can find out more at ingramspark.com.)

Although you will pay more for each copy you sell, you do not have to pay for, ship, or even stock quantities of books yourself. You can focus all your energies doing the single most important job you will have as a self-publisher . . . promoting your book. You will need to keep on hand only enough books to send to book reviewers, radio, and TV media and the like.

Going the route of print-on-demand also means that you can easily test the waters to see just how well your book will sell without making a major financial investment. If the book begins to take off you can then lower your per-book cost by having thousands of copies printed at a conventional printer. Or if you like, you can use the rocketing book sales as leverage in selling your book to a mainline publisher.

Why every how-to author should write at least one traditionally published book

No matter what your goal as a how-to author, I recommend you write at least one nonfiction book for a traditional publishing house. Why is this so? To begin with, you want to establish your reputation as a recognized expert in your field or topic. The prestige of having written a book for a "real" publishing house, large or small, does this faster and more effectively than self-publishing the book.

Second, writing the book and having it published gives you a product to sell and a source of revenue from advances and royalties.

Third, when magazine editors see you are the author of a book on topic X, they will be more likely to hire you to write articles or even a column on topic X.

Fourth, as mentioned, make sure your book contract specifies that when your book goes out of print, you can buy the remainders at low cost. Often, you can make more money selling the remainders of your book than you would when the book is still in print and earning you an 8 to 10 percent royalty on the cover price per copy.

Fifth, your book contract should also specify that when your book goes out of print, the rights revert to you. So when the publisher puts the book out of print, you can either sell it to another publisher, or you can republish it as an e-book, which you sell for a profit margin of close to 100 percent.

Coming up with the right idea for your first book

As a how-to writer, your first nonfiction book will naturally cover your core subject matter or niche. But what aspects of this topic will the book be about?

An obvious but often overlooked source of book ideas is your job. Thousands of excellent books have been written by authors about a skill, expertise, or career experience gained on the job.

This is how I came to write my first book, *Technical Writing: Structure, Standards, and Style*. My first job after graduating college was as a technical writer for Westinghouse Electric Corporation in Baltimore.

After several months writing technical materials, I began to feel the need for a writing guide to assist technical writers with matters of style, usage, punctuation, and grammar (for example, does one write "1/4" or "0.25" or "one-fourth" in technical documents?). Being book-minded, I went to the bookstores and found nothing appropriate.

My idea was to do a style guide for technical writers modeled after the best-selling general writing style guide, *The Elements of Style*, by Strunk and White. I wrote a content outline and book proposal, and I began to pursue agents and publishers.

In my case, I was extremely lucky: The first agent who saw my technical writing proposal agreed to represent the book, and within three weeks he sold it to the first publisher to look at it, McGraw-Hill. The advance was $8,500—not bad for a first-time author in 1981 for a short (100-page) book. More than four decades later, with some 150,000 copies sold, the book is still in print (with another publisher, Pearson) and continues to earn me thousands of dollars a year in royalties.

Not every book since has sold so quickly and easily. But subsequently, I have written a number of books based on skills and experiences gained in my various careers and jobs.

Do you hold a highly desirable position or do you work in a glamorous industry? If so, you can write a book telling others how to get into your line of work.

Have you developed specific and valuable skills such as selling, marketing, finance, negotiating, or programming—skills that others need to master? There's a need for a book telling them how to do it.

Another way to come up with ideas and content for books is by teaching. There are many opportunities for you to design and teach courses to other people: at work or at adult education evening classes at the local high school, community colleges, association meetings, and even university level.

If you get the opportunity to teach a course, keep in mind that the topic and content outline you develop for the course may have appeal to a publisher as the outline for a potential book on the same subject.

Example: A private seminar company offering low-cost public seminars in New York City asked me to do an evening program in marketing and promotion for small business. The pay was lousy, but I accepted. A year or so later, I took the course title and outline, turned it into a book proposal, and sold my second book, *How to Promote Your Own Business*, to New American Library, a large Manhattan publishing house.

So by developing and teaching the course, you will simultaneously be doing most of the legwork necessary to produce a book on the subject. Therefore, transforming the course material into a book is a relatively quick and easy next step (or at least quicker and easier than doing a book from scratch).

As a bonus, teaching the course positions you as an expert in the subject, making you more attractive to book publishers. They figure that anyone who can give a course on the topic must have a substantial amount of information and expertise to share. If you taught the course at a prestigious, well-known institution, that further boosts your credibility.

Why you should not worry about having your book idea stolen

There are three reasons why you shouldn't be overly concerned about copyrighting your manuscript if you want to sell it to a commercial publishing house.

First, if the publishing firm publishes your book, it will copyright it for you in your name.

Second, publishers are not interested in stealing your work. I don't have the space to go into all the reasons why this is so, but it is. So, as an author with 100 published books, I suggest you can trust me on this point.

Third, obsessive concern with copyright and theft of your material marks you to publishers as an amateur they don't want to do business with. Professional authors know that the publisher is not out to rip us off, and we do not decorate our manuscripts with copyright notices and warnings. To do so is a turnoff to potential publishers.

Self-publishing the work is a different story. If you are self-publishing your book, then it is up to you to register the copyright with the U.S. Copyright Office in Washington, D.C. The website is www.copyright.gov. A sample of the form you need, Copyright Form TC, is included in the appendix. Go to www.copyright.org for full instructions on its usage. Also, place a copyright notice toward the front of the printed book on a copyright page, similar to the one in this book.

Writing a winning book proposal

As for structuring your book proposal (see the appendix for a sample proposal), make sure it contains the following sections:

- *A title page.* The book's title and the name of the author are centered in the middle of the page. In the upper left corner, type "Book Proposal." In the bottom right, type your name, address, and phone number (or, if you have one, your agent's name and phone number).

- *Overview.* Summarize what your book is about: the topic, who will read it, why it's important or interesting to your intended audience, and what makes your book different from others in the field.

- *Format.* Specify approximate word length, number of chapters, types of illustrations or graphics to be included, and any unique organizational schemes or formats (for example, is your book divided into major sections? or do you use sidebars?).

- *Markets.* Tell the editor who will buy your book, how many of these people exist, and why they need it or will want to read it. Use statistics to dramatize the size of the market. For example, if your book is about infertility, mention that one in six couples in the United States is infertile.

- *Promotion.* Is your book a natural for talk radio or a prime-time TV show? Can it be promoted through seminars or speeches to associations and clubs? Give the publisher some of your ideas on how the book can be marketed. Do you have a website, blog, or e-newsletter that you can use to promote the book? That's something publishers look for. (Note: Phrase these as suggestions, not demands. The publisher will be interested in your ideas but probably won't use most of them.)

- *Competition.* List books that compare with yours. Include the title, author, publisher, year of publication, number of pages, price, and format (hardcover, trade paperback, or mass market paperback). Describe each book briefly, pointing out weaknesses and areas in which your book is different and superior.

- *Author's bio.* A brief biography listing your writing credentials (books and articles published), qualifications to write about the book's topic (for instance, for a book on popular psychology, it helps if you're a therapist), and your media experience (previous appearances on TV and radio).

- *Table of contents/outline.* A chapter-by-chapter outline showing the contents of your proposed book. Many editors tell me that a detailed, well-thought-out table of contents in a proposal helps sway them in favor of a book.

Finding and working with a literary agent

Many editors will not read your material unless it is submitted by an agent. Agents act as screening devices for editors. Although representation by an agent does not guarantee a sale (far from it), editors at least take the submission of your proposal seriously. The editor's logic in doing so is that if the agent thinks the book is good enough to represent, it is at least worth taking a look at.

As a rule of thumb, the larger the publishing house, the more vital it is to have an agent. The smaller the publishing house, the more likely it is to look at unsolicited proposals not represented by an agent. University presses can also be approached directly by potential authors without the benefit of an agent.

Another area where agents help is in negotiating favorable book contracts for authors. A book contract has dozens of clauses in fine print, each of which is negotiable and can greatly affect your total income from the book.

The basic function of an agent is sales. A good agent is one who is able to sell your writing and get you the best deal in terms of advance, royalty, publisher, promotional budget, and quality of editor.

The best place to start looking for an agent is with your own personal contacts. If you don't know someone who has published a book, chances are a friend of a friend, or a relative of a friend, may know someone. Ask that author for a referral. Does he have an agent he can recommend to you? Does he have any suggestions on which agents to contact?

Go to a bookstore or library and look at recent books on topics similar to the book you want to write. Now, read the acknowledgments at the beginning of the book. Many authors will thank their literary agents by name in the acknowledgments. Write down the names of these agents, look them up in a directory such as *Literary Marketplace*, and contact them. Another place to find agents is the American Association of Authors' Representatives, www.aaronline.org.

This technique of looking for agents in book acknowledgments works well. Reason: agents each favor different types of books. So an agent will be more receptive to your idea if it fits in with the type of books she likes to work with.

Send the agent a brief letter of introduction. Explain where you got their name, who you are, and briefly describe the type of book you want to write. If you have writing credentials or are an established expert in the subject matter of your proposed book, say so.

An agent collects a percentage of all advances, royalties, and other income (e.g., sale of serial rights, movie rights, etc.) generated by your book. Typically, this ranges from 10 to 15 percent.

Book marketing and promotion

Ostensibly, your publisher handles marketing and publicity for your book. But in reality, a publisher will do little of either. The reason is simple economics: Your book competes for the publisher's limited promotional budget and staff resources with all the other titles it publishes that season. Therefore, authors are expected to take charge of marketing for their own book.

Here is where the self-published author has the advantage. It takes just as much effort and money to market a self-published book as it does a traditionally published book. But when you self-publish, you get a better return on investment from your book-marketing activities, since you earn more money per book sold.

What's the most effective promotion you can do for your book? I recommend you publish an e-newsletter for readers in your niche about your topic and distribute it free, as I outline in Chapter 10.

By giving away valuable free content, you can get many thousands of readers to subscribe to your online newsletter. When you publish your book, promote it to your online subscribers as well as through other people's online newsletters that reach the same audience demographic.

By coordinating this promotion with your peers who also have large e-lists, you can sell hundreds or even thousands of extra copies of your book. Send emails to these lists promoting the book. Offer an incentive, such as a collection of free bonus reports to readers who order the book on Amazon on a specific date. This can help lift your book up to a top spot on the Amazon best-seller list.

The File Folder Method for Writing Your Book
I use the "file folder method" for organizing and writing my books. Here's how it works.

Create one or more hanging files for the book. Within those files, place one manila file folder for each chapter (see Fig. 7.2). Print the description of each chapter from your book outline and paste it to the front of the folder for that chapter.

As you go throughout your day, you will come across material that can be used in the book. Clip or print this material, note the source on the clip or printout, and drop it into the appropriate folder. If it's online, print a hard copy for the folder, also noting the URL where you found it. Then, when it's time to sit down and write the book, you pull out the folder and have plenty of great research material for each chapter on hand, eliminating the need to do frantic research to find enough content to fill the book.

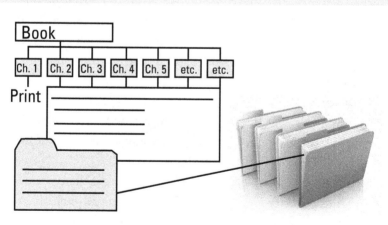

Fig. 7.2. The file folder method

8

Make an Online Fortune Selling E-Books

A re e-books profitable? For me, yes. And many writers and info marketers I know say the same thing. In 2019, e-books generated $1.94 billion
in revenue, according to the Association of American Publishers.

Although I have written and published 100 books with traditional publishers, I also make a six-figure annual income publishing and selling e-books
online. I really do believe that for the writer or information marketer who
wants to publish and sell his own work, there is no better format than e-books.
Read on to learn why.

Publishing Kindle e-books on Amazon

Yes, there are a few other brands, but Amazon's Kindle is the dominant
brand and format for e-book readers.

Amazon makes it really simple to upload your Kindle e-book file. It's a
very familiar process for most of us: when Kindle Direct Publishing (KDP)
prompts you to do so, you:

- Click "Browse."

- Navigate to the folder on your computer containing your book content file.

- Select the file you want to upload and click "Open."

Your file will now enter the conversion process to the Kindle format. Once your upload and conversion is complete, you will see a confirmation message letting you know the upload and conversion was successful and ready for review. You'll want to click on "Preview Your Book" to view your converted title.

You'll have the option to use either the "Online Previewer" or the "Downloadable Previewer" to see an approximation of how your content will look on various Amazon Kindle devices. (The online previewer is quicker and easier and emulates how most books will appear on Kindle, Kindle Fire, iPad, and iPhone.)

The book details (title, author, etc.) you provided for your book are not included in the Kindle Format 8 book file you download from KDP, and will not appear when you preview your book file using the enhanced previewer. Yet, not to worry, as the product details will be included with the book file when you publish it to the Kindle Store.

What about adding images to your Kindle e-book? KDP converts images right along with the text content you uploaded. The system can process graphics in the following formats:

- GIF (or .gif)
- PNG (or .png)
- BMP (or .bmp)
- JPEG (or .jpeg)

The Kindle book format supports JPEG and GIF image files up to 5MB.

An HTML image with an aspect ratio of 9:11 automatically displays with maximum screen coverage.

If your content contains embedded images (for example, in a Microsoft Word document), KDP extracts images from the content and replaces them with HTML <img> tags. Each image converts to a separate image file, which becomes a part of your content's publication package.

Digital Rights Management

Digital Rights Management (DRM) is intended to inhibit unauthorized distribution of the Kindle file of your book. Some authors want to encourage readers to share their work, and choose not to have DRM applied to their book. If you choose DRM, customers will still be able to lend the book to another user for a short period, and can also purchase the book as a gift for another user from the Kindle store.

DRM will NOT prevent pirating. It will, however, send a message to your readers: "It's my book even though you paid for it, and I'm going to control how you use it." Or perhaps it's sending a subtly different message: "I wrote this book and therefore I own the copyright. You bought one copy so please don't pass it on as though the copyright belongs to you now. It does not."

Pricing Kindle e-books

First, let's talk about the costs you've incurred in writing your e-book. Unless you had to purchase a computer or peripherals, purchased a relevant domain name, or hired professionals to assist you, you've probably spent absolutely nothing in the process of becoming a successful Kindle author.

But, you have committed valuable time—and as the old saying goes, "time is money." Certainly you'd like to at least compensate yourself for the time you've spent in researching and writing your Kindle e-book.

"No legal standard exists for setting the price of an e-book," writes Ali Luke, in *Publishing E-books for Dummies*. In fact, you can even let readers download your e-book for free.

I can imagine the question going through your mind right now: "Why would I want to do that?"

Well, are you looking to build a following? Do you want to promote your professional services? Then you may want to consider putting a $0.00 price tag on your Kindle e-book. You might also want to jumpstart or reinvigorate slumping sales. For example, pastor and author Brandon Clements (who really struggled to sell more than a few hundred copies of his novel in a year) decided to give away the e-book version. And in a week, over 60,000 people downloaded it. The next week, he sold another 2,000 copies.

"People really don't want to pay more than $2.99 for a digital book," declares Alex Foster, in his Kindle e-book, *Kindle Income: How to Make a*

Living Writing Kindle Books. According to him, it's only when you have a best seller or a large following that the price of $4.99 will be accepted in the market.

He acknowledges that the "norm" has really been established by Amazon as part of their royalty structure. "Amazon has kind of forced Kindle writers to sell at the $2.99 standard with the way they set up the 70% royalty bit." In short, guidelines for pricing your Kindle e-book look like this:

- $0.00: free access to establish your reputation, solicit reviews, and build a following

- $0.99: suitable for very short e-books, or to promote more sales

- $2.99–$4.99: it's the comfortable norm for Kindle e-books

- $4.99–$9.99: reserved for best-selling, well-known authors

The norm for a Kindle e-book should be $2.99, only dipping into the $0.99 category when sales have slumped, or you simply want to jumpstart sales initially. But many experts will tell you to be willing to experiment with your pricing just a little.

Kindle royalty options

When uploading your finished e-book to Kindle Direct Publishing, you'll have to choose between two royalty options: the 35 percent royalty option and the 70 percent option.

Most often you'll choose the 70 percent royalty rate and select your price, letting the international prices adjust based on the US price. Most e-books are priced $2.99–$9.99 (this is what is recommended to maximize your royalty rate).

David Wogahn, in the online article "Kindle E-book Royalties: 70% vs. 35% and 6 Essential Things You Need to Know," informs his readers that in order to qualify for the 70 percent option:

1. *You will price your e-book between $2.99 and $9.99.* You may have heard of different royalty arrangements for books priced higher than $9.99, and there are, but they aren't available to self-publishers.

2. *You will pay for file delivery.* Amazon is the only e-book retailer that charges publishers a fee to deliver their e-books to buyers. The price

for delivery to U.S. buyers is $.15 per megabyte; e.g. subtract $1.50 from your royalty if your e-book is 10MB.

3. *You won't get 70 percent in all territories.* In all others you get 35 percent. The territories where you get 70 percent are the U.S. and most of Europe.

4. *Your e-book must not be in the public domain.* In other words, you need to own the copyright if you want to get the 70% royalty.

5. *You agree to allow buyers to lend their copy of your book.* This is a one-time, 14-day loan each e-book license holder can make after buying your book.

Visit the help section on KDP's website—kdp.amazon.com—for more information on the program's royalty structure.

How to pick the right category for your Kindle e-book

"When you categorize your e-book," advises Ali Luke, in *Publishing E-books for Dummies*, "focus on its visibility." Certain categories are more popular than others; meaning there's a whole lot of competing titles within that category—which could result in a lower ranking for your e-book. In choosing a less popular category, your e-book has a greater chance of reaching a coveted position in the Top Ten e-books within that category.

In selecting your categories, you'll want to pick both a larger, more inclusive category, as well as a smaller, more specialized category.

You can only list your e-book in two categories when using KDP, but you can add categories by using tags. These tags serves as labels for your e-book that can relate to the content (let's say, online marketing), the style (first-person or action-packed), or any other aspect. You're not the only person who can tag your e-book; readers also have the ability to add a tag or tags to your book description.

For example, Dr. Alan Wolfelt, author of *Funeral Home Customer Service A–Z: Creating Exceptional Experiences for Today's Families*, chose Business & Money > Industries > Customer Service for his category. Compare that to Glenn Gould's decision to list his e-book, *Funeral Home Marketing—Moving the Bottom Line*, in Business & Money > Marketing & Sales > Marketing. (Interestingly, Gould priced his 335-page Kindle e-book at $52.50, which certainly limits his sales. And while it does give me the vague impression that his knowledge is valuable, I also see it as exclusive and well out of my price range.)

Complete your Amazon book listing

Never forget that your book listing page is intended to be a sales page. After all, the goal of the page is to convert a book browser into a book buyer! You really want your book description to be compelling enough to convince people to buy your e-book. For nonfiction books, you'll need to tell your prospects exactly how the book will solve a specific problem. And you'll want to use at least some of the top-performing keywords you discovered in the topical research phase (Amazon allows you to use up to seven targeted keywords).

Catherine Ryan Howard, self-published author of *Travelled: Tales about Not Staying at Home* (2013) and *Mousetrapped: A Year and A Bit in Orlando, Florida* (2011), offered readers a guest blog post, "The 11 Ingredients for a Sizzling Book Description," from best-selling writer Mark Edwards (author of *What You Wish For* (2014), and *The Magpies* (2013), among many other coauthored volumes). Edwards really has something to say about writing persuasive book descriptions:

- Make it clear. Your prospect needs to be able to quickly learn what kind of book this is, what it's about, and why they need to own a copy.

- Write in your genre. "Find some popular books in your genre and study the description. The backs of paperbacks can be better to study than self-published books, and first novels that were big hits are the best of all."

- Go ahead and reference other books or writers. Prospective buyers are looking for hooks that will inform them about what kind of book yours is. "If you've written a grown-up vampire novel you could do a lot worse than say that it's for fans of Anne Rice."

- Remember, the book is far more important than you are. Don't be tempted to boast about your own achievements or credentials.

PDF e-books

Why are so many e-books published as PDFs? For several reasons. With Adobe's free Acrobat Reader, virtually anyone with a PC can open and read PDFs, though you will occasionally run across someone who doesn't know how to do it. But buyers who can't handle PDF files are so rare nowadays that it's not worth worrying about.

The PDF format allows you to circulate an electronic document with a look and page layout similar to an actual book, rather than looking like another text or Microsoft Word file. In addition, the PDF file can be locked by you, its creator. This prevents people from altering or copying your e-book without your permission.

What makes PDF e-books special?

"Effective [PDF] e-books are single-problem oriented, with step-by-step, current, applicable solutions that justify the higher price," said Gordon Burgett, the author of dozens of books and e-books.

E-book marketers are "micro publishers," meaning they produce e-books addressing problems that are too highly specialized or narrow for a traditional publisher to publish a conventional book about.

For instance, one of my core topics is copywriting, and in 1985, a mainstream publishing house, Henry Holt & Co., published the first edition of my book on the subject, *The Copywriter's Handbook*. But copywriting is as narrow as they will go within this topic. I also publish a book of business forms for freelance copywriters, *The Copywriter's Toolkit*, but this is a highly specialized topic with a limited audience: freelance copywriters. Therefore, I publish it myself as an e-book.

The simplest of information products to develop is the PDF e-book. And, it is as close to a "perfect product" for internet marketers as you can get. Such e-books typically vary in length from twenty to a hundred pages (though some are longer), and the price ranges from $19 to $79. Exceptions? Of course.

The topics for PDF e-books are almost limitless, and thousands are published every year. You can write one about anything, but the best-selling e-books are usually oriented toward being instructional, informational, and full of how-to content: *You* know something that interests other people, and you can publish and sell an e-book sharing your knowledge for profit and fun.

A PDF e-book costs nothing to print because it is an electronic file. That also means that your e-book takes no room to store. There is no inventory, no hard copy, no printing and handling. The buyer can read it on the screen or print a hard copy, but that does not concern you, since you are not the one doing the printing.

Delivering your e-book to a customer is as simple and easy as attaching the file to an email. It can be even easier, as we'll explore later in the book, when you automate the purchase and delivery process using autoresponder and shopping cart software.

Zero printing costs, zero storage costs, and very low overhead costs give the PDF e-book a virtually 100 percent profit margin. The e-book is also easy to update, since it is a computer file and not a printed document.

Some disadvantages of the PDF e-book are that your customer has to use his own paper and ink (or toner) to print a copy—which many people still do—and that the e-book will be printed on loose, unbound pages. This makes it a little less convenient for the reader, and it makes an e-book less physically appealing than a traditional book. Self-publishing your writings as e-books is also not likely to bring you a lot of prestige, and book reviewers and the media almost always ignore e-books.

Tip: Do not use large areas of black either on the e-book covers or in the interior page layouts (e.g., bands of black or other dark color), as this consumes too much of the customer's ink when he goes to print the book on his laser printer.

By following the 21-step process presented in this chapter, you can create your own e-book, develop a website to promote it, and start getting orders for your PDF e-book within months or even weeks. These 21 steps can lead you to the successful marketing of your very first e-book, and to the beginnings of your own how-to information empire.

21 steps to writing and publishing your first e-book

Here's the step-by-step process I have used to create dozens of highly prof-itable e-books, which together generate literally hundreds of thousands of dollars of income online for me every year:

1. *Choose your topic.* Choose a topic that is specific and targeted to your niche market. Your first PDF e-book lays the foundation for an entire line of information products related to the topic of that first book. Use your very first e-book to establish yourself as an authority in your subject area.

   For instance, one of my core markets is freelance writers. For my first e-book, I collected columns I had written on freelance writing for *Writer's Digest* magazine. The advantage was that the material had already been written and I owned the rights. I titled the book *Write and Grow Rich*, so that it would appeal to the maximum number of prospects in my core market; what writer doesn't want to make more money? So far I've sold 1,673 copies of the e-book for gross revenues of $51,807.

2. *Use keyword discovery to make sure there is a market for your e-book online.* Be sure your topic is one people are searching for online. Use keyword discovery tools such as www.workdtracker.com (see Chapter 2) to learn how often, and which keywords, people are searching to find information on your topic.

3. *Create an outline.* The outline is your road map for completing this e-book and can serve as a template for future efforts. Effective methods of organizing how-to and reference books include alphabetical order, process steps, and Q&A. We covered how to create content outlines in Chapter 4.

4. *Research your topic.* Be organized when doing research. Use your outline to set up a separate file folder for each chapter. Store everything relating to your topic in the appropriate chapter file. Visit the library, surf the web, and comb bookstores for information related to your e-book. You might even consider interviewing experts to build on your own knowledge and the information you gather.

5. *Write your e-book.* You can write the e-book yourself or hire a freelancer to write it for you. A fast and efficient way to create e-books you can sell profitably online is to assemble them from content you have already written, such as articles, blog entries, and newsletters.

   In my information marketing business, I use a variety of means to get my e-books written. Some are assembled from articles and columns I have published and own the rights to. Others are edited from my out-of-print books, the rights to which have reverted to me. Some I write from scratch. I hire ghostwriters to write others under my editorial direction. For a few of my e-books, I found relevant articles written by friends, colleagues, or other authors, and I obtained permission to reprint them in the e-book. Usually, they granted permission for free, and in exchange I offered them a 50 percent commission on sales they made of the e-book from their website or as a result of adding it to their list.

6. *Create a few bonus reports to give away to your e-book buyers.* These reports are additional information you offer to your customers as an added incentive to buy your e-book now. They may be separate PDF files or sections within the main e-book PDF file. Chapter 9 offers guidelines on how to create bonus reports.

7. *Edit your e-book.* As with the writing, you can hire a freelance editor or you can do it yourself. I recommend that the writer and editor should be different people, as it's difficult to edit your own writing. Watch for spelling mistakes, readability, clarity, and completeness. Fortunately, as an electronic document, an e-book can be corrected even after it is released. Thus errors, while undesirable, are not as disastrous as they would be in a traditional book with a first printing of 5,000 copies, because e-books are essentially "reproduced" and sold one copy at a time.

8. *Create the front cover design and interior page layout.* Your best choice is to hire someone to do this work unless you are experienced in book design. Be sure to ask what is included before agreeing to any provider's price. You want a cover design, the pages laid out, and a book image (2- or 3-dimensional) for your landing page (the web page on which you describe and sell the e-book online; see step 12 below). To find a graphic designer to design your e-book cover and page layout, go to www.bly.com, click on Vendors, and then click on E-Book Graphic Designers.

9. *Proofread and lock the PDF file.* This is your last chance to spot mistakes before releasing the e-book. You can hire a freelance proofreader

or proofread it yourself. Once you have proofread the document and corrected mistakes, you can lock the PDF.

Locking the PDF prevents those in possession of the e-book from altering or stealing the content. When you lock a PDF file, you create an unlock code that only you know. Write down the unlock code and keep it stored in a safe place.

With the unlock code, you can unlock the PDF later to make changes if needed. For e-books of forms and other materials, you may want to sell the book with an unlocked PDF, enabling the buyer to cut and paste the forms he wants to use.

10. *Load your e-book PDF into a shopping cart.* Shopping cart software is going to collect payments, deliver the e-book and reports, provide you with an email autoresponder, and track your sales. Once you decide which shopping cart to use, loading your e-book into the shopping cart is as easy as attaching a file to an email. Popular shopping carts include Infusion, 1ShoppingCart, MailChimp, Aweber, Active Campaign, and ConvertKit.

11. *Reserve a domain name for your e-book.* Shorter is better. An ideal domain name is the keyword or phrase related to your topic or a short phrase that is easy to remember (e.g. www.myveryfirste-book. com). To check on the availability or to reserve a domain name, visit www.ultracheapdomains.com.

12. *Write and design a landing page to sell your e-book.* Now that your e-book is ready to sell, you need a landing page to do the selling. A landing page is a dedicated website—some call it a micro-site—that sells a single product. It is essentially a long-copy sales letter posted online. And, yes, you can hire a freelance copywriter to write this sales tool, or you can visit www.thelandingpageguru.com for help (the site user name is "user" and the password is "pageguru"). Also see www.myverfirste-book.com, which generated a 32 percent conversion rate selling a $19 e-book, as an example of a landing page format and design proven to work; I use this style and form in dozens of my own sales pages with good results.

13. *Arrange hosting for your landing page.* You need a reliable hosting service at a low cost-per-site hosting charge. Be sure your hosting

service package gives you enough space to hold all your files, that there is sufficient bandwidth to permit a high volume of downloads each month, and that you can add lots of new landing pages without increasing the total monthly hosting fee. My hosting service is www.hostwithstanley.com, which I highly recommend if you plan to have more than a few websites. I have dozens, and hosting costs me less than a dollar a month per site. A larger and more widely used hosting service is www.hostgator.com

14. *Capture the email addresses of landing page visitors who do not buy your e-book.* You want to capture the email addresses of people who click onto your landing page but leave without buying the product, so that you can continue to market to them in the future. The easiest way to capture the email addresses is to have a window pop up when a visitor leaves without making a purchase. The window offers a small free bonus report in exchange for an email address.

15. *Set up an autoresponder email series to convert non-buyers to buyers.* Once you have the visitor's email address, use an autoresponder email series to persuade him to come back to the landing page and buy your e-book. This is a sequence of prewritten emails that extol the virtue of the product in an attempt to get the visitor to click back onto the landing page and buy the e-book.

16. *Drive traffic to your landing page.* Use email marketing, pay-per-click advertising, videos on YouTube, banner ads, social networking sites, articles, affiliates, and other traffic-building methods to drive prospects to your sales page. My favorite method is to send a short email to my online subscriber list teasing them with a promise or benefit to entice them to click on the link and find out more about what I am offering; you can see a sample email in the appendix.

17. *Test, measure, and optimize your landing page.* There is always room for improvement. A/B split and multivariate testing can show which parts of your landing page are working well and which need tweaking. Testing can help you increase the landing page's conversion rate, thereby selling more e-books.

18. *Create a profitable line of e-books and related info products.* Internet marketing is direct marketing. You will make your greatest profit on "back-end sales" (sales to repeat customers), so you need to develop a line of related products you can sell to purchasers of your first e-books on an ongoing basis.

19. *Recruit affiliates to sell your e-books and other info products.* Allowing affiliates to sell your e-book can significantly increase sales and revenues. An affiliate is a person or company that agrees to sell your e-book to their prospects for a commission.

20. *Publish a free e-zine and drive traffic to the subscription page.* Offer a free e-zine with useful and relevant content to anyone who joins your e-list. This can increase sign-ups and also give you a vehicle for communicating with your online prospects and customers on a regular basis. My subscription page is www.bly.com/reports.

21. *Send regular emails to your opt-in subscriber list to drive additional sales.* Every time you have a new information product, tell your customers about it. You can use a service like Constant Contact, MailChimp, or Bronto to send emails to your subscriber list; a portion of the recipients will click onto your landing page and buy the new product.

Ideal word length for PDF e-books

I like to charge at least $29 or more for an e-book. My current e-books range in price from $19 for an introductory guide to online marketing to $59 for a library of sample email marketing messages and $79 for a book of business forms for freelance copywriters.

Why is $29 my preferred minimum price? Because you are only going to sell so many copies per email blast, and if the price is too low, your revenue from the email marketing message promoting the book will also be too low. I like to make at least $2,000 to $3,000 per email blast sent to my list, and that's difficult to do with a product that costs less than $29. Also, $29 seems to be a low price point for PDF e-books and overcomes any price resistance buyers may have.

To charge $29 for an e-book, it has to be a minimum of 50 pages. Fewer pages and the buyer will feel ripped off, believing that the book is too light in content. In an e-book format, figure 300 words per published book page. That means you need approximately 15,000 words to publish a 50-page book.

A traditional 200-page trade paperback like this one typically has around 75,000 words. So an e-book contains only one-fifth the amount of content as a conventionally printed book. Yet you can charge $29 to $39 or more for an e-book versus only $15 to $20 for a trade paperback. Therefore, packaging your product as an e-book lets you command a higher price for less content.

Why can you charge more for PDF e-books? Because they deal with one specific problem-solving topic. Remember the rule for pricing specialized how-to information: the narrower the topic, the smaller the potential audience, but the more you can charge.

Choosing e-book topics

In chapters 2 and 4 we talked about choosing a niche for your how-to writing and then coming up with book ideas and titles within that niche.

My rule of thumb for e-book publishing is as follows:

- If the topic is general and I can publish it in a couple of thousand words or less, I write a magazine article on it.

- For general topics that take multiple thousands of words to cover, I self-publish a white paper or special report, which is often a free bonus I give away to generate leads or sales.

- For broad and some specialized topics that take tens-of-thousands of words to teach adequately, I write a traditional book for a mainstream publisher.

- For specialized instruction on a narrow niche topic, I write and sell an e-book on the topic.

Related to narrowness or specificity of topic is audience size: If I think we can sell many thousands of copies and that people would look for this information in a bookstore, I write a traditional book for a traditional book publisher. If I think the market is only a few thousand copies, and that people would look online for this information, I write and publish an e-book.

Importantly, e-book buyers are not primarily looking to read about why they should do something or even what they should do; these readers expect to find out *how* to do it by reading your e-book—and the more comprehensible, clear, accurate, and actionable your instructions, the happier they will be.

Writing style for e-books

I'm not sure that there's really a separate writing style for e-books versus traditional books and magazine articles. But there are some minor differences I notice between the formats.

Editors at magazines want articles to be entertaining first and informative second. No editor has told me that, but that's the impression I get when reading magazines and writing for them, too. Some editors at certain mainstream book publishers are the same way; they want the book to be entertaining first and then have solid content second. One editor told me: "Above all else, make it a good read."

The e-book buyer wants to enjoy reading your e-book, but in how-to nonfiction writing in general and e-books in particular, content is king. The reader will forgive typos, misspellings, and lack of literary style as long as you deliver solid content.

Follow the writing advice in Chapter 5, in particular the "Three C's." Make your writing concise, compelling, comprehensive, and, above all, clear.

E-book page layout and PDF setup

I urge you to outsource the cover designs and page layouts for your e-books. Freelance graphic designers are plentiful and so affordable that it makes little sense to agonize over design work on your own. The professional will do a much better job and free you to concentrate on core activities—in particular writing and marketing.

You can find freelance graphic designers to produce your e-books on internet job sites such as www.elance.com or by Googling "e-book designers" or "e-book cover designs" or "book cover designers." Several are listed in the appendix of this book. Prices vary, but you can get an entire e-book designed, including front cover and page layout, for a couple hundred dollars or so.

Pricing and guarantee

As we mentioned, PDF e-books range in price from $19 to $79, with most falling in the $29 to $49 range. The customer pays online by credit card, and as soon as he does, a link to where he can download the PDF of the e-book is delivered automatically via email autoresponder. I give my customers a 90-day money-back guarantee of satisfaction. If they are not 100 percent satisfied, they can let me know within 90 days for a full and prompt refund of every penny they paid me.

Does the customer have to return the e-book to get the refund? Not really. The e-book is electronic, so what is there to return? Some information marketers tell customers who request a refund to tear up their print-out of the book and delete the PDF from their hard drive. Of course you can't make sure they have complied, so you put them on the honor system.

Since you don't benefit in any way by insisting on destruction and erasure of the e-book, why do it? My guarantee is that, even if they request a refund, they can still keep the e-book free—my gift to them—a nice extra that costs me absolutely nothing to offer. Once I started telling them "keep the e-book free no matter what you decide," my refund rates did not increase at all—meaning no one was taking advantage and ripping me off—but my landing page conversion rates increased 10 to 15 percent.

Technical glitches

There are a few common technical glitches in publishing and selling PDF e-books that you should know about.

The first is the customer who attempts to order the e-book but finds his credit card is declined because of an "AVS mismatch." This simply means some of the information he entered on the order page was incorrect or incomplete. You can solve this problem by contacting the customer and taking the order over the phone.

Another technical glitch occurs when the customer complains that he did not get the e-book. Since the e-book is delivered to the buyer via an automatically generated email message, the likely culprit is that the customer or his Internet Services Provider (ISP) has blocked your email with a spam filter or firewall. In this case, I call or email the customer and suggest they send me a personal email with the book title in the subject line. When I get it, I return their email with the PDF file for the book attached, and it always gets through.

A third glitch is the customer who gets the PDF but says they cannot open or read it. The likely cause is that the customer is using an old version of Adobe's Acrobat Reader. Tell the customer to go to the Adobe website and download the latest version of Acrobat Reader. It is free.

Updated and new editions

One of the great advantages of PDF e-books versus printed books is that when you spot an error or typo, or want to change or update something, it's relatively quick and easy to do. Just make the change to the PDF file and load the updated file into your shopping cart software.

From time to time, you may feel the desire to update one or more of your e-books by correcting dated, inaccurate, or incomplete information or adding new sections or chapters. I encourage you to do so, because keeping your material fresh and content-rich pleases your customers.

If your updates and additions involve more than 20 percent of the pages, you can advertise the revised book as an updated second edition; doing so can substantially increase sales. If you have expanded the number of pages by 20 percent or more over the original, advertise it as an "updated and expanded second edition," and consider raising the price by $5 to $10.

Your email distribution software or service provider can probably identify within your database customers who bought the first edition. You can send owners of the first edition an email offering the second edition at a special discount rate.

Also, a new edition should have the updated year of publication of the updated e-book on the title page. The older the copyright date of information products sold online today, the more your potential buyers will think the content must be out of date, even if that isn't true.

9

Special Reports, Booklets, Forms, Kits, and Other Short-Form Information Products

The how-to writer is not limited to book-length or even e-book-length form. Everything you write does not have to be your magnum opus. I recommend mixing books (traditional and electronic) with shorter formats.

Why should you produce a mix of both short-form and long-form how-to writings? A few reasons. To begin with, different subjects merit works of different length. Some topics can be covered adequately in an article, while others may require a large book or several books. When I wrote *The Advertising Manager's Handbook* for Prentice Hall to advise advertising managers what they needed to know, it was over 800 pages long and sold for $80—and that was pre-internet. Today, with all the new developments in marketing, it could easily be twice that length.

Second, *by writing in multiple lengths, you increase your publishing opportunities by opening up multiple markets.* If you can only teach an idea in 50 to 100 pages or more, you are pretty much limited to writing an e-book or maybe a traditional book (see Table 9.1). On the other hand, some ideas only warrant a couple thousand words (magazine articles) or even a couple hundred words (blog posts).

Third, I don't know about you, but as a writer I absolutely love variety, in both subject matter and word length, and, conversely, I deplore monotony. Stephen King has expressed a similar sentiment regarding variety in length. He says that after finishing a big novel, he wants to write a novella or short story before buckling down to write another novel. In my work as a copywriter, I love writing long-copy sales letters, but after I finish one, before starting another I'll do a few short-copy assignments in between, such as postcards or print ads.

Fourth, monotony robs you of stamina in almost every activity. Varying project length creates variety you will find fun and energizing. Some days you arise and are primed for sustained concentration on a single work; other days, your concentration is lessened, and you are more productive switching among several shorter projects.

Fifth, but perhaps most important, as a rule of thumb you can charge more for lengthy items (but not always) than for short items. Writing shorts as well as longer works enables you to develop a line of how-to information products that sells at different price points.

Table 9.1. Formats and Word Length

Length	Medium	Words or Character Count
Ultra-short-shorts	Tweets	280 characters
Ultra-short	Online articles, blog posts	100–300 words
Short	Tip sheets, press releases	300–800 words
Medium	Magazine articles	800–2,000 words
Medium-long	Special reports, booklets, white papers, monographs	1,000–5,000 words
Long	E-books	10,000–25,000 words
Ultra-long	Books	50,000–100,000+ words

Multiple price points and sales funnels

Have you ever hesitated to buy an interesting book in the bookstore because you hadn't read the author before?

Consumers prefer familiar brands. This is why the Dummies and Idiot's Guide books sell so well: The consumer trusts the brand.

Authors are also a brand. I will plunk down $25 for the new Stephen King novel because I am a fan of the brand. But I rarely will pay $25 for a hardcover book from a novelist I have not read before.

When a reader of your free e-newsletter sees you plug one of your $25 hardcover books, he might be more inclined to buy it than would a complete stranger whom you emailed out of the blue (not recommended, because it's spam). But still, the percentage of subscribers who buy the book will be relatively small, because they have no experience with buying your writings before.

The solution would be to sell them a $9 special report or a $7 booklet. Reason: The smaller the price tag, the more people are willing to take a chance on buying material from a new author.

Most writers are more concerned with their royalty or advance than the price their work is selling for. But that's a mistake. Ideally, you want your writings to be packaged in a variety of different formats, lengths, and prices in order to appeal to the broadest range of buyers.

As shown in Fig. 9.1, you can think of your product line as a funnel with four distinct levels. Customers enter at the top and then work their way down. The four levels are:

- Free products
- Low-priced products
- Medium-priced products
- High-priced products.

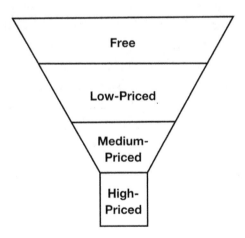

Fig. 9.1. Sales Funnel

At the top level of the pricing funnel are your *free products*. These include your online newsletter, blog, podcasts, and other content you give away, either to build your online subscriber list or to establish your reputation as a thought leader in your field. My monthly e-newsletter, "The Direct Response Letter," is packed with useful content and doesn't cost a dime. There is also no charge to read my blog at bly.com/blog.

The next content consumers encounter as they move further into your sales funnel is *low-priced information products*, which we can define as anything under a hundred dollars. Most e-books and traditional hard copy books fall into this category. With low-price products, we give readers of our free content an easy entry point to making the transition from freebie seeker to paying book buyer. For instance, the first product of mine that thousands of my e-newsletter subscribers have bought is a $19 e-book available at www.myveryfirste-book.com.

We can make handsome profits by cross-selling our customers many products in the lower price range. We know the buyer of a $39 book will spend at least $39 to purchase our how-to information and advice, so we can easily sell him $19 e-books and $25 paperbacks all day long.

However, a percentage of low-price buyers may be willing to spend at a higher price point to acquire our content. Therefore, you can increase your writing revenues by creating information products that sell at *medium and high price points*.

Getting buyers to move from free to low to medium and higher price points in buying your information is called the ladder or funnel. It works in the direct marketing of virtually any product category.

For instance, you've seen those magazine ads that say "Buy this gold or silver coin at our cost." Are they really selling the coin at their cost? Often, yes. Why? Because for every 10,000 customers that buy a $49 coin, they know they can get 1,000 of them to buy a $490 coin set. And for every 1,000 customers who buy the $490 coin set, they know they can get 100 to buy a $4,900 rare coin.

Table 9.2 shows the four price ranges you should have in your product line (free, low, medium, high) and the type of products you can offer within each.

Table 9.2. Pricing Your Information Products

Price Range	Products
Free	Blogs, social media, e-zines, online articles, bonus reports, podcasts
Low ($9–$99)	Special reports, booklets, e-books, books, teleseminars, webinars, single DVD
Medium ($100–$399)	Audio CD album, DVD album, loose-leaf manual, home study course
High (over $400)	Boot camps, training classes, seminars, coaching programs, consulting, multimedia programs, paid subscription newsletters and information services, membership sites (annual fee)

Booklets

One of the low-end information products you can price at the bottom of the range is a booklet.

In the pre-internet era, booklets were big sellers. A booklet is a small book—typically saddle-stitched (held together with staples through the spine)—that can fit in a #10 envelope; page size is approximately 4 by 9 inches. Depending on the number of pages, booklet prices can range from $7 to $19.

Why create a booklet? *A booklet is an ideal format for topics that you don't have enough content to fill a full-length book.* For instance, during the recession of the early 1990s, I decided to promote myself as a thought leader in marketing by publishing and promoting a book on marketing in a recession.

But when I sat down to write the book, I found I could come up with only 5,000 words on the topic of marketing in a recession, not the 70,000 or more I would need to fill a book.

Solution: I self-published my recession-proof business strategies as a booklet, priced it at $7, plus shipping and handling, and sold it by sending a press release (see Appendix B) to business magazines and newspaper business editors.

I mailed the press release to 300 editors at a cost of less than $300. The press release was run in nearly two dozen publications, giving me a huge amount of publicity which generated several consulting assignments and speaking engagements. In addition, I sold 4,000 copies of the booklet at $7 each to gross $28,000. And my printing cost was just 39 cents a copy.

Tip sheet

A tip sheet is a mini-report. It is published as a series of numbered tips printed on two sides of an 8½ by 11-inch sheet of paper (a sample is included in Appendix B). Tip sheets are great giveaways as premiums for paid information products, because people enjoy the quick-reading format. And for you as the author, they are quick and easy to create.

Seminar promoter Anvar Suleimen once created a series of mini-reports, each typewritten on two sides of a sheet of paper. He offered them as a bonus for attending a conference. He assigned a value of $2 each and, as I recall, he had around 40 of them. The 40 were bundled into a single document of 40 pages printed on both sides, and had a perceived value of $80—an effective incentive to entice people to register for the conference.

Forms kits

A great information product for the low or medium price range is a forms kit. As the name describes, this is a kit, or collection, of forms used in a particular business or activity. Socrates Media, for instance, publishes a set of forms for landlords, including model leases and eviction notices.

One of my core markets is freelance copywriters, and one of my most successful information products is *The Copywriter's Toolkit*, an e-book that is simply a collection of several dozen business forms and model documents I use in my freelance copywriting business. These include samples of my sales letters, sample ads, model invoices, collection letters, client agreements, and so on.

While most of my e-books are in the $19 to $39 range, the Toolkit is a brisk seller at $79 a copy. Forms kits are easy to sell because of the high perceived value. You can easily pay a lawyer $200 or more to draw up a model contact or letter of agreement. Therefore, if your forms kit has 50 forms, the perceived value of the content is at least $10,000, which at $79 for the entire collection makes it a bargain. To date, I have sold 2,534 copies of the Toolkit, generating gross revenue of $128,295.

In addition, forms kits are how-to writing at its highest level. Recall from Chapter 5 the three-level hierarchy: telling the reader what to do; showing him how to do it; and doing it for him. With a forms kit, you are doing it for the reader. Instead of just presenting a list of five things that must be in every copywriting contract, I give the reader a prewritten contract he can use "as is" or adapt to his own business.

Writing white papers for fun and profit

A white paper is a marketing document that helps sell a product by educating consumers about the application the product handles or the problem it solves. For instance, to help a technology company sell a business software package, I wrote for them a white paper on "Choosing Business Software."

As you can see, white papers are more often than not how-to in nature. I have written white papers on everything from how to safely dispose of industrial waste to how to make sure your computer software meets federal government standards for data security.

As a nonfiction writer, you can earn handsome fees writing white papers for companies that use them to market their products and services. "The demand for white papers has never been higher," says Michael A. Stelzner, executive editor of WhitePaperSource.com. "During business downturns, corporations rely more on marketing to help them acquire leads and establish thought leadership. White papers are the secret weapon for companies. Our organization has seen a major increase in white paper use among businesses of all sizes, but especially those selling costly or complex products."

A typical white paper is ten pages, or about 3,000 words long. You can charge clients $3,000 to $5,000 to write a white paper of this length. Do one a month and that's an extra $60,000 a year added to your nonfiction writing income.

In a survey of nearly 1,400 IT professionals, the majority said they were more likely to download and read white papers than product literature. Over the years, I've seen a number of direct mail and email tests in which offering a free white paper or other free content increased response rates 10 percent to 100 percent or more.

White papers work; more than half of IT professionals say white papers influence their buying decision. I do think, however, that we have to broaden our notion of how to use free content offers, which is essentially what a white paper is (free information designed to educate our prospects and motivate them to inquire about our product or service).

To begin with, I think it's not white papers themselves that are tiring, but the name itself. "White paper" signals to some prospects a document that is an obvious selling tool. And with virtually every white paper in the world available for free, white papers have a low perceived value as a giveaway.

The solution is to keep using white papers in your marketing portfolio but to call them something else. The mailing list broker Edith Roman used to publish a print catalog of mailing lists. But instead of calling it a catalog, her company called it the "Direct Mail Encyclopedia." Offering a free Direct Mail Encyclopedia helped generate more inquiries for their brokerage services.

Copywriter Ivan Levison calls his white papers "guides." Marketer David Yale uses "executive briefing." I'm partial to "special report." For consumer marketing, marketing expert Joe Polish suggests "consumer awareness guide," and for a B2B white paper giving product selection tips, I'd change this to "buyer's guide" or "selection guide." For a white paper giving tips or instructions on a process, I might call it a "manual." If you publish a print version that fits in a #10 envelope and is saddle-stitched, you can call it a "free booklet."

All of the above are variations on the free content offer. Direct marketers refer to free content offers as "bait pieces," because they are used to "bait your hook" when you go "fishing" for sales leads. Does what you call your bait piece really matter? I think it does, because calling it a report or guide creates a perception of greater value—after all, thousands of publishers actually *sell* special reports and booklets for prices ranging from $3 to $40 or more. I often put a dollar price for the guide or report in the upper right corner of the front cover, which strengthens the perception that the freebie has value; I don't think this would be credible on a document labeled as a white paper.

What about the complaint that prospects already have too much to read? I am reminded of a quotation from Rutherford Rogers: "We are drowning in information but starved for knowledge." There is more information on the internet than you could process in a thousand lifetimes. But good white papers don't merely present information; they offer solutions to business and technical problems. Virtually every B-to-B sale you make is because someone thinks your product or service is the solution to their problem. A white paper can help clarify the problem as well as convince the reader that your idea or method is the best of many options for addressing it.

Every marketing campaign has an objective, yet if you ask most managers what the objective of their white paper is, they probably couldn't tell you. Too many see white papers as an opportunity to merely collect and publish a pile of research material they found on the web using Google. *To make your white paper successful, you must define the marketing objective before writing a single word.*

For example, a manufacturer found that consumers were not buying their do-it-yourself (DIY) underground sprinkler kits, because homeowners perceived installing the irrigation system by themselves as too difficult. Solution: a free DIY manual on how to install an underground sprinkler system in a single weekend. Clearly written and illustrated, the manual overcame the perception that this was a tough project, making it look easy.

In the pre-internet era, bait pieces were mainly paper and ink. Thanks to the PC and the internet, bait pieces can now be produced as PDF files and can be instantly downloaded online. But at the receiving end, they are usually printed by the prospect and read on paper.

It may be that what's wearing out is not free content, but the standard white paper format: pages of black ink on 8½ by 11-inch sheets of paper. To make your bait piece stand out, consider using alternative formats: DVDs, CDs, podcasts, webinars, teleseminars, flash cards, stickers, posters, software, apps, and slide guides. (A slide guide is a cardboard promotional item with a moving slide or wheel that allows the prospect to perform some simple calculation, e.g., convert inches to centimeters or determine the monthly payments on a mortgage.)

Most white papers are six to ten pages—about 3,000 to 4,000 words—but you are not locked into that length. You can go shorter or longer, depending on the content you want to present and the marketing objective of the bait piece. The bait piece can be as short and simple as a list of tips printed on one side of a sheet of paper. Or it can be as long as a self-published paperback book.

Free content offers have been used effectively in marketing for decades, and rather than tiring, they have been given new life, thanks in part to the information-oriented culture spawned by the internet. "Every organization possesses particular expertise that has value in the new e-marketplace of ideas," writes David Meerman Scott in his book *Cashing In With Content.*

"Organizations gain credibility and loyalty with customers, employees, the media, investors, and suppliers through content."

Compiling and marketing directories, dictionaries and reference guides

Another lucrative market for the how-to writer is collecting and compiling information into directories, dictionaries, and reference guides. The king of this genre is Matthew Lesko, the guy you sometimes see on late-night TV infomercials selling books on how to get free money from the government.

The internet has somewhat diminished the market for directories and reference guides, but in many fields, they are still desired and can sell briskly. One of my colleagues sells a guide on where to buy merchandise at wholesale and close-out prices and resell it at a profit. It lists numerous sources for wholesale and close-out merchandise.

Years ago, pre-internet, I saw that a lot of valuable free information could be obtained by calling the toll-free 800 numbers of corporations, nonprofits, the federal government, and even local businesses. You could call Campbell's Soup, for instance, and they'd send you a free recipe book on cooking with soup. I compiled hundreds of these numbers and descriptions of the free information each company offered into a paperback book published by New American Library as *Information Hotline U.S.A.*

More recently, I published a guide on how to make money participating in market research studies. The guide has a few pages of instructions on how to be selected to participate in these studies for pay, but mainly it is a state-by-state directory of market research companies looking for study participants to pay.

Okay. Let's say you find an information niche in which you think there is demand for a directory. Here are some tips for selling your directory profitably year after year:

1. *Target previous buyers.* Mail to past buyers and tell them specifically why, although they already own a copy, they should get the new edition. For one directory, a test mailing to buyers from three years past pulled almost triple the response to a rented list.

2. *Play on your good name.* When Medical Economics successfully launched *Physicians' Desk Reference for Nurses*, direct mail copy

positioned it as "the PDR for nurses." If your flagship product or publishing company has name recognition, play off that name in promotions for other products.

3. *Offer a pre-publication discount.* The most effective incentive for any prospect to order now instead of later is a pre-publication discount. This can be an actual cash discount or free shipping and handling— or both.

4. *Stress the urgency and importance of having up-to-date information.* Many prospects don't ask "Why buy?" when they see your offer; instead they ask "Why buy now?" Demonstrate to prospects why they need or should want the most current data available. For instance, bringing a manager up-to-date on new safety regulations might help him achieve compliance at lower cost.

5. *Differentiate yourself from the competition.* If your data is approved by a regulatory agency, for example, then your advantage is that it's official. On the other hand, if your data is not reviewed by a governing body prior to publication, then you provide expert ratings, guidance, unbiased opinions, or some other advantages the "official" competitor does not. Identify what makes you unique and communicate it clearly in your mailings.

6. *Show the potential buyer how he or she can profit by putting your directory to use.* One obvious benefit is saving time. Your prospect knows that using old directories means wasted mailings and phone calls to update old listings and reach the right people. Position the purchase of the new edition as a drop in the bucket compared to time and money saved, as well as better results obtained.

7. *Talk about the important people or companies who rely on your book.* Communication Briefings uses this technique in direct mail selling their newsletters; half a page of the four-page letter is a box listing Fortune 500 companies that subscribe to the newsletter. Tell your prospect about the prestigious companies in his field that buy your directory, or about the important associations that endorse it.

8. *Quantify the improvements in the forthcoming edition.* Be specific. How many listings out of the total have been revised or updated?

How many are new? Give percentages, e.g., "25 percent of listings updated." The most important improvement buyers look for is new and updated core information. Second is expanded listings (e.g., more data on each company or product; email addresses added). Third is new features, such as photos, maps, guides, glossaries, background articles, etc.

9. *Spell out the negatives and penalties of working with old information.* A classic example is a mailing for *Physicians' Desk Reference* that warned buyers of older editions that the information in those volumes was now dated and should not be used when making clinical decisions. The mailing included a warning sticker the buyer could place on the cover of their old directory until the new one arrived!

10. *Test a guarantee.* A number of directory publishers are successful without offering a money-back guarantee. That may be the case with you; however, you should still split test no-guarantee versus 30-day, money-back guarantee (or even 60 or 90 days) if you are currently not offering a guarantee. Doesn't it make sense to confirm whether your current offer is the most profitable offer possible?

Collections, compilations, and calendars

One quick and easy information product for the how-to writer to produce is a collection compiled from previously published material.

I love this strategy for increasing my writing income, and here's why: Traditionally, when a writer writes an article, it is largely forgotten about once it is published. Therefore, any writer who has been active for any length of time amasses a collection of prewritten articles on his or her hard drive. By compiling them into a collection, you can create a saleable book, e-book, special report, or collection in a small fraction of the time it would take you to write an original work on that topic.

I have sold compilations of my articles to three different publishers who have brought them out in book form. I have also produced several highly profitable e-books. In one instance, a magazine publisher had already paid me $7,500 to write ten columns on freelance writing. After these articles had run in the magazine, they sat ignored in the publisher's back-issue archive and on my hard drive.

I compiled them into an e-book (at a total cost of $75 for a graphic designer to put them into a PDF document) and I sell the compilation for $39; to date I have sold 931 copies, earning an additional $36,309 from articles that otherwise would have not earned me one more dime.

This is an important point for how-to writers looking to maximize their income. While we get excited and enthused about writing new material, far more profit can be produced by recycling already published material into new information products and formats.

You can create and sell more collections of your previously published material—and make more money from your content—with far less work, simply by being organized. Keep an Excel spreadsheet or Word document that lists your published columns, articles, and other content by file name and topic. When you want to create a new information product, select a topic and then compile the best content you have already written on that topic. Using this method, I have produced 200-page manuscripts for new books and e-books, from start to finish, in a single afternoon.

Let nothing go to waste. Readers will buy in one format material that they have already bought or even received for free in another. One of my early mentors, the late Jerry Buchanan, published a monthly newsletter and had a profitable side business selling bound annuals (one year's worth of issues). Oddly, most of the bound issues were sold to people who already subscribed to the newsletter and therefore had received all of the issues that were included in the bound annual. When I asked Jerry about this, he said subscribers often didn't save their issues, and when they got his offer for a bound annual, the subscribers would buy them again to have them collected between hard covers.

An oft-overlooked format in the information product business is calendars. You can create a wall or desktop calendar and enhance it with content on your subject. I prefer a desktop calendar because there is more space for text on each day. Adams Media has published a desktop vocabulary calendar of mine annually since 2012.

I have been publishing my e-newsletter, "The Direct Response Letter," for years, and have always given it away for free, and will continue to do so. However, following Jerry's lead, I am collecting these newsletter articles in a series of e-books for which we will charge $29 or $39 each. Because the content is already written and on my hard drive, I can compile these volumes in just a few hours each. My first in the series, which now consists of half a dozen volumes, is titled *Don't Wear a Cowboy Hat Unless You Are a Cowboy: Grumblings of a Cranky Curmudgeon* (CTC Publishing).

Workbooks and study guides

I began my writing career as a technical writer with Westinghouse and my first book, still in print today, was a guide to technical writing, *The Elements of Technical Writing* (first published in 1982 under the title *Technical Writing: Structure, Standards, and Style*).

As a result of the book, I taught dozens of on-site, technical writing seminars to corporate clients. The book was not designed to be used in a training class, and so I compiled from the book and other sources a 50-page workbook, which I used in the seminar. I sold many copies of the workbook to companies that bought it for the attendees they sent to my technical writing workshop, but I also sold quite a few to companies that wanted to teach their own class but wanted to use my material as their workbook.

In the pre-PC days, you would print the workbooks and ship them to your corporate client; a typical fee was $29 per copy. Now you can email a PDF of the workbook to the client, let them handle printing and collating, and charge a small royalty per copy, or even throw them in with your training seminar as a free bonus.

A husband and a wife with a small home-based company specializes in educational workbooks for children in elementary school. In 2020, when the COVID-19 virus forced children to study and learn at home, sales of their workbooks increased 500 percent.

Information product merchandise

By information product "merchandise," I mean information published in nontraditional formats: board games, apps, flash cards, bumper stickers, toys, calculator wheels, slide guides, and other content-based merchandise.

When you package your content as "merchandise," you can charge ten times what it would sell for in conventional print format and often make 100 times more money from it.

One example is the famous Pet Rock. The Pet Rock was a rock sold in a cardboard "home." But what really made the idea work was the "care and feeding of your pet rock" booklet that came with the rock and container, and it made its creator a small fortune.

Another example of merchandise content is the game *Trivial Pursuit*. I have written nearly half a dozen books of pop culture trivia and earned only modest sums from them. But the creators of *Trivial Pursuit* put their trivia content into a board game and made millions.

10

Newsletters and E-Zines

Many information products are one-shot products, meaning the reader buys the book or report from you, and your revenue stream from the product ends there. You make no additional money from the reader until he buys another book or information product from you.

Most information marketers and how-to writers spend much of their time writing and selling one-shot products, and there's nothing wrong with that. However, this chapter will show you how your income will be higher and more consistent if you can create information products that give you a *recurring stream of revenue*. These can include membership sites, software, coaching services, and paid subscription newsletters.

Packaging and selling your how-to writing in a newsletter gives you a recurring source of revenue that, with renewals, can last for years. In this chapter, we cover the two types of newsletters being published today: free and paid.

The first is the free "e-zine," an online newsletter which is given away freely to anyone who wants it. If it's free, how do you make money writing it? You do so by using the free online newsletter to build a list of people who like your writings and will therefore be predisposed to buying your books, special reports, and other how-to information products.

The second type of newsletter is the paid subscription newsletter. This is a print or electronic newsletter that people pay for on an annual, quarterly, or monthly subscription basis. You continue to make revenue from it until the reader cancels or fails to renew his subscription.

One-shot products are profitable, but they produce an uncertain cash flow. On the other hand, if you have 10,000 paid subscribers to a $100 a year subscription newsletter, you have a recurring revenue stream of a million dollars a year.

How to write and design your free e-newsletter

For many writers and publishers, the fastest way to build a house list of opt-in email names and addresses—an important asset for online marketers—is with the offer of a free subscription to an online newsletter or e-zine.

The free e-zine is sometimes stand-alone; other times positioned as an online supplement to a print publication for which there is a subscription fee. But to lure potential subscribers into their database of online prospects, many publishers also offer the e-zine free to nonsubscribers as well.

A variety of online marketing tools are used to drive potential customers to a web page where they can sign up for a free subscription to your e-zine in exchange for giving you their email address. You can also ask for their name, which allows you to personalize future emails you send to them.

These traffic-building tools include such things as Facebook ads in e-zines reaching similar audiences, email marketing, Google Ads, and search engine optimization of the e-zine sign-up website. The acquisition cost per subscriber can range from $1 to $5 a name, depending on the method used and the market targeted.

Generally, the larger and more targeted your subscriber list, the more profitable your online marketing will be. After all, a click-through rate (CTR) of 1 percent per one thousand e-zine subscribers will bring just ten visitors to your landing page; however, if you have a million online subscribers, a 1 percent CTR will generate 10,000 visits.

For your e-zine to work as an online marketing tool, subscribers must not only sign up, they must also open and read your e-newsletters. If they don't open the current issue, they can't respond to any of the ads or offers you make in it. And if they don't read it on an ongoing basis, they will eventually unsubscribe, and you will lose them as an online prospect.

There are two basic types of e-zines:

1. *Digests.* In my experience, the best e-zines—those with the highest open, read, and click-through rates—are those that present useful

how-to tips or news in short, bite-size chunks. When the news stories deal with current events, open rates soar. And as for the tips, the more practical and actionable they are, the better.

2. *Email essays.* Your e-zine is not the place to teach difficult-to-master skills or explain complex processes; you can send your subscribers to web pages and downloadable e-books or special reports that cover those topics. Instead, e-zine readers love practical articles that tell them how to do something useful, and which do so in just a few concise paragraphs.

News can also serve as effective e-zine content, but by itself, news is not as potent as advice. The best way to use news is to link a tip or other advice to the news. For instance, if you are a financial publisher talking about $50-a-barrel crude oil, tell the reader which oil stocks he should own to profit from rising oil prices.

You don't need a news angle to make advice an effective content strategy for your free e-zine. However, as noted, if you can relate your tips to current events or news, do so; experience shows that this can potentially double your readership and response.

That being said, you never know what article is going to strike your e-zine reader's fancy. And it's often not the article you'd think.

For instance, a manager for a company that sells information on safety to human resource (HR) managers publishes a regular e-zine on safety and other HR issues. He reports that his best-read article of all time was, "10 Ways to Reduce Eye Strain at Your PC."

The eye strain article generated far more response than more specialized articles targeted to his HR audience. Go figure.

Here's what I've found makes the ideal e-zine article (many of these ideas are borrowed from my colleague, Ilise Benun, of www.artofselfpromotion.com):

1. Think of yourself as a conduit. Your job is to pass useful information along to those who can use it.

2. Pay close attention to questions, problems, and ideas that come up when you're doing your work or interacting with customers.

3. Distill the lesson (or lessons) into a tip that you can share with your network via email or snail mail, or even in simple conversation.

4. State the problem or situation as an introduction to your tip. Distill it down into its essence.

5. Give the solution. Tips are action-oriented, so make sure you give a couple of action steps to take. Readers especially love something they can use right away, like the ten tips article I mentioned on how to reduce eye strain while working at a PC.

6. Describe the result or benefit of using these tips to provide some incentive to take the action. If there are metrics readers can use to measure the results of your tip once they put it into practice, even better.

7. Include tips the reader can use without doing any work, phrases they can use verbatim, boilerplate clauses, checklists, forms, and so on.

8. List websites and other resources where readers can go for more info.

9. Put your best tip first, in case people don't read the whole thing— because sometimes even really short tips are too much.

Sample E-Zine Tips

Five ways to make a positive impression at work:

1. Keep your desk neat . . . tidiness conveys that you're organized and have things under control.

2. Be sincere and generous with compliments . . . people like to be told that you appreciate them.

3. Return phone calls and emails promptly . . . it makes co-workers and customers feel valued.

4. Be on time . . . being late shows that you think your time is more important than theirs.

5. Set a good example . . . find out what kind of behavior your managers and colleagues expect, and do your best to practice it.

Source: Words from Woody.

How to engage your e-newsletter audiences

Be aware that most free e-newsletters and e-zines have a dual audience consisting of: (1) prospects who get the free e-zine but not your paid subscription product and (2) subscribers who have paid for your magazine or newsletter and get your free e-zine as a supplement.

For reasons of economy of scale and simplicity of management, most publishers use one e-zine to serve both audiences. But you need to keep the different needs and perspectives of both groups in mind for your e-zine to be effective.

The first group of e-zine subscribers consists of people who have signed up for your free online newsletter. They do not subscribe to your paid subscription magazine or newsletter, and, in fact, they may not even be aware of it—or you.

Your goal with these subscribers is to (a) delight them with the free e-zine they are receiving and (b) upgrade them to the next step—a 30-day free trial to your paid service.

To accomplish these goals:

- Pack the e-zine with solid content. Nothing beats useful, practical how-to tips.

- Put a 100-word ad in each issue of your e-zine offering a free 30-day trial to your paid subscription publication, with a link to a landing page where the reader can accept such an offer.

- Send at least one solo email to subscribers between e-zine issues giving them a compelling reason to accept your 30-day free trial offer; this could be the offer of a free special report or other premium. Ideally, they can get the premium as a downloadable PDF after they register for it on your landing page.

The second group of e-zine subscribers are readers who have already paid for a subscription to your print magazine or newsletter. Your e-zine can do any or all of the following for your paid subscribers:

- Give them news updates, recommendations, and fresh ideas between monthly print issues.

- Highlight or expand upon ideas and tips already presented in their print issues.

- Bring them special discount offers on your other products: periodicals, conferences, seminars, master classes, databases, and whatever else you sell.

Can you stray from my formula of how-to advice and tips? Of course. My e-zine, "The Direct Response Letter" (available at www.bly.com/reports), uses many different types of articles, including book reviews, quotations, news items, and new product announcements.

But take a tip from me: When you're putting together your next e-zine issue, remember that nothing gains the reader's interest and attention like solid how-to tips.

Now, some authors and information marketers tell me they do not use e-zines because they simply do not have the time. Well, it only takes me two hours or less per month. Those two hours are some of the highest ROTI (return on time invested) writing hours I can spend. I hate to waste time, so I have come up with a simple formula for writing e-zines that anyone can follow.

For each issue, I write five to seven short stories about a topic, just one to three paragraphs per story. These include short tips, news items, reviews, and recommendations.

Since I use this ultra-short article format, my readers can get through each story in under a minute. You do not have an unlimited amount of time with your reader, so make sure he can read your entire e-zine issue in about five to seven minutes.

The next little tip might seem insignificant, but I think it is vitally important: Do not put any click-links to your stories; you do not want to give the reader's mind a chance to wander because they are waiting for another page to load. Many websites like to give you a brief description of the article and then ask you to click on a link to read the whole article.

That's just too many hoops to go through to read the story. Do not put in your newsletters only the story title and first paragraph with a link to the full article which is posted on the web. I like to write short articles and *include the entire article in the e-zine itself*, not a teaser or hyperlink.

Email distribution services

There is email distribution software you can subscribe to on a monthly basis. These "software-as-a-service" products include Mailchimp, Constant

Contact, Active Campaign, Infusionsoft, ConvertKit, Aweber, and others. The software can store your email subscriber list. It can also distribute your e-newsletter and any other emails you wish to send to your list.

How to design and format your e-newsletter

Should your e-newsletter be text or HTML? There is an ongoing debate about this among marketers and how-to writers. Personally, my e-zine is presented in text. That is mainly because text is quick and simple to edit. I like simple. Remember, your readers are only interested in one thing: information. If your reader wants the information, she doesn't really care what it looks like.

That being said, there do appear to be pros and cons to both text and HTML. With text, I can just type the e-zine, click a button, and it's instantly sent to my list. With HTML, I would have to learn HTML or hire a designer to do each issue, adding time and cost. HTML emails are sometimes trapped by some spam filters and ISPs, but text emails are not as frequently filtered because they are considered less spammy.

Text is better than HTML when the information does not require pictures to teach, the audience is accustomed to text, your prospects are information seekers, the subject matter is not visual in nature, and branding (e.g., a logo or color) is not important to you. For some information marketers, branding is important; example: The Motley Fool investment newsletters and their famous court jester logo.

HTML is better than text when the audience is accustomed to HTML, branding or image are important, the topic is "visual" (e.g., travel), or you want to track open rates. You can track open rates with HTML, but you can't with text.

While this list is certainly not all-inclusive, it should help you decide what format you would like to go with. Many writers say they do not publish an e-zine because they do not have the time or they question their technical ability to create one. You can easily overcome those issues with text, which is why I use it.

A text-based e-zine is very easy to design using Microsoft Word; there are only seven things to remember when you are designing it:

1. Set left margin at 20

2. Set right margin at 80

3. 60-character column width

4. Hard carriage return after every line

5. Dashed lines separate articles in the e-zine

6. Article titles are centered with asterisks on both ends (e.g., ***A Little Known Trick For Picking Effective Domain Names***)

7. Save as a text file.

Designing and publishing an online newsletter doesn't really get much easier than that. Fig. 10.1 shows the header of one of my newsletters.

Fig. 10.1. First Screen of My Online Newsletter.

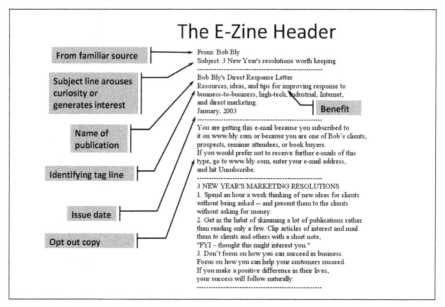

At the top of each issue are the "from" line and "subject" line required by email. First is the "from" line, and the newsletter "from" line should either be your name (e.g., Bob Bly) or the name of the publication (e.g., "The Direct Response Letter"). Use whichever is more familiar to your readers. Knowing that the email is from you and that they requested it will entice more recipients to at least open the email.

Next is the subject line: It should arouse curiosity and generate interest. It's the headline. After the subject line, place the title of the publication and an identifying tag line that is benefit-oriented.

Some people forget they had subscribed but your catchy title will jog their memory. Make sure to include a brief note on how to opt-out (unsubscribe) from your list. The next section is made up of the body. This is where you include all your articles, ideas, reader feedback, or whatever information you would like to share.

Now we come to the bottom of the e-zine (Fig. 10.2). This is where you make your close. This is also where you softly offer your services or your products; use no hard sell tactics here. Include complete contact information. Some readers may not want to visit your website and prefer to email you, phone, fax, or write. Giving readers multiple contact options helps them reach you with information requests, giving you an opportunity to cement the relationship and sell more products.

Fig. 10.2. Closing Page of the E-newsletter.

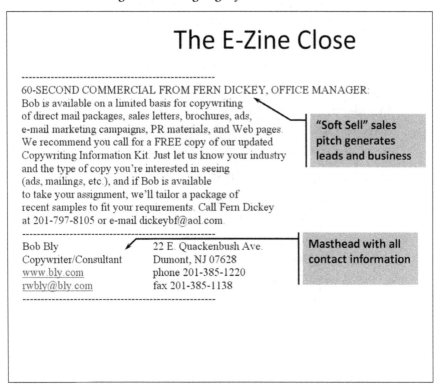

Fig. 10.3. Squeeze Page

"Free-on-Free Squeeze Page"

Get 4 FREE Special Reports from Bob Bly Worth Over $100!

Sign up for a free, no-commitment subscription to my monthly e-newsletter on direct marketing -- *The Direct Response Letter* – and get 4 FREE Bonus Reports ... 194 pages of valuable marketing advice that can double or triple your response rates:

FREE Special Report #1: How to Double Your Response Rates at Half the Cost

7 ways to build your e-zine subscriber list

1. Create a "squeeze page" (Fig. 10.3). This is a separate web page providing an online subscription form that visitors can use to request your newsletter.

2. Offer a free report or other bonus as an incentive to subscribe to your online newsletter. I do this on my squeeze page at www.bly.com/reports.

3. Include one or more links on your website home page to your e-newsletter sign-up box or page, so that site visitors can easily find the subscription form and sign up.

4. Have an exit pop-up on your site. When the visitor leaves the site, a window pops up offering him your free bonus report in exchange for opting into your subscriber list.

5. Use a floater. A floater, or "interstitial," is a window that floats over and blocks the user's view of your home page, and it promotes a subscription to your free e-newsletter. Because the interstitial is written in HTML code, separate from the actual website, it is displayed even if the user has a pop-up blocker. Tip: Make sure it's easy for visitors to close the floater window, as many of them are likely to already be subscribers to your newsletter.

6. Use Google Ads' pay-per-click ads to drive clicks to the squeeze page where prospects can opt into your list and subscribe to your newsletter.

7. Ask joint venture partners and friends to promote your free e-newsletter to their list. In exchange, you agree to promote their offer to your subscriber list. This simple technique can add many hundreds of new subscribers to your list at no out-of-pocket cost.

Upselling your free e-newsletter subscribers to a paid subscription

Remember, if someone is getting your monthly e-newsletter for free, you should upsell them to your paid subscription newsletter. Consider testing a paid subscription newsletter at a price point of $49 to $149 per year. This newsletter can be a traditional 8- or 12-page monthly print newsletter, or it can contain the same content delivered via email as a PDF file or HTML email. Obviously for the paid newsletter to be worth $50 or more a year, it must deliver valuable content, and *more* content, than your free online newsletter. Otherwise, if readers can get content just as good as the paid content offered in the free newsletter, why do they need to buy a subscription from you?

You can upsell your free e-zine subscribers to a paid subscription using email marketing messages sent to your subscriber list. The act-now incentive is usually a combination of a discount and a premium (free gift).

For instance, say you have a free e-newsletter on personal finance and investing. You want to upsell as many of your free subscribers as possible to a monthly newsletter on investing in small cap stocks. The small cap stock letter is priced at $99 for a year. In your upsell promotions, offer a one-year subscription for $49—a 50 percent discount off the regular rate—and give them a free report on "Three small cap winners you must buy now."

Will your paid subscription newsletter fly?

The failure rate among start-ups for paid subscription newsletters is high. A newsletter can be a difficult item to sell. Many people simply are not newsletter readers. With the proliferation of free online newsletters, some younger buyers do not understand that the content in paid subscription newsletters can have greater value.

To increase your chances of success in publishing a paid subscription newsletter, here are the most common reasons why newsletter ideas and promotions don't work, and one good way to overcome each:

- *Lack of a "Big Idea."* With so many information sources today on virtually every topic, why create yet another? To establish its place in the market, your newsletter must have a clear "reason for being"—a reason why it should exist and why people would want to buy it, even though other publications already exist.

  What's the "Big Idea" behind your publication? What is its unique selling proposition (USP)? For an investment letter on cryptocurrency, the "reason for being" is to help investors (the audience) increase their profits (the benefit—what it does) by trading Bitcoin, Ethereum, and other cryptos.

  Here's how to counter the lack of a Big Idea: To create a strong USP, clearly identify the audience, the benefit, and how you achieve the benefit differently than other information sources. If the USP is weak, no promotion, no matter how strong, is likely to work.

- *Bad fit.* You may have a clear promise or big idea, but what if it's not something the reader cares about? Then you are doomed to failure.

In his 1960 bestseller, *Reality in Advertising*, Rosser Reeves identified the three factors needed to have a strong, effective USP:

1. Each advertisement must make a proposition to the consumer. Each advertisement must say to the reader: "Buy this product, and you will get this specific benefit."

2. The proposition must be one that the competition either cannot, or does not, offer. It must be unique—either a uniqueness of brand or a claim not otherwise made in that particular field.

3. The proposition must be so strong that it can pull over new customers to your product.

The third item mentioned above means that the big promise must be a good "fit" with your audience. It is something they want and care about.

What does your audience really want? You can make an intelligent guess, but you really don't know. That's why smart publishers do A/B split tests comparing different USPs, themes, or creative approaches.

Often you can test selling propositions inexpensively online with split tests of emails and landing pages, with one set reflecting sales appeal A and the second based on sales appeal B. Many of the popular email distribution software and services mentioned earlier have functionality that allows you to do A/B split tests with email marketing.

Selling newsletter subscriptions online

Here is a proven strategy for selling paid newsletter subscriptions online:

1. Build a website that positions your newsletter, editor, or publishing company as an expert or guru in your field or topic. This is the "base of operations" for your online marketing campaign.

2. This website should include a home page, an "About the Company" page, editor bios, and a page with a short description of each publication (each product or service overview can link to a longer document on the individual newsletter or advisory).

    Allow the visitor to read, print, and download a PDF of the most recent issue. Also, post the current control promotion (typically your direct mail package converted into a long-form landing page linked to an order form).

3. You should have an "Articles Page," where you post a few select articles taken from your newsletters that visitors can read and download for free. Don't give away everything from your newsletters for free, of course. But give them a taste.

4. Write a short special report or white paper relating to a hot topic in your field, and make this available to people who visit your site. They can download it for free, but in exchange, they have to register and give you their email address (and any other information you want to capture).

5. Consider also offering a daily, weekly, or monthly online newsletter or e-zine. People who visit your site can subscribe for free if they register and give you their email address. You may want to give the visitor the option of checking a box that reads: "I give you and other

companies you select permission to send me email about products, services, news, and offers that may be of interest to me."

6. The more free content on your site, the better. More people will be attracted to your site, and they will spend more time on it. They will also tell others about your site.

   In time, your site will be regarded as the place to go online for information about your topic. The more people who visit for the free content, the more likely they are to read sample issues and sign up for your paid products.

7. The key, however, is to drive traffic to your site where you get them to sign up for either your free report or free e-zine. Once they register, you have their email address and you can now market to them via email as often as you like.

   With this approach, you can market as many offers as you want, whenever you want, to your house e-list at virtually no cost. Therefore, even if the promotion pulls a very small response, it can still be immensely profitable. You can test quickly and inexpensively, and read the results within 48 to 72 hours.

   How often should you email to your house file? Some publishers are having success with frequencies as high as two times a day. To test this, increase your frequency. When the opt-out rate suddenly increases, you know you have reached your maximum frequency.

   Whenever someone clicks onto the landing page and order form for one of your paid products but does not buy, they should get a pop-up screen as they click off. The pop-up invites them to sign up for a free report or e-zine on the same topic. This way, you capture their email address whether they buy or not.

8. The bulk of your online leads, sales, and profits will come from repeat email marketing to this "house" e-list of prospects. Therefore, your goal is to build a large e-list of qualified prospects as quickly and inexpensively as you can.

9. There are a number of online marketing options that can drive traffic to your site or newsletter subscription page. These include free publicity; email marketing; online advertising; affiliate marketing; search

engine optimization; articles in other e-zines; cross-promotions with marketers reaching your audience; and e-zine text advertising.

Provide your subscribers with these value-added extras and bonus gifts

Offering one or more premiums—free bonus gifts given as an incentive to subscribe—is a standard ploy in direct mail used to sell newsletter subscriptions. But what premiums work best? Here are a few of your choices:

- *The super-premium.* A super-premium is a special report that delivers all or most of the information, secrets, or strategies promised in the landing page selling the publication.

- *The owner's manual.* An owner's manual advises the subscriber how to use the service for maximum results and benefits. An options trading course, for instance, will typically have a premium explaining terms (e.g., "puts" versus "calls") and the types of trades the service makes (e.g., "straddles").

- *The vertical premium.* A vertical premium is an in-depth report covering one specific area the newsletter deals with rather than the bigger picture. A newsletter on information technology, for instance, might have a special report on supply chain management or enterprise resource planning.

- *The resource guide.* A resource guide is typically an online directory of vendors, suppliers, associations, websites, and other resources of interest to the newsletter's target audience. Be sure to include addresses, phone numbers, email addresses, and web URLs for listed resources.

- *Surveys.* The results of subscriber surveys are of great interest to potential subscribers. When a business-to-business newsletter targeting hospital admitting managers added the offer of a salary survey premium, response to its control jumped 50 percent.

- *Best of's.* If you have a regular column that is highly popular with subscribers, collect a dozen of them or so in a "best of" premium. Newsletters covering regulatory or legal issues have done this with monthly columns on court cases and their outcomes (e.g., "The Best of 'You Be the Judge'").

- *E-Alerts.* Some newsletters offer periodic, unscheduled emails when there is important news or instructions that cannot wait for the next issue. If you do this, position it as a value-added premium service.

- *Online archives.* Access to your password-protected subscribers-only website is a bonus for subscribers to your print or online newsletter. One feature subscribers look for is an online archive of back issues. If they are searchable by keyword, even better.

- *Forums and chat groups.* Hosting a forum, chat group, or other online community where subscribers can network and share best practices is another nice little online extra. Reading the postings is also great research for your marketing and editorial people.

- *Conference invitations.* You can offer potential subscribers invitations to exclusive live or virtual conferences, workshops, and seminars. They should get these invitations early, before the general public, and a subscriber's discount on the registration fee wouldn't hurt either.

- *Transcripts.* Transcripts of conferences, seminars, speeches, lectures, or even TV or radio appearances by the editor can make attractive premiums.

- *Webinars.* You can offer your subscribers either free webinars only for them or a hefty discount on paid webinars you market to a larger audience.

11

Recurring Revenues with Membership Sites and Private Facebook Groups

Paid subscription newsletters can be fun and profitable to write. Newsletter readers look to the editor as their guru and advisor. Therefore, you can write in a highly personalized, opinionated, and authoritative voice (see Chapter 5 for a discussion of voice in how-to writing). Few other media give you as much editorial freedom and flexibility or are as powerful a bully pulpit for your views.

The drawbacks of newsletters are twofold. First, newsletters are not an easy product to market. Second, when you publish a paid subscription newsletter, you live with constant deadlines: As soon as you put this month's issue to bed, you have to immediately get started on next month's issue. And it never ends.

The most profitable and enjoyable online information publishing vehicle that generates recurring revenues is a paid membership website— and any how-to writer can produce one. Unlike a newsletter, which is published on a strict schedule that cannot be altered, your membership site can be launched and updated at your convenience, and readers and customers can be alerted to your more important content updates by email or by an RSS feed.

However, for brand-new writers, a paid membership site is not the place to start your how-to writing or information packaging career: It requires a lot of content, and you probably don't have enough of it yet. But if you have been writing for a while and you are an experienced expert in your subject, and you have a lot of articles and other content on your hard drive, a membership site may be the perfect vehicle for profiting from your writings and knowledge—and for bringing them to a wider audience.

What are membership sites?

Many writers, publishers, internet marketers, and entrepreneurs have successfully launched "membership websites," also known as subscription websites. These websites are packed with valuable content and tools on a specific topic, which can only be accessed by users who pay a subscription or membership fee. For an example, see my membership site at www.infoproduct-central.com.

Membership sites are an ideal way to provide great how-to resources. Available content can include audio programs, e-books, special reports, blogs, forums, streaming video, online calculators and other tools, and newsletter archives. The membership fee is usually monthly, though some membership websites offer an annual option, and others allow you to buy content piecemeal.

Peter Schaible, founder of SWEPA, a professional organization focusing on membership websites, and now merged with the Mequoda Group, offers the following suggestions for launching and marketing your own membership site (assuming you have already selected a content area around which you want to build your site):

1. Write a 25-word, promotionally oriented description of your site, e.g.: "Vintage Ford, Mercury owners and admirers, www.shoeboxford.com is your complete, one-stop source for 1949–1951 Ford/Mercury news and information. Need parts now? We're your site!"

2. Submit your 25-word descriptions to website directories relevant to your topic. To find these directories, search Google for your topic's most basic keyword phrase, plus the word "directory." For our shoebox example, our Google search might read: "Vintage auto directory."

3. Write a press release announcing the launch of your site and email it to relevant media. The press release should be pasted into the body of the email, not sent as an attached file. Continuing with our shoebox

example, you might mail your press release to editors at automotive magazines.

I am guessing you already know how to write and distribute press releases. If not, see the book *Public Relations for Dummies* written by Eric Yaverbaum, Ilise Benun, and myself. Also see the sample press release in Appendix B.

4. Compile a list of e-zines that reach your target market. To find these e-zines, search Google for your topic's most basic keyword phrase plus the word "e-zine." For our shoebox example, our Google search might read: "Vintage auto e-zine."

    Also check out such sites as www.ezine-universe.com and www. freezineweb.com.

5. Write short articles (100 to 200 words) and tips on your topic, and submit them to e-zines. Always include a link to your membership website. You are offering these articles free to the e-zine publishers in exchange for them promoting your membership site to their subscribers by including its URL when they run your article.

6. Add the name of your membership website, its URL, and a one-line description of its purpose and contents to your email signature file. For our example of www.shoeboxford.com, the one-line description might be, "We find the parts—you build the car!"

7. Join online discussion groups that talk about your topic and get involved in the discussion. Many of the people in the group who read your emails will click on the URL link in your sig file, generating hits to your website.

8. Add a "Links" page to your membership website and place on it links to as many related websites as you can find. The more links you have, the higher your rankings with the search engines will be.

9. Submit your site to the major search engines, including Google, Bing, and DuckDuckGo.

10. Continue all these activities to generate site traffic and positive press for your membership website. Periodically develop and submit new press releases and free articles to keep the buzz going.

To Peter's list I add a few more suggestions:

- Measure the conversion rate of your traffic (the percentage of visitors who become paid subscribers).

- Test your home page and sign-up page copy to increase your conversion rate.

- Use keywords in your home page's title and body copy to optimize it for search engines.

- Offer a free bonus for immediate sign up, such as a free e-zine or free content in a downloadable PDF; see www.bly.com/reports as an example.

- The narrower the focus of your membership website's topic, the more you can charge—and the lower your "abandon rate" (number of subscribers who drop out) will be.

- Update and add content to your site frequently—weekly at least and preferably daily. If the site content does not change, subscribers have no reason to continue subscribing once they have accessed all of the existing content.

- Add useful online calculators, content libraries, and other helpful tools which visitors will want to use again and again, and must remain members to do so.

Membership site software

A membership site needs specialized software to run on. There are a few major membership site software packages available. The major ones are Membergate and aMember. Of these, Membergate is the market leader. The functionality these software packages provide for your membership site includes the ability to:

- Post and make accessible content in multiple media formats and in many different categories—for instance, have an archive section of teleseminar audios downloadable as MP3s and a special reports library downloadable as PDFs.

- Have a method your members can use to contact the membership site owner (you) directly from the site online, such as a button that allows members and visitors to send you an instant email from the site.

- Maintain a database of members with their email addresses.

- Broadcast emails to your members: both online newsletters as well as invitations and announcements (e.g., inviting them to a members-only teleseminar).

- A shopping cart that allows nonmembers to enroll and pay for their membership online using a credit card or PayPal.

- Divide content areas on the site into (a) free to any visitors versus (b) for paid members only.

- When a nonmember attempts to access paid content available to members only, a button or window should lead him to a sign-up page where he can buy a trial membership and, upon doing so, instantly obtain access to the content he wants.

- On the sign-up page, offer a choice of different membership levels (see the next section for details) at different price points. Also offer different billings options, such as monthly versus quarterly versus annual.

- A content management system that makes it easy for you or your webmaster to post new content on the site. You can see as an example my membership site www.infoproductcentral.com. As you look at it, notice some key features on the home page:

- Expert bios: Membership sites are content-rich, members-only websites that typically contain the writings of a single expert or a group of experts. The bios of these experts should be prominent on the home page of the site.

- Positioning statement: The positioning of my membership site with Fred Gleeck, www.infoproductcentral.com, is that we teach internet information marketing in a hype-free and honest fashion. This is communicated on the home page copy.

- There are two buttons that give you access to the full site. The "current member" button gives members access when they input their user names and passwords. "Join now" takes you to a shopping cart where you can buy a membership.

When you log in as a member, you go to a menu page that shows you all the stuff available on the site for members. On www.infoproductcentral .com, this includes a list of content by topic; an article library; downloadable MP3 audio files; streamlining videos; and downloadable PDF files. There are special sections highlighting software; a reports library; guest contributors; new topics on the forum; and the latest articles, audios, and videos posted.

Membership pricing and terms

What can you charge for a membership to your website?

Website memberships are typically billed monthly to the member's credit card or PayPal account. The monthly membership fees typically range from $9 for a general topic to $49 or higher for more specialized topics.

Some membership sites offer monthly, quarterly, and annual billing options. Since the annual option improves your cash flow, you may want to offer a discount on that option versus the regular monthly rate. Commonly, a one-year subscription costs the equivalent of 10 months, so if the monthly membership fee is $29, the annual fee would be $290.

On www.infoproductcentral.com, Fred Gleeck and I offer three levels of membership. For the $29 a month basic level, "silver" members get access to all content on the site. The gold membership, at $49 a month, gives members everything available to silver members plus a free monthly teleseminar. The $79 a month platinum level gives everything in the gold membership, plus email access to me and Fred for asking us questions and receiving our answers.

Tip: Why offer three levels of membership at three price points? When you offer only two levels, most people take the cheaper. However, when you offer three levels, the average order is for the middle level, giving you more revenue per member.

How to quickly and easily create a high-value paid membership site

The idea behind a membership site is actually quite simple: rock-solid, useful content, and a ton of it.

This is why I think it's difficult for a new or young how-to writer to put together a membership site, though plenty have done it. To sit down and create enough content to fill a membership site from scratch is an enormous undertaking.

An easier way to build such a site is to wait until you have been writing for a few years. You'll have built up a library of content to which you own all the rights. When it's time to build your membership site, load up the site with all of that great content, and your members will be getting their money's worth.

My partner Fred Gleeck and I did not start our membership site until we were both 50. Combined, we had hundreds of articles and countless hours of audio and video, so when the site was launched, new members were dazzled by the sheer volume.

One mistake we made that you should avoid is not labeling the content clearly. For instance, "September 2021 Writer's Conference Speech" as a title for an MP3 audio file may be clear to you, but the member has no idea what the speech is about. A better label would be a descriptive title; e.g., "Six Ways to Earn Six Figures as a Freelance Writer."

Since new content is important for membership retention, all new content posted on the site should be made available in a special section highlighting the material as new. Otherwise, if you just add material without pointing it out to members and segmenting it as new content, it loses much of its marketing value to you.

Do you own your content?

Always make sure you control the rights to your writings, speeches, audios, and videos by following these three simple tips:

1. Never sign any form giving up all rights to audio and video recordings of presentations you give for associations or other groups. Specify that both you and the event sponsor jointly own the rights, and you can each do with the recording as you please. Also insist on getting a master of the audio or video.

2. When writing articles for magazines, newsletters, or websites, type "First rights only" in the upper left corner of page one of the manuscript. Do not sign or accept an agreement that asks you to give up your other rights.

3. In book contracts, make sure there is a clause saying the rights to the book revert to the author when the book goes out of print.

Marketing your membership site: the 1,000 member goal

Your number of memberships and income goals for your membership site can be whatever you want them to be. The important thing to realize is that you do not need a massive number of people to join for your membership site to be immensely profitable.

Let's say you charge $29 a month, or $290 a year. If you have only a thousand members (and remember, I have 80,000 subscribers to my free e-zine, so a thousand members is an ambitious but achievable goal), you will gross $290,000 a year from membership site fees, all collected automatically via the internet.

Many freelance writers I know have annual incomes of less than $40,000 a year. I am sure having a recurring passive income stream of $290,000 a year would considerably relieve financial pressure and give them a great cash cushion against the vagaries of the freelance writer's life. I would guess it would for you too, yes?

No matter what you charge for monthly membership, there is some price resistance: People are wary of giving you their credit card to be billed monthly with no foreseeable end. To overcome this, I offer a 10-day trial period. The new member enters his credit card on the membership site shopping cart. But we do not bill him for the first 10 days.

During those 10 days, the new member can theoretically extract from the membership site virtually all the content there, downloading all the special reports, printing all the articles, listening to the audios or burning them onto CDs for later listening. He knows this, and so he is eager to accept the 10-day no-risk trial.

What happens, of course, is that he doesn't want to spend 10 solid days on the site, but would rather go through the material at his own pace when time permits. Therefore, if the content is good, he will not cancel and we will start billing his credit card the monthly membership fee.

How to keep paid members from unsubscribing

One of the biggest challenges for the how-to writer running his own membership site is retaining members. There is really only one strategy that can prevent your members from leaving: continuously posting fresh content on the site.

What typically happens is that the writer creates the membership site using Membergate or another software package and then dumps everything he has ever written or recorded into it. This is actually not a bad strategy: For a membership site to be worth the monthly fee, there has to be a lot of content in it.

However, after a week or a month or two, the member will have worked his or her way through the site several times, read or listened to or watched everything of interest, and then concluded there is nothing else for him, at which point he cancels the membership.

The solution is to always have fresh content on the site. There are several ways to make sure your site retains members with a steady stream of new content. These include:

- Hold a monthly members-only teleseminar or webinar. Post a recording of the teleseminar on an archive audio section on the site after each event.

- Write columns and articles for other publications. Retain all rights. After the articles are published, post them on your site.

- Have one or more members-only blogs and post to at least one blog at least once or twice a week.

- Record and post a short video message or tutorial for your members once a week.

- Post excerpts or chapters from books and e-books currently in progress. Some authors have found this to be an excellent way to receive knowledgeable input on their works-in-progress.

- Have one or more "What's New?" sections on the home page and menu page that clearly indicate what content is new and make it easy to click on and download.

Another great membership retention strategy is to put up a members-only forum and work hard to make it very interactive, useful, and essential. Send emails encouraging members to use the forum. Get involved in the forum yourself so members can communicate with you more easily and directly. If the forum becomes an important resource and networking tool for them, many will stick with their membership just to continue their access to the forum alone, even if they no longer feel a great need for the website's other content.

Private Facebook groups

Another venue for bringing customers and content together online is a private Facebook group.

Facebook allows you to create a group and then restrict access, meaning it's up to you whether a person is allowed into the group.

There are two basic variations on the closed Facebook group: free and paid.

The objective of the free Facebook group is to build an online community where you, as the group moderator, are front and center stage. People know it's your group. Some join it because of the opportunity to connect with you or get one-on-one advice.

The paid Facebook group is typically offered as a supplement or adjunct to another paid information product, most often a big-ticket training course, of which the Facebook group is one of many benefits or features of membership in the class.

12

Speeches, Presentations, and Workshops

Most people, especially introverted writers, rank public speaking high on the list of things they don't like to do. The late author George Plimpton said, "One of life's terrors for the uninitiated is to be asked to make a speech." Making presentations is an unavoidable part of corporate life, so why not make the best of it? The following may help you prepare a more interesting, informative, and persuasive talk the next time you're asked.

Public speaking is great for building your reputation as an expert in your field, and it's also a lucrative profit center in its own right. Many experts and professional communicators earn mid to high six-figure incomes primarily through their public speaking, and the top speakers can hit seven figures. I have been paid more to give a seminar than the advance I have received on certain books!

How to give great talks

Experience shows that 20 minutes is a good length for a presentation. Less seems insubstantial; more is boring. An hour is the maximum. If you're asked to speak for a longer time, stop after an hour and give your audience a break.

Since the average person speaks at a rate of about 100 words per minute, a 20-minute talk is 2,000 words long. This translates into eight pages of double-spaced typewritten copy (on the basis of 250 words per page). *A good pace for matching visuals with your narration is one visual for every minute you're speaking.*

It is important to know your audience, since different people are interested in different aspects of a subject for different reasons. Let's say, for example, that the subject of your presentation is new advances in pump design. Engineers would be interested primarily in the capabilities of the available equipment, while plant operators would want to learn how the systems work and how to troubleshoot them. Purchasing managers, on the other hand, would be interested in their cost.

Many subject matter experts, when faced with giving a talk, do so with a minimum of preparation, perhaps because they feel that the topic is so cut-and-dried that a straightforward recitation of the facts is sufficient.

But it isn't. If your voice drones along in a monotone, or if your talk is dry, or if the content lacks excitement or new or useful information, your audience will be bored. And you will lose them early in the speech. "Everything God created has a kernel of excitement in it, as has everything civilization invented or discovered," observes Joseph J. Kelley, Jr., who was speechwriter to President Eisenhower and many other political figures.

His statement applies to technical presentations as well as political speeches. Technical topics are not dry and dull in themselves. Rather, whether a subject makes for an interesting talk or a boring one depends on the style of the speaker and the content of the lecture.

Make your topic fascinating by digging for useful applications, immediate benefits, new developments, or little known facts. Read popular science magazines, the better trade journals, and science stories in newspapers to see how skilled writers turn highly technical material into interesting reading, and employ these same techniques.

How much time goes into researching, writing, and preparing for a speech? According to *Best Sermons*, a religious magazine, it takes clergymen about seven hours to prepare a 20-minute sermon. Terry C. Smith, a presentations expert and author of the book *Making Successful Presentations*, says that to give his best effort requires one hour of preparation for every minute he will talk.

Of course, the time you must spend preparing your talk depends on several factors: your experience and skill in public speaking; your knowledge of the topic; whether assistance for research and visual preparation is available; and the importance of the talk. Also, it takes considerably less time to brush up an old presentation than to create a new one.

The point, however, is that preparing a memorable address requires many hours—much more time than inexperienced speakers ever dream would be required. Plan your schedule accordingly so you can give your talk the attention it deserves.

In a 20-minute, 2,000-word presentation, there are limits to the amount of information that can be transmitted. To ensure a meaningful, informative talk, focus on a narrow, specific subject rather than a broad-based area. For example, "Chemical Process Equipment" is too broad a topic for a presentation, but 20 minutes is just the right amount of time for giving a useful lecture on "Seven Tips for Sizing and Selecting Static Mixers."

Write for the ear, not the eye

A speech is just that—speech. And writing a speech is not the same as writing for the printed page. Words intended to be spoken must sound like conversation, or else the talk will seem stiff and stilted.

To ensure a good talk, read your rough draft aloud first to yourself, and then to others. Rewrite any sentences that sound awkward or unnatural until they roll off the tongue (and into the ear) smoothly and naturally.

A little humor can help lighten a heavy technical talk and prevent your audience from drifting off. But overdoing the humor can ruin an otherwise fine presentation and erode your credibility.

The best way to handle this is to *pepper your talk with tidbits of warm, gentle, good-natured humor. Be wary of using outright jokes, unless you are a natural-born comedian.* Do not use off-color humor at any time, because what is funny to one person is offensive to another. Never lead off with a prepared joke. If it fails, it turns off the audience, and you look like a clown.

You are probably knowledgeable about the topic of the presentation, or you wouldn't have been asked to talk. But this doesn't mean you know everything about it or even enough to put together an engaging lecture.

Good speakers supplement their own knowledge and experience with outside research and examples. The internet and the library are two good places to start. Books, magazines, newspapers, trade publications, websites, and user forums can provide a wealth of data, ideas, advice, and anecdotes. Interviews, informal chats, and letters exchanged with colleagues and experts in the field can add further to this information base.

Sample Speech Outline

Title: Generate More Leads and Sales with Free White Papers

Description: Offering white papers and other free content as premiums—known as "bait pieces"—can double the response to your marketing campaigns. In this presentation, you will learn how to create free content offers that generate more leads while achieving other marketing objectives, such as gaining a reputation as a thought leader in your industry.

What You Will Learn:

- Five reasons to offer free white papers in your marketing
- Choosing white paper titles and topics with the strongest appeal to prospects
- How to catch more prospects when fishing for sales leads
- Generate twice as many leads at half the cost
- The four characteristics of a successful offer
- How to interest the prospect in your product and not just your white paper
- Increasing perceived value with electronic information premiums (CDs, DVDs, flash drives)

Gather about twice as much material as you need. Then, when drawing on these data, you can be choosy, selecting only the best stuff. The process of doing research will also act to permanently increase your own knowledge, and this is a real confidence-builder to a speaker. As Cicero once said, "No man can be eloquent in a subject he does not understand."

The best way to organize your thoughts is to make notes on index cards. Jot down one idea or one piece of information per card. You may also want to make a rough outline of your talk, and then arrange the cards according to the topics on the outline. This helps you arrange the material in logical sequence, and it also reveals which areas require further research.

Every talk has three parts: beginning, middle, and end. In the beginning, you state your purpose and provide a preview of what will be covered. This preview is a quick summary of the outline of your talk. In the middle, you go through the outline point by point. Be sure to cover every topic promised in the preview. In the end, you sum up your talk and ask for any appropriate action (for example, a scientist might ask top management for funds to pursue a particular avenue of research or a salesperson might ask a group of prospects for an order).

Overcoming stage fright

According to an article in *Science Digest*, psychologists estimate that 80 percent of the population suffers from stage fright. What can you do to overcome butterflies?

Practice helps. The more speaking experience you gain, the less frightening it seems. There are also seminars that teach stress relaxation and confidence-building techniques designed to reduce nervous tension.

However, many professional speakers would advise you not to eliminate stage fright. A little anxiety, they say, is a good thing. It pumps you up, keeps you sharp and alert, and helps you "get psyched," so you can do your best.

While talking, make eye contact with individuals in the audience. Look at a person and act as if you're speaking directly to him or her. After a minute, pick someone else. Doing so helps you communicate with the audience rather than just read to them.

Speak loudly enough that people in the back of the room can hear you. If people are too far away, ask them to move closer before you start. Use gestures, tone, and volume to emphasize key points. Stick to your main points as outlined in the visuals and your notes. Don't wander off on tangents.

If you intend to distribute a leave-behind (such as a bound booklet containing copies of the visuals or a reprint of the speech), say so before you begin your talk. That way, the audience knows they don't have to take notes and they can sit back, relax, and enjoy the speech. But don't hand out the leave-behind until after the presentation. If you distribute it before or during the talk, people will read it and ignore the speaker—you.

Leave time for a question-and-answer period. Take all questions only after your talk, rather than allowing interruptions. At the conclusion, summarize your main points and tell the audience what action they should take, or at least what you expect them to have learned, or want them to believe.

Using visual aids

Visual aids have become standard in public speaking, and with good reason— visuals reinforce the presentation and help the audience remember your talk after it's over. Visuals also serve to focus audience attention on the speaker.

There are other benefits. According to a study by the Wharton School, the use of visuals results in a greater percentage of the audience agreeing with the speaker's point of view. *When visuals are used, participants come to a decision faster. And they perceive the speaker as more professional, more credible, more interesting, and better prepared than speakers who don't use visuals.*

With today's modern computer graphics, visuals are affordable to firms of every size. Media include PowerPoint presentations, images, videos, slides, overhead transparencies, and flip charts. When preparing your visuals, select the format that will convey your message most effectively. The basic types of visuals used in technical presentations and the information they best serve to communicate are listed in the table below:

Table 12.1. Types of Visuals

Visual	This Visual Shows
Photograph or drawing	What something looks like
Map	Where it is located
Diagram	How it works or is organized
Graph	How much there is (quantity)
Pie chart	Proportions and percentages
Bar chart	Comparisons among quantities
Table	A body of data

The key to creating successful visuals is not to cram too much onto a single slide. Each slide should contain no more than one simple graph or chart, or five short lines of text.

Note: When creating PowerPoint presentations to be used in webinars, make sure the slides are legible. View your sides in PowerPoint at 40 percent to simulate the reading experience your attendees will have. Use larger type than you would when creating PowerPoints for an in-person audience; 18-point type is recommended.

Arrive early to check out the room and the equipment. Anyone who doesn't think this is important hasn't heard the words, "But no one said you wanted a projector!" If possible, run through the talk in the conference room before the audience arrives.

How to use PowerPoint effectively

PowerPoint has become the de facto standard for making presentations in the corporate world today. Yet everyone—even Dilbert!—talks about how boring PowerPoint presentations can be. Why is that?

To begin with, relying on PowerPoint takes the focus away from where it should be—the content, message, and audience—and puts it on the technology. It's like telling a writer, "I don't care how good the piece is, as long as it's in the latest version of Word."

Second, it encourages a conformity that can rob speakers and presentations of their individuality. At many multi-speaker conferences, all the PowerPoint presentations tend to look somewhat alike.

Third, it is boring. Many bad presentations have been prepared with PowerPoint. I believe the very use of the medium can itself be a signal to some audience members that says, "Prepared to be bored."

Fourth, it renders many speakers ineffective, or at least less effective. When the speaker is focusing on his clicker, keyboard, or computer screen, he is not focusing on, or interacting with, his audience, a key requisite for a successful talk.

Fifth, it locks the speaker into the prepared slides, reducing spontaneity, ad-libbing, and the valuable ability to adjust the presentation in response to audience reaction and interest—another requisite for a successful talk.

Sixth, it can literally put the audience to sleep. What's the first step in preparing an audience to view a PowerPoint presentation? To dim the lights, an action proven to induce drowsiness.

Can you really give an effective presentation without building it around PowerPoint? Of course. But let's say you are putting together a presentation for an event that requires speakers to use PowerPoint. What can you do to make it more effective? Here are four suggestions.

First, don't have the projector on all the time. Use PowerPoint selectively, not throughout the entire presentation. When there's a valuable picture to show, show it. When you're through with it, turn off the projector and turn the lights back on. The brightness rouses the audience out of their darkness-induced stupor. In a darkened room, it's too easy to close your eyes and nod off.

Second, use visuals only when they communicate more effectively than words. If you are talking about quality, having the word "Quality" on the screen adds little to your point. On the other hand, if you want to explain what an aardvark looks like, there are no words that can do it as effectively as simply showing a picture.

Third, consider adding other media as supplements or even alternatives to PowerPoint. When I taught telephone selling, the sound of a ringing telephone and a prop (a toy telephone) engaged the trainees in a way computer slides could not.

Fourth, design your presentation so that, if there is a problem with the computer equipment, you can go on without it. There's nothing more embarrassing than to see a speaker fall apart because he can't find the right slide. Use visuals as an enhancement, not a crutch.

When and where to speak

Unless you are sponsoring your own seminar, you will need to find appropriate forums at which you can be invited to speak. How do you go about it?

First, check your mail and the trade publications you read for announcements of industry meetings and conventions. For instance, if you sell furnaces for steel mills and want to promote a new process, you might want to give a paper on your technique at the annual Iron and Steel Exposition.

Trade journals generally run preview articles and announcements of major shows, expos, and meetings months before the event. Many trade publications also have columns that announce such meetings on both a national and a local level. Make sure you scan these columns in publications aimed at your target market industries.

You should also receive preview announcements in your email. If you are an advertising manager or the owner of your own small business, professional societies and trade associations will send you email messages inviting your firm to exhibit at their shows. That's fine, but you have another purpose: to find out whether papers, talks, or seminars are being given at the show, and, if so, to get you or your people on the panels or signed up as speakers. If the show email doesn't discuss papers or seminars, call up and ask.

Propose some topics with you as the speaker. Most conference managers welcome such proposals, because they need speakers. The conference manager or another association executive in charge of the "sessions" (the usual name for the presentation of papers or talks) will request an abstract or short 100- to 200-word outline of your talk.

Because many others will be pitching speakers and presentations to the conference manager, the earlier you do it, the better. Generally, annual meetings and conventions of major associations begin planning eight to twelve months in advance; local groups or local chapters of national organizations generally book speakers three to four months in advance. The earlier you approach them, the more receptive they'll be to your proposal.

You can "recycle" your talks and give them to different groups in the same year or different years, tailoring them slightly to fit current market conditions, the theme of the meeting, or the group's special interests. When you create a description, outline, or proposal for a talk, keep it on your hard drive. Then, when other speaking opportunities come your way, you can quickly edit the file and print a customized proposal or abstract that you can fax or email to the person in charge of that meeting.

Since one of the goals of speaking is to build your reputation as a top expert in your topic, you want to pick a topic that relates to and helps promote your business but is also of great interest to the group's audience. Importantly, the presentation does not sell you directly, but sells you by positioning you and your company as the expert source of information on the problem your product or service addresses. As such, it must be objective and present how-to advice or useful information; it cannot be a sales or product presentation.

One last tip: If you are not on an organization's mailing list to receive advance notification of meetings and conventions of your industry associations, subscribe to the organization's e-newsletter on their website. Or call or write a letter. Their names and addresses are listed in *The Encyclopedia of Associations*, published by Gale Research and available in your local library.

So where can you speak? Almost anywhere. Associations, clubs, religious organizations, civic organizations, charitable groups, chambers of commerce, community centers—any might be open to a program that would be entertaining, informative, and relevant to its members. To get paid well for a talk, market yourself to meeting planners at national associations. You can earn $1,000 to $10,000 for a one-hour keynote presentation at a national meeting; at local chapter meetings, speakers are usually vendors speaking for free to pitch a product or service. You need not be a Winston Churchill, Erma Bombeck, or Orson Welles to succeed as a speaker. A florist can demonstrate the art of flower arranging; a karate instructor can demonstrate the art of self-defense; an art-gallery owner can give pointers on buying sculpture; a dentist can talk about saving money on major dental work.

Make a list of societies and neighborhood groups you belong to, adding the names of local clubs that might be attracted to what you have to say. The next step is to contact the program chairman and propose your program.

Don't expect to be paid for your efforts at local meetings. Comparatively few speakers are paid at this level. Of course, if you were being paid, you'd probably be restricted from mentioning your own business—no one likes paying for a commercial. As a speaker who is not being paid, you should ask yourself several questions:

- *How many people will attend?* The more people, the more prospects. Make sure that if your speech includes visual elements, they can be seen by everyone.

- *What else is on the club's agenda?* As we mentioned, the event may be the incorrect forum for your product or service. You want to speak to people who want to hear what you have to say, not just people who happen to be members and are showing up merely to socialize with other members.

- *Do you expect to take orders after the speech?* At some gatherings, it is perfectly acceptable for a speaker to hand out promotional information after a speech. However, many organizations feel this is too blatantly commercial, and they will forbid you to hand out promotional material or even refer to your business directly. Find out how the program chairman of the organization you're interested in feels about your blending information with salesmanship.

- *Can I get an info product out of this presentation?* Is your talk being professionally recorded on audio, video, or both? If not, will the organization let you digitally record the audio or video on your own, at your expense? If they are recording it, will they supply you with a master for duplication and permission to use it as an information product?

Screening speaking opportunities

On occasion, meeting planners and conference executives may call to ask you (or a representative from your firm) to speak at their event, rather than you having to seek them out and ask them.

This is flattering. But beware. Not every opportunity to speak is really worthwhile. Meeting planners and committee executives are primarily concerned with getting someone to stand at the podium, and they do not care whether the speaker will benefit in any way from the exposure. So, before you say yes to an opportunity to speak, ask the meeting planner the following questions:

- What is the nature of the group?

- Who are the members? What are their job titles and responsibilities? What companies do they work for?

- What is the average attendance of such meetings? How many people does the meeting planner expect will attend your session?

- Do they pay an honorarium or at least cover expenses?

- What other speakers have they had recently and what firms do these speakers represent?

- Do they pay those other speakers? If so, why not pay you, too?

If the answers indicate that the meeting is not right or worthwhile for your company, or if the meeting planner seems unable or unwilling to provide answers, thank him or her politely and decline the invitation.

Negotiating the speaking contract

Since your goal is not *only* to make money as a speaker, but *also* to promote yourself as a guru and sell more of your other info products or services, you can use the group's lack of payment for your talk as a weapon in negotiating for concessions: extra things it gives you that can help maximize the promotional value of your talk for your firm. Here are some things you can ask for.

You should get all or at least some of them, in addition to the opportunity to address the group:

- Tell the meeting chairperson you would be happy to speak at a reduced fee or no charge, provided you receive a list of the members and their mailing addresses. You can use this list to promote your company via direct mail before as well as after your presentation.

    A pre-talk mailing can let people know about your upcoming talk and be a personal invitation from you to them to attend. A post-talk mailing can offer a reprint or audio recording of your presentation to those who missed it.

    At larger conferences and conventions, the conference manager provides attendees with show kits, which may include a variety of materials, such as a seminar schedule, passes to luncheons and dinners, maps, tourist sights of interest to out-of-town visitors, and the like. These kits are either mailed in advance or distributed at the show. You can tell the conference manager, "I will give the presentation at no charge, but in exchange, we'd like to have you include our company literature in the conference kits mailed to attendees. Is that possible? We will supply as many copies of our literature as you need, of course." If he or she agrees, you get to have your promo pieces mailed to hundreds, even thousands, of potential clients *at zero mailing cost.*

- You can request that your presentation be videotaped. Ask for a copy of the master as well as rights to use the video for your own purposes. A speech is an effective way of getting yourself known to a particular audience (the members of the organization and, more specifically, those members who attend your presentation). But as you know, making a permanent impression on a market segment requires a series of contacts, not a single communication.

You can easily transform a one-shot speaking engagement into an ongoing PR campaign targeted to the membership of this particular group. One way, already discussed, is to get the mailing list and do your own mailings, plus have the sponsor include your literature in their mail-out kit.

Another is to have one or more PR placements in the organization's newsletter or magazine. For instance, tell the meeting planner you will supply a series of articles (your current press releases and feature articles, recycled for this particular audience) to run in the organization's newsletter before the talk; this makes you known to the audience, which is good PR for your firm but also helps build interest in attending your program.

After your talk, give the editor of the organization's newsletter the notes or text of your speech, and encourage him or her to run all or part of it (or a summary) as a post-talk article, so those who could not attend can benefit from the information. Additional articles can also be run as follow-ups after the talk to reinforce your message and provide additional details to those who want to learn more, or to answer questions or cover issues you didn't have time to cover.

If the editor will not run a resource box with your website address with the articles, talk to the meeting planner about getting some free ads for your product or service. For a national organization that actually charges for ads in its magazine, the value of your free ad space should be approximately twice what your fee would be if you were charging for your talk.

The organization will do a program or mailing (or both) with a nice write-up of you and your talk. Usually it prints more than it ends up using, and throws out the extras. Mention that you would be glad to take those extra copies off its hands. Inserting those fliers is a nice touch in press kits and inquiry fulfillment packages.

A professionally done audiotape or video of you giving a seminar can be a great promotional tool and an attention-getting supplement to printed brochures, direct mail, and other sales literature. But recording such presentations in a studio can be expensive.

One way to get an audio or video produced at low cost is to have someone else foot the bill for the taping. If an organization wants you to speak but cannot pay you, and especially if its audience is not a prime market for you, say, "I'll tell you what. Normally I charge $X for such a program. I will do it for you at no charge, provided you can arrange to have it professionally videotaped [or audio recorded, or both] and give me a copy of the master."

If the organization objects to the expense, say, "In exchange, you can copy and distribute the video or audio of my speech to your members, or even sell it to those who attend the meeting or belong to your group, or both, and I won't ask for a percentage of the profits. All I want is the tape master when you are through with it."

At many major meetings, it is standard practice for sponsoring organizations to audiotape all presentations and offer them for sale at the conference and for one year thereafter in promotional mailings. If you are being taped, tell the sponsor you normally do not allow it, but will allow it as long as you get the master. Also make clear that, while you will allow the sponsor to sell it and will waive any percentage of the profits, the copyright is to be in your name.

If the group is a local chapter of a national organization, ask the meeting chairperson for a list of the other state or local chapters, along with addresses, phone numbers, and the names of the meeting organizers for each of those chapters. Then contact these chapters and offer to give the talk to their members.

The TSR = SR + PS + CB seminar profit formula

As we've been discussing throughout this chapter, not all of your how-to writing need be delivered in print. Don't neglect oral presentations; you can get paid ten times more for delivering a piece as a speech than publishing it as a magazine article.

What you do need to realize is that the speaker's income is often not solely, or even primarily, from getting paid a speaking fee. The income also derives from sales of books, audio albums, coaching, consulting, and your other products and services at the event, determined by this formula:

TSR = SR + PS + CB
Where:
TSR = total seminar revenue
SR = seminar speaking fees
PS = product sales
CB = consulting and coaching business

Some speakers prefer a business model where the revenue is primarily SR: They get $5,000 to $10,000 for a speech, so they're earning a handsome fee and don't bother to sell anything else (other than more speeches). These fee-based speakers typically market their services to corporate and association meeting planners, as well as speakers' bureaus. Often, they build their reputations when they are just starting out by speaking for free at small local meetings (Elks Club, Chamber of Commerce).

On the other hand, some of the most financially successful speakers charge a small fee and in some cases even no fee for speaking. The bulk of their revenue comes from PS: selling their information products from the platform. Their market is associations as well as conferences, workshops, seminars, and boot camps sponsored by entrepreneurial seminar promoters. Selling products enables you to speak at other people's public seminars when they don't offer you a speaker's fee and still make it pay off.

13

Colleges, Adult Education, and Public Seminars

In addition to giving speeches and presentations for corporations and associations, don't neglect the continuing education market: adult education, college extension courses, and public seminars.

All of these venues are rich in opportunity for the how-to writer and information marketer. To begin with, they can be quite profitable in their own right, especially when you sell your existing information products from the back of the room—or, the college makes your book a required textbook. In addition, audio and video recordings of your classes can be turned into new information products you can sell to the public online.

While the corporate and association markets pay higher speaking fees, the drawback is that your attendees have been required to attend your session by their boss, and they did not for the most part elect to go on their own. Therefore, the audience can sometimes be indifferent to the subject matter or even adversarial, because they resent being forced to attend.

With the adult education market, your attendees, with rare exception, are there because they want to be there. They are attending on their own time, and spending their own money to do so. They want to learn and are eager to soak up your wisdom. This makes them an easier audience to please. And they are also much more likely to buy additional information products from you after your talk.

In addition, teaching adults is, in my experience, much easier than teaching kids, who are anywhere from kindergarten to college seniors. Again, the adult learners want to be there. When you teach elementary through high school, you have to deal with immature and disruptive behavior from the more troublesome students. College students, though not disruptive in class, also present frustrating challenges for the professor—today much of it in the form of texting, social media posting, or watching videos on their smartphones.

The most well-behaved and easiest audience to teach is adults who have completed their formal education and degree. They are taking your class for a variety of reasons:

- Interest in learning the subject matter for pure enjoyment or intellectual stimulation.

- To get up-to-date on new technologies and knowledge.

- To master new skills that can make them more employable or enable them to go up in pay grade and position.

- To accumulate continuing education credits on an ongoing basis as required by their professional status, trade association, or employer.

Continuing education credits may be earned by students in a variety of accredited educational venues including universities, colleges, trade schools, associations, or other institutions; requirements for accreditation of the teaching organization are set forth in 34 CFR Part 602 Subpart C.

Public seminars–private and college

Producing your own public seminars can be lucrative, but it is also risky, labor-intensive, and expensive. An alternative to running the seminar yourself is to find a sponsor. This might be a public seminar company, adult education center, community college, continuing education program, YMCA, or local university—any place that gives courses aimed at adults instead of regular students. I have given workshops and taught classes at the YMCA, a big public seminar company (the Learning Annex), a local college (New York University), and elsewhere.

The first step in getting hired is to send a description of your program. If interested, they will contact you. Then it is up to you to negotiate your fee.

You might ask for a flat fee or per diem—anywhere from $300 to $1,000 per day. Or, you might be paid a percentage of the registration fees, anywhere from 15 to 50 percent. There is no standard. It is really up to you to negotiate. However, your goal should be to make at least $500 to $1,000 per day for your efforts.

When I taught for the Learning Annex decades ago, the pay was pretty sparse—around 20 percent of the registration fees. Still, if you drew a big crowd (100 attendees or more), which I did at times, the check could be respectable.

Teaching at New York University in the 1980s paid a small hourly rate, which covered only classroom time, not course preparation, grading papers, or commuting; they didn't even cover my travel expenses into and out of New York City. But I would recommend landing a college teaching gig if you can, because of the prestige associated with it.

The biggest public seminar companies and organizations include the American Management Association (AMA), Fred Pryor Seminars, and CareerTrack. These firms regularly hire speakers, both to present topics they already have, as well as to create new programs. If they want you to teach a topic they already offer, they will provide a prewritten course, including a teacher's guide and handouts, and they will expect you to give *their* course, not yours. The average training contractor working for Pryor earns around $72,000 a year.

A former executive at the American Management Association told me, "We get some top speakers at these rates because it's great exposure for them. Although they are not allowed to promote themselves outright at the class, they often are hired for nice fees by attendees to give private in-house classes at the attendees' companies."

I have spoken with a couple of the big public seminar organizations and found, to my surprise, that even for an experienced speaker or established subject matter expert, they are pretty inflexible about fees. They seem not willing to pay a premium for a more qualified presenter, and they prefer to hire someone who is competent, not necessarily great, but who will work within their fee structure.

The pay to develop a new course for these organizations is better—several thousand dollars—but still not great compensation for the work involved. An ancillary benefit is that some of these companies, most notably Career-Track, will produce and market a video of you talking about your topic, if they like you as a speaker. This adds to your prestige and helps attract new customers to your products.

Since these firms are flooded with applications from candidates who want to present for them, your odds of becoming their next presenter for an established topic like business writing or stress management are slim. A better strategy is to obtain and study their course catalogs. Look for new topics or niches within existing categories, then offer to create and give a program to fill that need. The AMA wasn't interested in having me do a generic selling course, but their interest was piqued when I suggested a specialized program on the selling of services (the topic of one of my books), as opposed to the selling of products.

Another way to break into the public seminar market is to offer to do seminars for specialized associations or for seminar and conference companies catering to specialized markets. The competition is less fierce than with the big-name CareerTrack and AMA. The association executives feel obligated to bring education to their members and are more open to new ideas, especially innovative programs that target their niche needs.

For instance, writer Steve Manning got the ICLE (Institute of Continuing Law Education) to sponsor a seminar on how to write a book. Why would a seminar sponsor catering to lawyers sponsor such a topic? The idea was that writing a book is a good way to promote your law practice. (Look at Alan Dershowitz and Gerry Spence, to name two lawyers whose fame is partly owed to being authors.) If you can show how your topic benefits a particular audience, seminar sponsors that target those audiences may hire you.

In many cities, you will find catalogs of courses distributed on street corners or mailed to residents. These may be from the local YMCA, a town adult education program, or a private seminar company such as the Learning Annex in New York, San Francisco, and Toronto. Contact the program director and see whether the seminar promoter might be interested in having you do a class on your topic.

The pay again is extremely modest, but it's good exposure and good practice. For a year or so, I gave monthly seminars in two topics—how to write a book and get it published and how to make a six-figure income as a freelance writer—for the Learning Annex in New York.

Doing the Annex was fun and there were several benefits. I was able to take my course handouts for "how to write a book," turn them into a book on that subject, and sell it to a small publishing house. So even though I no longer give the seminars, I now get royalty payments on the book sales. I also recorded the seminar and sold it as a six-cassette audio album for $97.

Another large market is the adult and continuing education market, which focuses on teaching adults and is often sponsored by a local college or university. If your town or city has continuing education programs, you no doubt have seen their mailings and catalogs. If not, you can see whether there are such programs near you by contacting the American Association for Adult and Continuing Education and the National University Continuing Education Association.

There is no better education for the new speaker than to present classes to adults at the continuing education college level. You learn how to teach and deal with "adult learners," as the grown-up students are referred to in the continuing education world. And you learn how to prepare, organize, and present a full-length modular course. Best of all, you are being paid while you are learning, and you have an eager group of students upon which you can practice. Their feedback tells you what works in the classroom and what needs to be fixed.

Adult and continuing education programs are constantly in need of teachers. It is usually not difficult to get hired. The reason: Turnover is high. People agree to teach for the prestige, because it sounds fun, or for other reasons. When they realize how much work it is, they don't come back next semester. Or, if they return for each next semester, most become burned-out within a couple of years and quit.

Also, the world is changing rapidly, so there is always a need for new courses to address these new topics. If you can't get invited to teach one of the existing courses, propose a new one. If it fills a need or a gap in the course offerings, the institution will be glad to take it.

When my first book—a how-to book on technical writing—was published, my coauthor Gary Blake and I asked New York University if it would be interested in having us teach an adult education course in its School of Continuing Education. This we did for several years until we grew tired of it.

Then I wanted to teach copywriting, but NYU already had a copywriting course. I suggested a course on my specialty, business-to-business copywriting, which was agreed to and which I taught for several more years.

Eventually, I took the material from the copywriting course and turned it into a book. In the course, students completed assignments and brought in samples of copy they were producing for their companies: I used these (with their permission), both in my book as well as in copywriting seminars I did for corporate clients. In fact, I turned both my NYU courses—technical writing and copywriting—into seminars that I gave to corporate clients at a rate of up to $6,500 a day. You can see the course descriptions online at www.bly.com/newsite/Pages/seminars.php.

12 tips for getting hired by public seminar firms and continuing education programs

1. Prepare a one-page fact sheet on each program you want to offer.

2. Contact the dean of the continuing education program or the president or program director of the public seminar company. Call first to get the person's name, so when you write you can directly address correspondence or email to the correct individual.

3. Ask if an instructor is needed for an existing course that you are qualified to teach. Give your qualifications and send your bio or resume.

4. Review the course catalog and suggest new courses that complement existing programs. For instance, if you speak on e-commerce and the organization has a course on building your website, suggest a complementary course on increasing website conversion rates and sales.

5. If the organization is not interested in the class you propose, ask what it is looking for. If a course it wants to do sounds interesting to you, suggest that you can create and teach the program for the sponsor.

6. Be willing to accept the standard fees, terms, and conditions. Arguing or insisting on compensation above the usual pay scale will make the sponsor disinclined to work with you. Remember, you are taking this gig not to get rich, but to get established.

7. Do not be a prima donna. Follow the sponsor's procedures: Collect registration cards, grade homework assignments, hand out and collect any forms the sponsor wants the student to complete, provide materials and information requested—neatly, accurately, and promptly—and treat the sponsor like a client. Don't be difficult or argumentative.

8. If you are hired to teach a course, do whatever you can to help the sponsor get attendees to register for your program. Promote the course

on your website and link to the sponsor's website for online registration. Do a special mailing of the course promotion to your mailing list.

9. Supply the sponsor with an updated bio. Any new achievements (e.g., a new book you have written on your topic) may help draw students to your class.

10. Never say anything bad about the sponsor in front of your class (e.g., "We would have had textbooks but the college goofed on ordering").

11. Cross-promote in your class other classes the sponsor offers, if appropriate (e.g., "That topic is covered in Advanced Direct Marketing Methods 102.").

12. Never badmouth another instructor or criticize his or her course content. If your viewpoint is different, just explain so, and say you are teaching the methods that have worked best for you. Don't say the other instructor is wrong or his or her information is incorrect.

14

Audio Conferences, Teleseminars, Podcasts, Radio, Internet Radio, and TV Interviews

If you like the idea of speaking and teaching but hate to travel or stand in front of a group, you can disseminate your how-to content electronically and remotely via audio conferences, webinars, podcasts, radio, internet radio, and TV interviews.

Audio conferences

An audio conference, or teleseminar, is a seminar, speech, or other educational format delivered to a group on the phone via a shared conference line. The presentation is often in what is called "lecture mode," and the presenter is the only one who can talk for most of the program, and the other people on the call, the audience, can just listen. On some calls, a moderator takes questions from callers who can be selected to speak by pressing a key on their phone, as instructed by the moderator. Usually, the presentation, including the question-and-answer period, is 60 minutes.

Audio conferences are suitable when:

- You have such a large number of attendees that using Zoom or Microsoft Teams would be unwieldy.

- The information can be well-presented verbally and does not require accompanying visuals.

- The speaker is comfortable with not being able to see the audience and their reactions to the presentation.

The basic premise of hosting an audio conference is that you are an expert in your field and have useful information to provide to your listeners. Think about it: You're asking for people to commit time, and perhaps money, to hear what you have to say about the topic.

Based on that premise, it's easy to see who would promote and produce teleconference learning programs: organizations or individuals who have useful, insightful information to share. In doing so, you can accomplish many beneficial things:

- Brand yourself as an expert

- Create interest in your field

- Bring in clients for your services

- Bring in customers to purchase your how-to products

- Bring in new e-zine and newsletter subscribers

- Increase public awareness of yourself, your services, and your products

- Build long-standing relationships with your clients

- Have more personal satisfaction and more free time

- Make money selling your content in the teleseminar format

- Generate sales leads

- Build your online subscriber list.

There are many benefits to creating and presenting teleseminars, above and beyond the obvious one of making money. These advantages include:

- No travel: unlike that required of "in-person" presentations

- Can do them from anywhere—including home

- Present them to anywhere, and from anywhere, in the world

- Can use free teleseminars to build your list

- No need for computers, as opposed to webinars which require internet access to view a PC presentation

- You can sell the recording and transcript as an information product.

Some information packagers burn the mp3 files of teleseminars onto audio CDs. Yes, you can also give your audience access to the audio via streaming or downloadable mp3 files. And these days, more often than not, that's what I do. That being said, CDs have a couple of advantages over digital files.

To begin with, as a physical object, the audio CD has a higher perceived value than the digital mp3 file, though the content is identical. Also, audio CDs and other physical information product formats (e.g., DVDs, paperbound books) are more attention-getting than the same content transmitted digitally.

Years ago—pre-internet and pre–audio CD—I did a teleseminar on "Ten steps to selling software with direct mail" for the Software and Information Industry Association. I duplicated it on audio cassette and offered it for free, through a blurb in my e-zine, to any software companies interested in doing direct mail. The objective was to promote my software copywriting services. Within 48 hours I received 200 requests for the free tape, many from qualified prospects, resulting in more than $12,000 in copywriting assignments! My cost of duplicating and mailing 200 tapes? Only about $400.

Teleseminars are also a relatively inexpensive way to practice and refine your material, providing you with an audience and feedback (in the form of questions and answers held during the teleseminar, and through follow-up emails). If you have an idea of a marketable service or product, perhaps it's time to present it to a willing audience—but make sure you're ready for the response of the listeners!

The uses of audio conferences are limited only by your imagination. Take a moment to brainstorm ways *you* could use teleseminars to build your business—you'll be amazed at the list you can create. You can use teleseminars to:

- Make money selling content delivered as a lecture or conversation over the phone

- Get a transcript you can sell as PDF content

- Get an MP3 you can post as content accessible on your website
- Create and sell a CD of the content
- Generate inquiries by offering the free CD or PDF
- Make money by selling the CD or PDF as a product
- Use the PDF or CD as bonus for other products you sell
- Educate or train association members or company employees
- Educate or train distributors or agents
- Build your e-list by inviting people to listen to a free teleseminar
- Generate qualified prospects you can up-sell to as a paid product or service on the same topic.

Teleseminars are used by individuals like you and me, as well as major companies and associations. These groups often have a series of teleseminars, which is something you could consider doing if your topic is too large for a one-shot presentation.

One entrepreneur has a wonderful book on the many uses of common North American plants. He makes weekly phone presentations to landscape gardeners, nursery owners, organic farmers (both large agribusinesses and small home-based growers), as well as entrepreneurs interested in the marketability of plant-based products.

Every week his calls attract an audience of people fascinated by the subject, and you can bet he sells copies of his books, fertilizers, and gardening tools, all because of the human connection he has made with the listeners, not to mention the excellent deals he makes with them on consulting (landscape and farming) services.

So . . . what's your specialty? What do you want the world to know about you and your services or products? How can you best transmit this information to your waiting public?

You guessed it: through your spoken voice. Unlike the printed word, the inflections in your speech, your auditory emphasis on important concepts, the humor you deploy, and your valuable experience comes through the phone lines most powerfully.

Another advantage is that it takes much less time and effort to do a tele-seminar than to write an original book or report on a particular topic. And, it's easier to accomplish for those people who are reluctant writers.

Also, audio content can often be sold at a premium price compared to print. A one-hour audio recording on average has 7,200 words of content, and it can be sold for $29 to $149, depending on content and market. By com-parison, a 200-page book selling for $29 has 70,000 words. What's more, audio albums containing multiple CDs can sell for $29 or more per CD. So you can charge over $170 for a six-CD program. I have sold thousands since 2007!

How do you find good topics for teleseminars and audio conferences? What topics are the most in demand? To find the answers, all you have to do is com-plete an internet search using the keyword "teleseminars" (or "tele-seminars," with a hyphen) and you'll quickly learn that there are presentations on every topic imaginable. Just try it. What you'll find is that people are thirsty for information that will help them solve problems in their personal lives or with their finances; or they're looking for information on how to increase their sales, put money in their pocket, or find the perfect partner.

I even found a teleseminar to help people through the emotional roller-coaster ride of Valentine's Day! This particular teleseminar was one in a series of presentations on "getting through the holidays." Each of them was 60 minutes long and free to attend. The point I'm making here is that people want what you have: your knowledge, your experience, and (most espe-cially) your strategic solutions to their problems.

So, remember your target market. Research their problems and offer solutions. If you are unclear about your target market group, take the time to define them clearly.

Always bring your true sense of self, your unique marketing plan, and your values to every internet marketing endeavor. Develop a passionate relationship with your prospects and work to honor their time, energy, and money. After all, a teleseminar is the great virtual medium for developing a strong bond with your prospects and customers. Build loyalty to one another and you've created a lifelong customer.

With that said, I'd like to offer you some time to write down what you are going to offer in your teleseminar, and to define who the "ideal" listener will be; in other words, who are the members of your target market, and what do you want to say to them? And last, but by no means least, what will be your "call-to-action"? So sit down with pen and paper and brainstorm away!

But first, let me say "think big"! See this first teleseminar effort as part of a larger plan of action. Don't think of it as an isolated event, but part of a whole marketing plan. I either use the teleseminar to bring people into a sales funnel for my more expensive products and services. Or I sell the audio content for money.

OK. You've decided on the target market, you know the topic of the presentation, and you've decided on the product or service you're promoting. After all, that's what it's all about, right? That is, providing enough information to make it worth the participants' time, exciting them about the solutions you are offering, and presenting them with a powerful call-to-action ("buy this product" or "subscribe to this service").

How to create a teleseminar

Now we come to the nuts-and-bolts of the process of teleseminar creation. It seems as if everyone has an opinion about what type of presentation is best. Some people are bored silly by a straight lecture format, unless the speaker is extremely engaging or humorous. Others are intimidated by a question-and-answer-based event, where they feel crowded into the background.

This can be especially true in a teleseminar, when you are actually sitting alone in your room, listening to others. I know that when I first started listening in on telepresentations I was extremely shy, never choosing to participate at all. By the way, there are tricks and strategies to use as a presenter to draw people out of their shell—usually they amount to being friendly, personable, and in control of the event.

Think back for a moment to your best classroom experience. We've all had that one teacher who was wonderful and that (hopefully only) one teacher who was the exact opposite.

How can you emulate the wonderful teacher, and avoid the pitfalls of the poor soul who left such a bad impression? Easy! By good planning and solid scripting of the call.

Essentially, there are three standard formats, with possible minor variations or combinations: lecture, interview, and audience participation:

- *Lecture*—delivered mostly one-way; you speak and the audience listens. Often combined with a question-and-answer period near the end of the call, this is a standard teleseminar format. Sometimes, pre-event questions submitted by participants are dealt with at the end of the call, rather than opening up the telephone conference lines for audience participation. This is done to avoid "losing control of the call" through unpredictable audience behavior. Pro: Ideal for large group presentations or where you need to deliver lots of information. Con: Can be boring (or frustrating) if the speaker rambles or speaks too fast.

- *Interview*—here, someone interviews you, or you interview another expert. Pro: Can be good if your audience in your niche market has similar problems, and if the expert is really able to share solutions (and not just grandstand about his or her achievements and reputation). Con: If the questions aren't good, the call can get boring. You must have great interviewing skills, and you must be really willing to probe and ask good questions. And you must ask questions that are relevant and interesting to your audience. One additional con: From a logistical point of view, it's sometimes difficult to get guests to commit to a date and time for an interview.

- *Participatory*—this format is great for a small group interactive workshop or a subscription-based mastermind group. Here a shared phone line becomes a roundtable discussion between the participants, facilitated by the presenter. Pro: Here the attendees pay attention and feel connected, getting to know one another and sharing experiences. Con: Such small groups offer a limited financial return to the presenter, unless the call is part of a series of calls.

I think what you're looking for as a presenter is control over the phone call, so make it work for *you*, and the participants will be happier. I've been on some participatory teleseminars as a listener where the presenter had no way of handling intrusive or overbearing listeners, and it spoiled the event for the rest of us. Monopolization of the time by call participants who were asking too many questions or otherwise being rude made the experience a miserable one for everyone. I'll offer suggestions on "crowd control" later; just be sure you are comfortable with the format before you begin.

Should you produce a single teleseminar or a series? The overriding issue here is the depth and breadth of the topic you are presenting. Many calls I've been on are only designed to introduce a tele-course of eight or more "classes," and as such, they are only "single event" material.

Pricing is another issue. In a series, some people charge one price per call, say $79, but the first call, the introductory call, is offered at a discount price—let's just say $29. Also, in a series, the client typically get a discount by buying all calls in the series versus buying them individually.

Designed as a teaser to create interest in what you are offering, the consensus is that 60 minutes is the perfect amount of time to present information, build interest, and initiate the sales pitch. Ninety minutes also works. Anything less than that just doesn't give you enough time to engage the listeners and build the trust level required to make the sale—whether on the call, or later in follow-up emails.

At freeconference.com, as at other conference call services, a variety of slot length options are offered; you can arrange for calls to last from 25 minutes to two hours and 55 minutes. Naturally, it will take planning and rehearsal to know exactly what the best length of time is for your topic and your audience, but the consensus is that 60–90 minutes works well.

For example, you could set up a "teaser" call to recruit participants for your teleseminar series on a given topic. You present the product—the teleseminar series, with all its features and benefits for the attendees—and then address any questions the listeners may have in the last 5–10 minutes. Give attendees a strong call-to-action at the end of the call; something like this, for example: "Anyone who registers in the next 30 minutes will receive the recordings for 50 percent off the list price."

Here is how it works for one of my clients who currently provides in-person seminars to their prospects: The teaser calls address the concerns of the audience regarding price, content, and quality of presentation for what would normally be a live, in-person seminar. The series then replicates the number of hours of live presentation, broken down into shorter (easier to digest) components, spaced over a number of days or weeks.

Frequency is an issue when you are planning a teleseminar series. If there will be "homework" assigned to the participants, you need to give them adequate time to complete the work, without giving them so much time as to allow for procrastination.

One series I've seen has one class per month, for eight months; personally, I feel this is too lengthy—people will lose interest and the series will lose momentum. (And one entrepreneur interviewed stated that long series teleseminars increase the refund rate; people expect their money back when they lose momentum or the desire to attend.) The standard is to offer weekly calls, but again I have seen teleseminars series where the calls are monthly.

Experiment with various schedules, query your preview call participants to see what they would like, and then be willing to make changes. Flexibility is important in this endeavor, as in any other!

How do you know what questions to ask and answer in your teleseminar? You can ask your prospects what material they'd want to have covered. How should you proceed, if you're unclear as to the nature of their "problems"? For example, if I wanted to do a teleseminar about writing e-books, how could I know what specific problems exist for people under the umbrella of that topic?

It would be necessary to ask questions. But how? If you don't have your own mailing list, created from e-zine sign-ups or website visitors, then I heartily advise checking out web-based groups, forums, blogs, and bulletin boards. Doing keyword research can lead you in the right direction, too. Let's look at what I came up with when using the above example, "writing e-books."

First, I used that phrase in a search engine and got over 192 million listings! Hard to believe, isn't it? Certainly, reviewing the top 100 is sufficient to see what people need or want: e-book writing software, e-book writing tips, and e-book promotion.

I suggest the following when using groups as a research resource:

- First, determine how active the group is—some groups are completely inactive.

- Then read some of the postings before joining.

- Next, set up a special email address to use for group membership email delivery. Opt in to receive daily digests of messages, as individual emails can be overwhelming.

These groups are perfect places to ask questions or to post a survey link. Only use those groups that are most active. The questions I'd create would revolve around the major topics of interest noted in the search engine listings: software solutions, writing tips and strategies, and e-book promotion.

See how easy it can be? The good thing about joining groups is that you then have a group of people to invite to your presentations or to subscribe to your e-zine. This is exactly how I build a strong list of subscribers to my e-zine, *E-Writer Bulletin*. Having used list-building services for other e-zine projects, I learned the hard way that it's better not to pay for subscribers.

Produce your own podcasts

Eighty percent of Americans have smartphones and more and more smartphone users are listening to podcasts.

- There are a million podcasts in over 100 languages and more than 30 million podcast episodes.

- Nearly a quarter of a million Americans listen to podcasts weekly, tuning into an average of seven different shows.

- Nearly seven out of ten consumers say podcast ads make them aware of new products and services.

- More than nine out of ten podcast listeners are active on at least one social media channel.

There's obviously something to take note of: Podcasting, as well as social media in general (more about that later), offers a huge opportunity to you and your business.

A few technical notes: A podcast is a digital audio file that you upload to your server for your target market to download, either to their computer or smartphone. They will be able to listen to it, and to your valuable how-to information, at their leisure.

There are a number of different types of audio files, but the most common are Wave files (.wav) and MPEG Layer-3 files (.mp3). The way the audio is compressed and stored is called the codec and this determines how small the file size is. Some file types always use a particular codec. For example, ".mp3" files always use the "MPEG Layer-3" codec. Some file types just contain the audio. But other file types can contain additional header information, which can contain other information about the file. We're most concerned here with .wav and .mp3 files.

The .wav format is a standard audio file used mainly in Windows PCs. Commonly used for storing uncompressed (PCM), CD-quality sound files, which means that they can be large in size—around 10MB per minute of music. It is less well known that wave files can also be encoded with a variety of codecs to reduce the file size (for example the GSM or MP3 codecs).

The MP3 or the MPEG Layer-3 format is the most popular format for downloading and storing music. By eliminating portions of the audio file that are essentially inaudible, MP3 files are compressed to roughly one-tenth the size of an equivalent PCM file, while maintaining good audio quality.

How will your audience find your podcast? It's easier than ever for podcasters to reach new audiences, now that most smartphone podcast player apps include a podcast directory. If you get your podcast listed on the major podcast directories, listeners will be able to find your podcast with a simple search. (Make sure your podcast description includes the right search keywords to make your podcast more discoverable.) The 300-pound gorilla of podcast directories is Apple Podcasts, and it is essential to be listed there. Other important podcast directories are Google Podcasts, Spotify, Stitcher, iHeartRadio, Pandora, Overcast, and Downcast.

The advantages of podcasting are many:

- It's portable
- It's personal
- It's entertaining
- It's accessible
- It's cooperative: listeners *choose* to listen. Selecting and downloading your podcast means listeners have a *commitment* to participation.

Why should you create a podcast? "To be successful on the web, you need new thinking," says content marketing guru David Meerman Scott. "The web is not about buying lists. Instead it is about publishing great content."

Be a featured guest on dozens of TV and talk radio shows this year

Today we live in an age of electronic information, with people reading less and watching and listening more. Therefore, getting on radio and TV enables you to reach additional prospects, who may not read the newspaper or magazines. But there are many other reasons why radio and TV publicity is so desirable.

"Radio and television are intimate media," says marketing expert Dr. Jeffrey Lant. "You have the chance to lower the buyer's anxieties about you and get them enthusiastic. Properly handled, your appearance on the media enables you to come across as a friend, and as a benefactor to your prospects. You can speak to them honestly, directly, sincerely, and get them genuinely enthusiastic about your offer. No paid ad is ever as direct and warm as a media appearance, and ads don't make you famous, while media appearances do."

Note that you do not have to be a celebrity to be a guest on radio or television. The media directories in the appendix list thousands of radio, broadcast, and cable shows in need of interesting, informative guests. While celebrities do get lots of airtime, at least as much airtime is given to people who, like you, have knowledge of a specialized subject of interest to a partic-ular audience and can who communicate this knowledge in an interesting, enjoyable, and clear manner.

"Talk and interview shows are a great way to get your message to the world, since talk shows are always looking for interesting guests," says David Yale, author of *The Publicity Handbook.* According to Yale, 30 percent of radio and TV producers say they are interested in booking guests who speak on topical issues, 16 percent are interested in having people speak about new products, and 12 percent like to book authors.

Spend some time boning up on your topic before you go on the show. A radio or TV appearance is the ultimate think-on-your feet challenge. No matter how well you prepare, callers will ask a host some questions on highly specific situations that require you to work out an answer instantly, on the spot, and then present it in a clear manner, without hesitation, in 30 to 60 seconds.

Spend an evening reading through your press releases, press kit, book, article clippings, brochure, annual report, or whatever source material is the basis for your topic. Take notes on some interesting highlights, and jot these key facts and figures on a few index cards or a sheet of paper. Take this material with you. You can study it while you wait to go on the air and, on radio, you can refer to it without the audience knowing you are using a crib sheet.

The listener and host expect you to be an expert in your topic; that's why you are there. However, part of being an expert is to know how far your expertise extends and where it ends. This honesty impresses hosts and viewers, rather than turning them off. I have two specific strategies for handling questions that throw me off balance and to which I don't have a good answer (or can't come up with one on the spot).

The first is to decline to answer based on limits of expertise. For instance, on a recent radio appearance where I was talking about how to be a more effective salesperson, a caller asked about managing a sales force and specifically about whether I knew compensation schemes that would reward salespeople for getting repeat business from existing accounts. I immediately answered, "Michael, I'm sorry, but my expertise is selling techniques, not management of salespeople. I know nothing about management and have no idea how to compensate a sales force. You might try asking colleagues who are sales managers at other companies in your industry."

The second strategy is to say, "I don't know the answer to that question, George, but if you call me at my office tomorrow we can discuss it further. I will research it and get the answer for you or put you in touch with someone who knows. Mr. Host, may I give George my office number?" This demonstrates that you are a helpful source of information and gets you off the hook of having to know it all.

Being a guest on a radio or TV talk show is not always a winning situation. It takes lot of effort and time to get on the show, prepare, and do the actual interview. For us small businesspeople, time is money. So, unlike many people, we don't do it for the fun or glory or to feed our ego. We do it for the sole purpose of publicizing our product or service, generating leads, enhancing our visibility and reputation, and making more sales and profits.

When I am interviewed on a radio show, I ask how long the interview will be. If it is a half-hour or longer, I know I can make an audio program. I don't do the interview unless the producer agrees to give me an audio file of the interview and permission to use it as I please. I often burn these onto CDs and use the radio interviews as free bonuses for my regular audio CD programs.

When we go to all this trouble and the media appearance doesn't work out, the tendency is to get upset and angry. But don't let it show. Instead, handle the situation gracefully, never yell or scream or complain, and always leave people thinking well of you. This positive behavior increases your chances of getting more and better media opportunities; negative behavior will give you a reputation as a difficult person and make media people want to avoid you.

Most media appearances do go well, but there are horror stories. One friend recalls driving two hours in torrential rains to keep an appointment to appear on a radio show. When he arrived, another guest was sitting down in the interviewee's chair. "Whoops," the assistant program manager told him. "I must have forgotten to make a note after we talked, and I guess I forgot to schedule you in. Can you come back next week?"

And of course, we've all heard about authors and other "last guests" on the *Tonight Show*, who know they're going to get bumped if the celebrity on before them has a big mouth and is in a talkative mood. Can you imagine being ready to appear on the *Tonight Show*, then watch the final minutes of the show tick by as Kim Kardashian or Kanye West keeps yakking? I was once bumped by a host because Chris O'Donnell showed up unscheduled and wanted to talk.

Another horror story happened to my friend Richard Armstrong. He was thrilled when his publisher booked him on the Bob Grant show, a top-rated talk show in the New York City market, to discuss his new book on politics, *The Next Hurrah*.

Unfortunately, when he arrived he discovered that he was not the sole guest but that another author would be on at the same time. The author was celebrity George Plimpton. Worse, Plimpton had just written a book on baseball, and wanted to discuss baseball, not politics. The show made absolutely no sense, with Plimpton talking about baseball and Bob and Richard discussing politics (with Plimpton also commenting on politics, but obviously disinterested in doing so); however, Richard performed like a pro and did well.

Bumping has never happened to me on an internet radio show. The producers book you because you have interesting or valuable information to share, and they are happy to get you. Today there are around 100,000 internet radio stations, which means plenty of venues where you can be a featured guest. Many internet shows cater to smaller special-interest audiences, so there is almost endless opportunity to share your content.

Most experts tell you, "Plug your product or service when on the air." I disagree. People don't want to hear about your book or video or accounting firm; they want to get solutions to their most pressing problems. So rather than talk about you, your product, your service, or what you know, focus on the listeners—what they need, what they want, what their problems and concerns are.

Example: I was a guest on a number of call-in radio shows to promote my book *Selling Your Services: Proven Strategies for Getting Clients to Hire You (or Your Firm)*. Repeatedly, the host would ask, "Tell us about your book, Bob."

The late Isaac Asimov, prolific author of more than 400 books on science, history, science fiction, literature, and other topics, tells an amusing story about the media's expectations of an "expert."

He was booked on a radio talk show by his publisher to promote his latest book, *The Human Brain*. When the interviewer asked him a question about the brain, he answered, "I don't know."

"What do you mean you don't know?" asked the interviewer. "You wrote a book on the human brain!"

"Yes," Asimov replied, "but I've written hundreds of books on dozens of topics, and I can't be an expert on all of them. I only know what's in the book, and in fact, I can't even remember all of that!"

Exasperated, the interviewer asked, "So you're not an expert on anything?"

"Oh, I'm an expert on one thing," said Asimov.

"On what?" asked the host.

"On being an expert," Asimov replied. "Do you want to talk about that?"

I'd answer, "I'd be happy to talk about the book, Mr. Host. But what I'd really like to do is to help your listeners overcome their fear of making cold calls, overcome all the objections they are getting from prospects, and feel more confident about selling and getting better results. So, those of you listening out there, when you call, we'll go through your particular selling situation and solve the problem right over the phone!"

The host was delighted with this approach, as were the listeners. I created a much more interesting, useful show by working with the listeners as if they were clients, rather than saying "my book this" and "my book that," as 99 percent of authors do. And what about promoting the book? No problem: The host did that for me, because he was enthusiastic about my information and wanted to help listeners get more of it.

The benefits were twofold. First, I came across as a credible, respectable expert, not a self-interested author trying to get the listeners to buy a book. Second, the promotion of the book by the host was more effective than me saying good things about it, since it amounted to a third-party endorsement.

Notes Jeffrey Lant: "You must personalize what you know, reach out and talk directly to your prospects as a friend, entirely honestly, as if you are having a conversation. The fact that you can't see the person you are talking to is irrelevant. That person must feel the force of your personality."

Whenever possible, get a copy of each radio and TV appearance you make. These copies have a number of uses. You can use them to convince producers of other radio and TV shows that you will be a good guest: entertaining, pleasant, bright, and informative, with information relevant to their audience.

Producers are somewhat reluctant to book guests who are experts but have no or little experience in broadcast media. Offering an audiotape or videotape of a good performance eliminates that reluctance.

Listening to your tapes help you improve your performance so you are better next time. You can use the tapes as marketing communications tools. For example, if you are a consultant specializing in quality and you are interviewed on a cable TV business discussing quality, make copies of the video and send it to clients and prospects.

How do you get a copy of your appearance? Before my scheduled interview, I call up the producer, say who I am and when I am scheduled to be on the show, and then I say, "May I ask a favor? I would love to get a recording of the broadcast. If I send you payment, would you be willing send me an audio file? If not, no problem, of course." Most will agree and, further, will not charge you for it (but you should always offer payment).

15

Training, Coaching, and Consulting

As a published how-to writer, you possess both valuable content and a reputation as an expert in your topic. You can multiply your profits by also offering your information in the form of high-priced training, coaching, and consulting services, and your reputation as a writer will enable you to close those deals with relative ease.

Your goal is to transform your expertise into profitable live teaching. Internet marketing expert Perry Marshall explains:

> Between the ears of every company's employees is knowledge and expertise that goes largely untapped. When I worked for a high-tech firm selling networking equipment, I realized that customers desperately needed to know what my own support staff knew. That's why they were calling for support. Furthermore, I knew a service/installation company in Pennsylvania that literally had more experience with this than any other company in the country.
>
> With the company in Pennsylvania, I assembled a training program and we sold it to our customers for $1,500 a head. Every $1 we spent mailing our customers flyers about our training events brought us $8 in sales.
>
> Please understand, before we did this, we were not even remotely in the training or seminar business. Our gig was selling industrial

equipment. But the training created an extra revenue stream for us and it also did something else: It positioned us as Grand Central Station for training on this technology in our industry.

How to make $6,500 a day training corporate employees

My main market for speaking is corporate training. A lot of speakers do corporate training, but most of them I meet prefer to target association and corporate meetings, rather than in-house corporate training classes. Why is this so?

Speakers like meetings—keynotes in particular—because the pay is higher and the sessions shorter. They can go in, speak for an hour in front of a large group that applauds at the end, collect a check for $2,500 to $9,500 or more, and leave.

Corporate training, by comparison, is more intensive and in-depth. On average, these workshops last one or two days, not an hour. Your audience is only one or two dozen people, not hundreds.

Still, I prefer corporate training because, in my opinion, you can deliver more benefit to your audience and make more of a difference in their businesses, their jobs, and their lives. In a one-hour keynote, you may motivate and even fascinate. But how much real learning takes place? How much do listeners get that they can take back to the office and actually implement the next day?

In a one- or two-day in-house class of limited size, you do more than entertain; you actually teach and transfer knowledge and skills from yourself to the audience. Training is closer in format and approach to a college course than it is to a speech, except obviously the time frame is compressed and the content is practical, not theoretical.

My primary offering is a one-day on-site seminar for corporate clients. I teach copywriting, marketing, and technical writing. The training day is about six hours. For a class of 10 to 20 trainees, my current fee for the day is $6,500 plus expenses. Depending on your topic and your reputation in your subject matter, expect to earn between $2,500 to $8,500 a day.

Reaching the corporate market is a little bit tricky because it is not always clear who hires you. However, there are generally two different groups of training buyers within a large corporation.

Zoom and Microsoft Teams

The use of virtual meetings, training, conferences, webinars, events, and distance-learning—especially as an alternative to live meetings—has been steadily increasing for years, but was accelerated greatly by the coronavirus pandemic.

The advantages to information marketers of offering virtual workshops include:

- Virtual events are less complex to plan and coordinate
- Less financial risk for the promoter
- Elimination of food and lodging expenses
- Protecting of your audience and presenters from the coronavirus
- Elimination of travel hassles and time, especially during COVID-19 restrictions.

The three most widely used platforms for virtual information marketing are GoToWebinar, Zoom, and Microsoft Teams. Zoom and MS Teams are especially popular with information marketers and customers, many of whom are now using these platforms with increased frequency, fluency, and comfort. Free versions of both platforms are available.

The good part of all this is that coronavirus worries have created more widespread willingness of learners to participate in programs remotely. So digital learning is certainly here to stay. Most likely, the future will consist of a mix of both virtual and live events.

The first are training professionals: In many large corporations, seminar leaders are hired either by a training manager who works in the human resources (HR) department or, if the company is not large enough to have a training manager, by the HR director or another HR manager. These folks are training buyers, not end users. They are not buying your program for themselves. Instead, like a purchasing agent, they are buying your services for someone else in their corporation, such as an executive who wants to train his or her team to improve their skills.

The second market for training is line managers, typically at the vice president or department-head level, in charge of departments or functional areas. These are the end users of training, the managers who will send their staff members through your program. The sales manager, for instance, might want someone to train the sales team in closing skills. A vice president of engineering or manufacturing might need a consultant to teach a seminar to the staff on new changes in ISO 9001 quality standards.

Which audience—the training department or the functional managers—is better? You can market successfully to either or both, and I have. Having done that, however, I will go out on a limb and say that it's usually better to target the functional managers directly.

A few years ago, I did a little telemarketing test for my small training firm to generate prospects with an interest in having us do an in-house seminar in effective technical writing.

The training directors were interested, but their main goal was in getting our literature to put into their files for future reference. If they did not have a request on the table that day from a manager who wanted a technical writing seminar, there was nothing we could say to create that need or make it more urgent for them. Clearly they functioned largely as purchasing professionals filling requests from their "clients"—the managers throughout their organizations whom they serve.

Vice presidents and department managers were different. They may not have ever thought about doing a technical writing seminar, so we asked them, "Do your engineers write as clearly as you want them to? Do they struggle with their writing, and take too much of their time to write and to edit their work?" That got the attention of many of the managers we spoke with. It started conversations about their writing problems, and it resulted in several engagements for us.

Selling yourself as a trainer

1. Understand the training department's buying cycle and process. If they do not have a need from someone in the company for a seminar on your topic, you cannot create the need for them. The training department buys to fill requests, not to solve business problems.

2. Should you go over the training department's head directly to the end users? Don't make it confrontational. Market to both the training department and the end users. Training directors are just as happy to have end users come to them with both a request for a program as well as the name of a trainer to handle it. The training department has no proprietary interest in searching for and finding a speaker; if the client wants you, the training department would just as soon hire you and make everyone happy. In fact, this is advantageous for the training professional: It's less work than having to go out and search for a trainer. And, if the program is not well received, the training department is freed of blame because the user was the one who selected you.

3. Speak their lingo. The first thing a training professional will ask you about your program is, "What are your learning objectives?" This is fancy language for what the course covers and what the students will be able to do after they take the program.

4. The premier society for training professionals is the Association for Talent Development (ATD). If you intend to do frequent work in the corporate training market, membership is very worthwhile. The members are mostly training managers, so the membership directory makes for a good prospecting list. You can find ATD online at www.td.org.

5. Get involved with your local ATD chapter. See if you can get on the program to speak on your topic at one of their meetings.

6. Since training managers often collect information on consultants for future, rather than immediate, needs, they are receptive to an offer of a free package of information on your program.

7. If you specialize in a narrow topic and receive requests for other topics you don't handle, make a list of speakers who do handle those topics that you can refer prospects and clients to. Whenever a training manager has a need you can't fill, refer him or her to the appropriate person. If they see you as a resource, they'll be more likely to favor you with their business when requests for your topic arrive on their desks.

8. Training managers are sometimes treated as low on the corporate totem pole by their own organizations, but you should treat them with respect and as the professionals that they are. When you are hired, ask the training manager about the idiosyncrasies of the organization and attendees as they relate to the seminar you are giving. This inside view will help you give a better session, and the manager will appreciate the fact that you asked.

9. Ask if there are controversial topics you should avoid. My preprogram questionnaire has a space for the training manager to indicate these topics to me. Do not spend time on subjects the training manager has asked you to avoid, even if you feel they are important.

10. Do not fight or argue with trainees. If a particular attendee is giving you a problem, quietly notify the training director during a break.

11. Corporate managers do not want to buy "training." They want to solve business problems. If you can prove that your seminar can help solve that problem, the manager will hire you to teach a class for employees.

12. Corporate managers hate the jargon training professionals use. Do not use educational lingo; use down-to-earth language. Avoid talking about "learning objectives." Tell the prospect: If you hire me to do this seminar, you can expect this result.

13. Do research to document the importance of solving the problem your seminar addresses. The prospect has many difficulties to solve, and assigns priority based upon the urgency and importance to the organization of getting results in that particular area. When I offered my seminar on "Effective Technical Writing" to the pharmaceutical industry, I did not say that good technical writing makes web pages easier to read; I pointed out that FDA submissions rejected by the Food and Drug Administration because of unclear writing delayed time-to-market, potentially costing the company millions of dollars.

14. The more you can tie in your program to the company's bottom line, the easier it will be to persuade managers to hire you. That's why sales training is an easier sell than business writing. A 10 percent increase in sales ability can mean an extra one million dollars in revenue for a

company with $10 million annual sales. It is more difficult to demonstrate the return on training investment for a business writing seminar that teaches managers how to avoid grammar mistakes.

How to become an independent consultant in your field

The *American Heritage Dictionary* defines *consultant* as "a person who gives expert or professional advice." The consulting business, though, has received a bad rap in recent years because of the number of people getting into consulting who really don't know what they are advising about. This is the result of unknowledgeable people hanging up their shingle but not spending time to learn their chosen profession properly.

Yet thousands of more conscientious consultants do practice their trade daily, which wouldn't be the case if they were not satisfying some clients at least some of the time. Consultant Andrew S. Linick says, "Having a consultant who will take you through the business minefields safely will greatly increase your chances of a super successful landing with your business intact."

Today we live in an age of specialization. In 1945, the amount of information in the world doubled every 25 years. In the 21st century, the amount of information in the world doubles every 12 hours, as incredible as that sounds. As a result, you can't know everything, or even most things. So naturally we seek outside help and expertise to supplement our own.

Consultants exist to guide people and solve problems in areas their clients don't know well. For example, an engaged couple, overwhelmed by the details of planning a lavish wedding for 200 guests, might hire a bridal consultant. The owner of a small trucking business, knowledgeable about trucking but computer-phobic, hires a computer consultant to create a billing, accounting, and fleet management system. The CEO of a corporation, seeking to improve efficiency and streamline operations, hires a "re-engineering" consultant to advise her on managing the restructuring process.

Given today's information explosion and rapidly changing marketplace, more and more organizations are hiring consultants to provide guidance, answer questions, give second opinions, train employees, and serve as sounding boards against which executives, managers, and entrepreneurs can bounce ideas, plans, strategies, and thoughts.

Individuals are hiring "life coaches" to help them make important decisions and manage their relationships, careers, and businesses. As a result of this explosive demand, the consulting profession is booming. In the United States, companies and individuals spend $58.7 billion annually buying consultant services.

We often hear today about how *knowledge* has become one of the most valuable business assets. To the consultant, knowledge is the *single most* valuable asset. Since most knowledge can be gained through experience and study, virtually anyone can acquire specialized knowledge which he or she can sell as consulting services.

Combined with the low start-up costs, this makes consulting an ideal business for self-employed how-to writers. Many consulting firms consist of one or two people, and these can be run from home in a very efficient manner.

Becoming an independent consultant

Making the transition from corporate employment to self-employment as a consultant can be scary. It seems to be a little easier for young people who don't have heavy financial burdens, and also for older workers who could afford to retire but want something to do. It can be more nerve-wracking for people in the middle of their careers who have to continue to earn a living after leaving the security of their corporate job.

Many of us feel that the pull of being an entrepreneur, and the lure of doing something different than the usual nine-to-five routine, can be strong. One powerful reason to consider consulting as a career is to do work you like.

Life can sure seem better when you look forward to going to work in the morning every day, especially if you only need to walk around the corner to the next room in your own home. Sales trainer Paul Karasik observes, "What motivates people is doing what they love." When you're a consultant, you can make money by practicing a skill or dealing with a subject that interests you most.

A book review published in the *National Home Business Report* quoted best-selling author Richard N. Bolles as saying, "What the world needs is more people who feel true enthusiasm for their work. People who have taken the time to think out what they uniquely can do and have to offer the world."

In an issue of *Words from Woody*, David Wood quotes Michael Korda as saying, "Your chances of success are directly proportional to the degree of pleasure you derive from what you do. If you are in a job you hate, face the fact squarely and get out." Timothy Butler, a director of career development at Harvard Business School, says, "Vocation has to do with your calling. It's what you're doing in life that makes a difference for you, that builds meaning for you."

For those of us who are not destined to climb the highest rungs of the corporate ladder and become the CEO, being an entrepreneur offers an opportunity to make more money than we might as an employee. As an independent consultant working from home or a small rented office, you have the potential to make $100,000 to $500,000 a year or more, while keeping your business relatively simple and small. Most consultants I know say they make at least twice as much money as they did when they had a regular job. Some make more.

For some people, being downsized or laid off is the impetus to take a closer look at consulting as an employment alternative—when you work for yourself, you can't be fired.

While money and autonomy motivate many of us to start consulting businesses, others do it because they like the lifestyle it offers. According to an article in *The Winner's Circle*, 77 percent of Americans have as a goal to spend time with family and friends, and 74 percent want to improve themselves intellectually or otherwise.

As a consultant, I can spend my time on things that stimulate me intellectually and are deeply rewarding to me. When I was a corporate manager, by comparison, I spent most of my time doing things I didn't enjoy: meetings, paperwork, budgets, plans, forecasts, project management, and administrative tasks. Writing in *Story* magazine, Brian Fleming notes: "Labor for no important purpose dulls the human spirit and lays waste to the soul."

For others, the urge to escape corporate life is even stronger: They feel uncomfortable in the corporate environment, don't fit in, and feel another setting is their real calling.

In *The Moon and Sixpence*, W. Somerset Maugham writes: "Sometimes a man hits upon a place to which he mysteriously feels that he belongs. Here is the home he sought, and he will settle amid scenes he has never seen before, among men he has never known, as they were familiar to him from his birth. Here at last he finds rest." This describes the comfort and contentment many people experience when they make the transition from corporate employment to self-employment.

When asked what they *miss* most about the corporate world, 68 percent of entrepreneurs interviewed cited office socializing. Other things missed include pension plans, company-paid health insurance, weekly paychecks, and access to resources.

According to an article in the *Daily News*, a poll of 202 small business owners showed that while they enjoy the freedom of being their own bosses and setting their own hours, they also feel pressure to work long hours and are anxious about making ends meet.

David Wood writes in *Words from Woody*: "An entrepreneur is the kind of person who will work sixteen hours a day just to avoid having to work eight hours a day for someone else."

Why consulting is more competitive today than ever before

Although the market for consulting services seems to be expanding, many consultants say it's tougher than ever to get and keep good clients. These consultants say that while they're busy and making good money, the business environment is more competitive and demanding than five or ten years ago.

One reason is the economy. The recession of 2020 transformed many service industries, including the majority of consulting specialties, from a seller's market to a buyer's market. Fees stagnated that year, or even dropped. Clients learned that they had a choice and became more particular.

Clients are not afraid to ask for what they want or to shop around. Even on smaller projects, clients who would in the past have simply called you with an assignment are getting quotes from several firms before selecting a consultant for the job. Consultants find more and more of their time taken up with prospecting, quoting, preparing proposals, following up, and maintaining good relationships with clients.

Clients are choosier and more demanding than ever. It's no longer enough to be technically competent or solve client problems. Your interpersonal and customer service skills must be excellent. Clients have their choice of consultants to work with, and most people prefer to work with people they like or at least feel comfortable with.

If you have been a consultant for several years, you may find yourself spending more time on building and nurturing client relationships than in the past. Lord Chesterfield advised, "Cause the other fellow to like himself a little bit better, and I promise you he will like you very well indeed."

In 2020, the U.S. economy was weakened by the coronavirus pandemic and the resulting workplace shutdowns, unemployment, stock market volatility, and recession. Money became tighter than it was prior to 2020. Since the recession hit, budgets have gotten smaller, clients spend more cautiously and more wisely, and buyers shop around more to get a good price.

At the same time, the buying authority of clients in large organizations has been reduced. Most purchases above $1,000 are made by increasingly larger and slower-moving committees. Some corporations have approved vendor lists or long-term contractual relationships with large vendors that make it difficult for them to purchase services from smaller, independent consulting firms.

The global population increases by 220,000 people per day. This means more potential clients for your services, but also more people entering the job market, including the consulting market.

Many people see consulting as desirable and even glamorous, and so they are drawn to the profession in greater numbers. Downsizing has left tens of thousands of skilled white-collar workers without employment and with uncertain job prospects. For many, hanging a shingle as an independent consultant is a convenient and attractive solution.

The five key consulting activities

Although there are many variations possible on these categories, most of the work done by most of the consultants today falls into one or more of the following five areas:

1. *Advisory services.* In the cartoon strip *The Family Circle*, a mother tells her son: "You misunderstand. I'm a homework consultant, not a homework subcontractor." She means she'll advise him on how to do his homework. But she won't do it for him.

   Most consultants act as advisors. They give recommendations and suggestions. But they don't implement their ideas, and they aren't the ones who decide which recommendations will be put into action.

   The client makes the decision, and a lot of what you recommend won't be done. That's typical, and it is no reflection on the soundness of your ideas. There are many reasons a client won't try a good idea. Maybe they tried it already and it didn't work. Perhaps it's against corporate policy. Or maybe they just don't have the resources to implement it.

Don't be put off when clients thank you for, pay you for, but don't do a lot of what you suggested. It happens all the time.

2. *Implementation services.* Some consultants actually implement the solutions they (or others) come up with. An accountant, for example, not only shows you ways to get a tax refund, but he also completes your return. A computer consultant, in addition to recommending a computing solution, may assemble the components, install and integrate them at the customer's site, do the custom programming, train the client to use the system, and even provide ongoing maintenance and support.

It's an odd fact, but giving advice often pays better than implementation. Those who tell others what to do frequently are paid more than those who actually do the work. An information systems consultant, for example, might get $2,000 a day or more to advise chief information officers on high-level computing issues. But a freelance programmer writing code for an application may earn a far more modest rate of $400 to $500 per day.

One-on-one consulting pays well and can be effective, but it has its limitations. One-on-one consulting is the most expensive form of information delivery, and the amount of such services most organizations can afford is limited. It also requires the consultant's individual attention, and with only so many hours in a week, there's only so much one-on-one consulting you can do.

3. *Training and development.* Many consultants specialize in training the employees of client organizations in various job-related skills. About half of the nation's annual training budget goes toward basic and "soft" skills (business writing, customer service, teamwork, leadership, management, time management), while the other half is spent training employees in technical and "hard" skills (local area network troubleshooting, Microsoft Office, sales forecasting, compensation management, regulatory compliance).

"Feed a man a fish and you feed him for a day," goes the old saying, "but teach a man to fish and you feed him for a lifetime." In theory, the skills a trainer teaches can last throughout a career and increase the productivity of every employee who takes the course for decades to come. For this reason, trainers are well paid, earning $1,000 to $4,000 a day, or sometimes even more, for classes presented in-house to an organization's employees.

4. *Publishing and product development.* The late consultant Howard Shenson said, "Publishing is every consultant's second job."

Much of the information disseminated through consulting can be packaged and sold as "information products," including books, audios, workbooks, software, forms, checklists, phone support lines, internet support, newsletters, and reference guides. So there is an opportunity for almost every consultant to package part of his or her expertise as information products.

Howard Shenson observed that consultants have limited income potential from rendering one-on-one service, because of the limited number of hours you can work each week. He likened the independent consultant to the independent dentist, who continually has to "drill and fill" before he can bill.

Becoming a producer of information products frees you from the limitations of rendering service on an hourly basis. If you bill $1,000 a day for market research, the most you can make for a day of research work is $1,000.

But what if you packaged your market research and sold it as a $1,000 report? You can just as easily sell ten reports in a day as you can one report. Or even 20 or 30! The "drill, fill, and bill" limitations on your income fall away.

Many consultants produce information products to generate revenue beyond their daily consulting service. These products can range from a $1 booklet to a $49 e-book to a $100,000 software package. Having a series of products, especially in the $10 to $1,000 range, enables you to package and sell your expertise to clients who cannot afford or do not want custom one-on-one consultation, further expanding your revenues.

5. *Contract and temp consulting.* Contractors and temps usually operate somewhat differently than a traditional independent consultant. The contract or temp typically works full-time on the client's premises, devoting all or most of their week to that client for as long as they are on the assignment. They perform a variety of tasks rather than just give advice, often working as part of a team comprised of both consultants and staff workers.

When you do consulting work, your final deliverable to the client often takes the form of a written report. Save all your consulting reports on a subdirectory labeled "consulting reports" in your hard drive. While the reports contain custom advice and confidential information, many sections are semi-boilerplate; these typically contain standard advice you give to multiple clients on a frequent basis. The boilerplate sections of consulting reports can easily be turned into articles or special reports.

Tip: When accepting contract or temp work, be sure to consult your accountant. Often contractors and temps are treated, from a payroll point of view, like staff employees rather than freelancers or vendors. They get a W-2 or W-4 instead of a 1099 and may be subject to withholding.

16

Physical Audio and Video Information Products

Now you are ready to multiply your public speaking, teleseminar, and live seminar profits by selling your how-to content as audio and video information products. You have two choices when producing audio and video information products: You can record at a live event or in a studio. For the latter, you can rent time in a professional sound studio or buy the equipment yourself and do it at home.

I have taken both approaches, but my favorite method of producing audio and video products is to give a talk in front of an audience and use that recording as the product. For my 16-DVD Internet Cash Generator product—my most expensive video set, selling for around $800—my business partner and I promoted a two-day weekend seminar on internet marketing with me as the sole speaker. While we made money from the event, the main purpose was to get the recording and make a product out of it.

What about a digital format? These days, I often offer the buyer the option of either physical products—DVDs or audio CDs—or streaming mp4 and mp3 files.

Some of my readers believe DVDs and CDs are outdated, and that one should offer only a digital version. But today I am still active helping a number of publishers, both large and small, sell physical video and audio products, including audio books and training videos.

Why do I love live recording? Several reasons. First, it eliminates the need to write a word-for-word script for the product. I produce PowerPoint presentations and speaker notes, and then speak extemporaneously from there. The result may be a bit unpolished, but it avoids the dullness of reading a script.

Second, the live recordings have a high energy level that studio recordings rarely match. Presentations in front of a live audience are just more entertaining and interesting to watch or listen to. They are also more fun to do: Reading a script in a studio is boring!

There *are* times when I choose to do a studio recording. My method here is again to avoid reading from a script. Instead, I use an interview format: Either I interview a subject matter expert, or an interviewer conducts a discussion with me as the topic expert.

The preparation for doing studio recordings for audio products using the interview method is easy. There is no script. Just make a list of questions you want to be asked and give them to your interviewer. Keep a copy for yourself. I put answer prompts in square brackets next to the question on the list when I want to be sure of covering a specific tip or idea, or telling a particular story, in my answer.

Check Google for "audio recording studio" in your area. You can typically rent studio time for $50 to $75 per hour, usually with a two- or four-hour minimum. The studios are equipped to do music, so their equipment is more than sufficient to handle spoken word audios, which are less demanding than music.

You can also record at home, thanks to the availability and affordability of professional-quality microphones. The microphone is connected to your computer. Use Audacity, GarageBand, or other software for storing and editing audio on your PC.

Alternatively, you can buy a good brand of digital recorder—I use Morantz—and record the audio directly into the recorder, bypassing the computer. Given the cost and inconvenience of studio time, buying a digital recorder or PC microphone and doing it yourself at home is by far the more economical alternative for how-to writers and information marketers who plan to do audio products on a regular basis. If you only record audio once in a blue moon, you may find that opting to use a studio is the way to go.

How to professionally record a one-hour audio at zero cost

Another alternative for producing audio products is to use recordings of live audio conference calls, teleseminars, radio interviews, and podcasts, as noted in chapter 14. When you use a conference service like www.freeconferencecall .com to provide the telephone lines needed for the teleseminar, the service allows you to digitally record the teleconference at no charge. You can access the audio file after the call, download it to your hard drive, and post it online or burn it onto a CD to create an instant audio product.

Your first audio product can be a single audio CD selling for anywhere from $29 to $49. A price point less than you charged for the live teleseminar is particularly appealing to your buyers. To create a multi-CD audio program, conduct a series of one-hour teleseminars; each becomes a different CD in the album. When I sell my audio CD courses online, I give the customer a choice of a CD set and also MP3 files that can be streamed or downloaded. We typically charge $97 for an album with two or three audio CDs and $47 for the digital version.

Produce a three-CD audio album in less than half a day

Going back to the interview format, this is the method my partner Fred Gleeck and I have used to develop over a dozen multi-CD audio programs, which sell for $100 or more a pop.

Here's the secret to producing audio programs quickly and easily: Do it in one take. We don't rehearse. We don't re-record. In fact, we don't even edit! Fred and I sit down and do the interview. The recording is captured on a digital storage device, which we FedEx to our duplication and fulfillment house. The fulfillment house burns the CDs, designs and affixes labels to them, packages them in a vinyl album, and designs and puts a front and back cover on the album.

When we sell the audio programs, we give the order information, including the customer's name and address, to the fulfillment house (we use Speaker Fulfillment Services; go to www.bly.com, click on Vendors, and look under Fulfillment Services). The fulfillment house picks the right audio albums off the shelf, puts them in an envelope, and ships them to the customer, for which they charge me a shipping and handling fee. I charge an extra $8.95 per order to my customers, which covers my shipping and handling costs.

I have also turned live seminars and workshops into audio or video information products. Many of my classes are a full day. So when I give the workshop, I divide my presentation into modules which are typically no longer than 50 or 60 minutes. A full-day workshop with eight hours of presentation translates into an eight-disk set.

Each module covers one topic. That way, it's easy to label disks by topic, so the buyer can easily find and watch the lecture module she is most interested in.

Here's an info product packaging tip for audio and video. If the course had eight CDs, don't advertise it as an eight-CD program for $X. Instead, say it is a six-CD program selling for $X that also includes two extra free bonus CDs. The latter offer typically outsells the former offer, even though they are in fact identical products selling for the same price. The reason the second offer sells better is that people love to get free bonuses.

Where to find the vendors you need

To write and produce many of the how-to information products discussed throughout this book, you will need the help of vendors. For audio products, those vendors can include recording studios, audio conference services, CD and DVD duplication houses, and fulfillment houses.

The best place to find vendors for everything you need is on my site. The direct URL link to the vendor page is www.bly.com/newsite/Pages /vendors.php.

Note: My vendors page is a free service provided for your convenience. I do not take responsibility for your satisfaction or lack thereof with the vendors you select.

Overcome the objection, "I'd rather read a book than listen to an audio CD"

Earlier in the book, we discussed the need to produce how-to information products that appeal to all four learning modalities: watching, listening, reading, and doing.

Obviously audio is for people who learn by listening. But at times a potential buyer who would rather read a book than listen to an audio asks if you can sell the audio as a printed product.

You can and should do this. It's easy. First, give the digital audio file to a professional transcriptionist (you can find several listed on the Vendors page of www.bly.com). Pay the vendor to transcribe the audio. Now, have a graphic designer put the transcription into a nice PDF page layout. Have her add an attractive cover.

Here is how you should price audio products. At minimum, the price of the CD version should be eight to ten times your manufacturing cost. Therefore, an audio CD set that costs $8 to reproduce per unit should sell for at least $64 to $80. The more valuable and specialized the content, the more you can charge.

Make a downloadable PDF of the transcript of the audio recording. Give this away as a free bonus item with the CDs. This helps provide instant gratification to your buyers: While they have to wait for the CDs to be shipped, the transcript is delivered instantly over the internet, so they can read the information immediately.

You can also offer the audio as a downloadable MP3. This allows the buyer to listen to the audio on their CD or download it to their computer or phone. It would also include the free transcript. The price of the MP3 download version should be 50 to 75 percent of the price of the physical CDs.

Occasionally a customer will say, "I don't care about the audio CDs; can I just buy the transcript?" The solution is to sell them the downloadable version of the product, which includes the PDF transcript (which they want) and downloadable MP3 files (which they can listen to, or not).

If you do offer a choice between hard copy CDs and downloadable MP3 files for your audio information products, you can add value by including the downloads as a free bonus to buyers of the CDs. Again, this gives them instant gratification as they wait for the CDs to be delivered.

Videotape your speeches for free

Hiring a skilled professional video crew to record one of your talks or seminars for a DVD or streaming video information product can be expensive. Recently, I was giving an afternoon workshop on a topic I wanted to sell as an information product. To hire a videographer to record and edit the program cost me over $2,000.

Fortunately, there is a way to get a professional videographer to tape a video of your presentation for free: Speak at a conference or other event where the sponsor records videos of the speakers. Prior to the event, make this arrangement with the seminar sponsor: You get a master of the video recording and the right to sell it as an information product or use it in whatever other way you wish—and they can sell or give it to their members and keep all revenue from member sales.

In addition to their profit potential as information products, video recordings of your lectures have another use: online video. Thanks to YouTube, more and more internet users today like and look for online video clips on websites; 500 hours of video are uploaded to YouTube every minute.

Extract short segments of one to three minutes from your videos to post on YouTube and also on your website. We have used both Vimeo and Viddler for posting short videos on our website and sales pages.

For videos on your website or landing pages, you can either require the viewer to click a button to run the video or set it for autoplay, so that when a user comes onto your page, the video plays automatically.

When you turn your lectures into DVDs or streaming video, what do you show on the screen? Part of the time, it's you at the lectern talking. You can cut to the audience and show them attentively listening, applauding, or laughing, but you need a signed release from your attendees to do so.

In the studio or while shooting, scenes of you and the audience should be interspersed with full-screen images of your PowerPoint slides. Each slide should be shown long enough for the viewer to clearly read and absorb the content on the slide. At the same time, don't overload your slides. Keep it to one dominant graphic or image. Word slides should have no more than five words per bullet, and no more than five bullets per slide.

17

Make Money Selling Software

Of all the information products available for repurposing your how-to information, software has the highest perceived value and the greatest long-term profit potential. But you don't have to be a programmer to create and sell your own software products. If you know something, you can hire a programmer for peanuts today to package that knowledge or skill as a useful software product you can sell for hundreds or even thousands of dollars. Websites for finding programmers include www.upwork.com and www.freelancer.com.

Alternatively, you can look around for a piece of software you think would be valuable to your readers in their pursuit of the skill or process (e.g., running a home business, preparing tax returns) that you write about or teach. This is often the best way to go, as it avoids the hassle and expense of developing, duplicating, shipping, and supporting a software product—a business you may not want to be in.

Back in the day, software was sold as a physical product on magnetic or optical media (floppy disks or CDs) at high per unit prices. Today, software often resides on a server and you access the functionality over the internet; this is known as SaaS or "software as a service."

The advantage to the consumer of SaaS is that instead of a large up-front purchase price, the user pays a more modest monthly subscription fee. The advantage to the seller is that SaaS gives you a nice recurring monthly revenue stream.

Marketing software

Most buyers of most software are not techies. And these nontechies care about different things, and respond differently, than the traditional Information Technology (IT) buyer.

Nontechies are results-oriented, interested in the ends rather than the means, the bottom line rather than the process. They lack interest in the details, preferring to focus on the "big picture." Most nontechies simply want to resolve problems, while engineers, scientists, and programmers enjoy actually working on problems.

The result is that nontechies are more interested in benefits, business results, and the reputation and credibility of the vendor. IT buyers, by comparison, tend to focus on technical issues, including platforms, scalability, interoperability with existing systems, reliability, specifications, limitations, and ease of implementation, operation, and maintenance.

Price and value

When generating leads for software, quote the price in the terms that seem most palatable to the customer; for instance, in some circumstances a per-user license is more appropriate than a site license, and sometimes the reverse is true. Demonstrate, if you can, the rapid return on investment your software will provide.

For example, a mailing for an application that monitors and controls employee internet usage in organizations informed the recipient that surfing the internet for personal rather than business reasons costs $300 per employee per week; the sales letter noted that four out of five hits to the *Playboy* website are from Fortune 500 companies. The letter then positions the license fee of a few dollars per user as a drop in the bucket compared to the savings the software can generate.

For selling high-end software, which represents a major corporate investment, the goal is often to get an appointment with the decision-maker. The offer then becomes, in essence, not the software, but rather the initial meeting, which is frequently positioned as a needs analysis or assessment, to be followed by recommendations. Of course, the seller's goal is to gain the information needed to provide a quote or proposal the buyer will accept.

For both lead generation and mail order, premiums are proven response-boosters. Premiums that have worked well for technology marketers include white papers, computer books, free software, free support, free training, seminars, and electronic conferences that the user accesses via telephone (for voice) and the web (for visuals).

Select a premium that is highly desirable and ties in with your product or service. A website design firm, for instance, offered "four free digital photos of your key staff, postable on your website." When the rep visited the prospect, she carried a high quality digital camera, took the photos, and immediately gave the flash drive to the prospect. Of course, the prospect wanted the photos posted on their website, something which could be done as part of the "website makeover" service the web consulting firm offered for a fee.

Response mechanisms

There are four basic response mechanisms for direct marketing of software: paper reply forms (fax-backs, reply cards, and reply envelopes), online (email or logging on to a website), phone, and fax. Since you never know which reply method a particular prospect prefers, why not offer them all? At a recent marketing conference, one software executive said, "Every software prospect is on the internet today. It's a waste of time to offer any other response mechanism." A colleague from his company disagreed. "I don't want to send email if I'm not already online just to respond to an ad or mailing," he said, insisting that for him, a toll-free number or reply card is more convenient.

While it's generally safe to assume IT professionals and many consumers are comfortable responding by going to your website, don't make that assumption with nontechies or aging Boomers. Some can access the web but are not comfortable with it and prefer not to use it. Others, amazingly, don't even know how to get onto your site!

Tip: *Always* offer the web as a response option. If you sell software such as the latest antivirus or spyware program, prospects may want to try your product immediately, so make it available for downloading from your website. You can let prospects download a demo version for free or the full program if they supply credit card information.

10 steps for marketing software products

Are you planning to test a new online promotion or direct mail package to promote your software? By using the following ten simple steps, you can avoid common mistakes, increase response rates, and tip the odds of having a profitable mailing in your favor:

1. *Clarify your product.* What are you selling? A stand-alone PC application? An enterprise-wide system, such as supply chain management (SCM) or customer relationship management (CRM)? A web application that must be integrated with back-end systems?

   Study the promotions from successful software companies in your category. Do you sell tax or accounting software? Reply to an Intuit mailing and see what happens. Selling databases? Check out what Oracle is doing.

   Analyze the structure, format, and content not only of the initial direct mail piece, but also of the entire marketing campaign, from generating the inquiry to closing the sale.

   Chances are that companies with products similar to yours, especially the successful ones, have developed these marketing models through expensive trial-and-error testing. Why not copy what works and avoid the cost of going down the wrong path?

   Things to study when modeling your efforts after the marketing campaigns of successful software publishers include elements of the sales funnel: offer, pricing, media, formats, the mix of online and offline marketing methods, lead qualification, the discrete steps that take a potential buyer from an inquirer to a closed sale, and the number and types of communications used in each.

2. *Develop the offer.* What offer would work best for your software? For low-priced products costing under $500, the mail order model—selling the software directly from the promotion—is possible and should be tested. If it works—if the promotion generates sales that are 1½ times or more of its total cost—then you have a winner.

   If the product is enterprise software or other applications selling for $15,000 or more, you will probably need to use a two-step, or lead-generating, direct mail model. The direct mail piece or email generates an inquiry, which is then fulfilled and followed up by mail, phone, autoresponder emails, in person, or some combination of these. The sale is closed in the follow-up, not in the initial mailing.

If the price of your software is between $500 and $5,000, you are in a gray area and you will have to experiment to see whether you should go for sales or leads.

One thing that works with a $5,000 product is to offer a "Small Project Version" or other limited-functionality version for a nominal fee, say $50 or $99. The small version has all of the features of the full product, but it is limited in some way; for instance, the "Small Project Version" of a project management program may only allow up to ten tasks in a project plan. If the customer decides to buy the full version, the money he paid for the small version is credited toward the purchase of the complete program.

When generating leads, offering a premium usually increases response. "White papers on websites, informative online newsletters, shareware, even thinly disguised bribes such as free USB sticks, are used to prompt dialog," says copywriter George Duncan. Other premiums that have worked well for software marketers include printed white papers, CD-ROMs, software utilities, ROI calculators, checklists, and "needs assessments," such as forms that can be used to evaluate whether there is a need for the software or how to plan for its installation and deployment.

3. *Hone the price.* Direct mail is a medium that works well when special offers, such as discounts, are used. Do you want to get $300 for your software? In the marketing, say that it is regularly $399 (yes, supermarket pricing works below $1,000), but if they buy now it is only $299. A $100 savings is a proven offer for mail order software marketing.

For more expensive software, state the license price per user. "Just $50 per user for 100 desktops" sounds more affordable than "$5,000 for up to 100 users." For an annual subscription of $350, say "less than a dollar a day."

Software with a high price often causes sticker shock. To offset this, show a strong ROI (return on investment). Example: A direct mail package for the previously mentioned program that monitors employees' internet access, noted that if an employee wastes an hour a day on non-work-related web surfing, and their time is worth $60 an hour, the cost in lost productivity is $300 a week, which amounts to a substantial $15,000 per employee per year. The copy then contrasted the elimination of that lost productivity with the mere $2 per user licensing fee.

4. *Analyze the audience.* Understand the audience's needs, interests, problems, concerns, awareness of the problem your software solves, level of PC literacy, and business sophistication.

"With end-to-end productivity solutions, you have two audiences: executive management and information technology," notes George Duncan. Executives want to know the business benefit: lower costs, increased productivity, improved customer service, higher profits. IT wants to know whether the software is compatible and easily integrated with its existing systems.

A helpful exercise is to analyze what is known as the buyer's "core complex," abbreviated BFD for beliefs, feelings, and desires. These are the attitudes, aspirations, and emotions that drive your prospect:

- *Beliefs.* What beliefs or attitudes does your audience possess about themselves and their customers? What is their attitude toward your product and the problems or issues it addresses?

- *Desires.* What do they want? What are their goals? What change do they want in their lives that your product can help them achieve?

- *Feelings.* How does your audience feel? Are they confident and brash? Nervous and fearful? What do they feel about the major issues in their lives, businesses, or industries?

For instance, we did this exercise with IT people working for a company that gives seminars in communication and interpersonal skills for IT professionals. Here's what we came up with in a group meeting:

- Beliefs: IT people think they are smarter than other people, technology is the most important thing in the world, users are stupid, and management doesn't appreciate them enough.

- Desires: IT people want to be appreciated and recognized. They also prefer to deal with computers and avoid people whenever possible. And they want bigger budgets.

- Feelings: IT people often have an adversarial relationship with management and users, both of whom they service. They feel others dislike them, look down upon them, and do not understand what they do.

Based on this BDF analysis (particularly the clarification of feelings), the company created a sales letter that was its most successful ever to promote a seminar called "Interpersonal Skills for IT Professionals." The rather unusual headline was: "Important news for any IT professional who has ever felt like telling an end user, 'Go to hell.'"

Before writing copy for a software ad, direct mail package, or landing page, write out in narrative form the BFD for your target market. Share this narrative with your team and come to an agreement on the items. Then write copy based on the agreed BFD.

5. *Select the right medium.* The choice of medium depends on the available list, the offer, the product, and the audience.

Is your audience very internet-oriented (e.g., webmasters)? Can the buyer gain access to the software online? Ask your list broker for recommendations on e-lists to reach this group.

On the other hand, sometimes a physical mailing can outpull an online promotion. A good example years ago was America Online, which had great marketing success sending disks in the mail; the prospects could use the disks to sign up for the service. But the physical disk, then a direct mail novelty, was a real attention-getter.

For a product with broad appeal and a potential market in the hundreds of thousands or millions (such as software used to prepare a will or to make greeting cards), marketing channels that you might test include Facebook advertising, Google ads, and even newspaper ads.

On the other hand, if you have a narrow audience of only a few hundred potential buyers (e.g., software for robot manufacturers), telemarketing may be the way to go.

6. *Determine the format.* Say direct mail is the medium of choice. What format will work best for you?

"When you want to drive prospects to a website where an uncomplicated transaction can take place, oversized postcards are frequently effective," advises George Duncan.

When designing a postcard, offer response via either a toll-free number or a landing page. Put both the 800 number and landing page URL in large, bold type.

7. *Acquire lists.* Contact one or two list brokers and ask for recommendations on both postal and email lists. Each list has its own "data card"—typically a single-page PDF describing the number and type of people on the mailing list.

Always go to a list broker for list recommendations. Do not call the list owner directly. If you call the list owner (e.g., a computer magazine), they will want to rent you their list, whether it's the best for your offer or not.

List brokers, by comparison, do not promote a specific list, and their advice is more objective. Their interest is in getting you the lists that will work best for you, so you will come to rely on their list recommendations and rent more lists from them.

Many software marketers do not realize that the services of a list broker are free. There is no charge to get list recommendations.

You pay the list broker only when you rent names from the lists they find for you. They do not mark up the lists. The list owner pays their commission. That means you pay the exact same price as if you rented the list directly from its owner.

The mailing list is the most important element in a direct mail marketing effort, affecting response rates up to 900 percent or more! And with more than tens of thousands of lists available, only a professional list broker has the time to keep up-to-date on what's available . . . and what will work for you.

8. *Define the USP.* With so many software products on the market today, how do you make yours stand out? By defining your product's USP—its Unique Selling Proposition. This is the reason why the customer should buy your program instead of your competitor's.

Many marketers have heard of the term USP, but very few remember the three characteristics of a successful USP. As mentioned earlier in the book, these were first defined by Rosser Reeves in his 1961 book *Reality in Advertising*:

- Each advertisement must make a proposition to the consumer. Each advertisement must say to the reader: "Buy this product, and you will get this specific benefit."

- The proposition must be one that the competition either cannot or does not offer. It must be unique: either a uniqueness of brand or a claim not otherwise made in that particular field.

- The proposition must be so strong that it can move the mass millions; i.e., pull over new customers to your product. (In the case of software, this may be the mass thousands rather than millions, but the idea is the same.)

Why is having a USP so important? Think about it: If you don't know what sets your product apart from the competition, or why people should buy your program instead of theirs, how do you expect to persuade complete strangers to do so?

9. *Develop the big promise.* Samuel Johnson said, "Promise, large promise, is the soul of an advertisement."

Once you have defined a USP, convert it into a big promise— a succinct, compelling statement of why the prospect should buy your product. The big promise can usually be stated in 15 or fewer words, and it can be used as the headline of an ad or HTML email. For instance: "Develop Clipper applications 4 times faster—or your money back," for an application development tool.

The headline is the most important part of any promotion, so once you have written it, see if you can make it even better and stronger. One useful technique for this is the "4 U's." That is, ask yourself whether the headline is urgent, unique, ultra-specific, and useful (that is, it promises a clear benefit).

A software marketer sent out an email marketing message with the subject line "Free White Paper." How does this stack up against the "4 U's"?

- *Urgent.* There is no urgency or sense of timeliness. On a scale of 1 to 4, with 4 being the highest rating, "Free White Paper" is a 1.

- *Unique.* Not every software marketer offers a free white paper, but a lot of them do. So "Free White Paper" rates only a 2 in terms of uniqueness.

- *Ultra-specific.* Could the marketer have been less specific than "Free White Paper"? Yes, he could have just said "free bonus gift." So we rate "Free White Paper" a 2 instead of a 1.

- *Useful.* I suppose the reader is smart enough to figure the white paper contains some helpful information he can use. On the other hand, the usefulness is in the specific information contained in the paper, which isn't even hinted at in the headline. And, does the recipient, who already has too much to read, really need yet another "Free White Paper"? I rate it a 2. Specifying the topic would help, e.g., "Free White Paper shows how to cut training costs up to 90 percent with e-learning."

Rate your Big Promise headline in all four U's on a scale of 1 to 4 (1 = weak, 4 = strong). Then rewrite it so you can upgrade your rating on at least two, and preferably three or four, of the categories by at least one point on the scale. This simple exercise may increase readership and response rates substantially for very little effort.

10. *Refine the content.* "Content" refers to the rest of the copy. How much copy should there be? What information should it present, and at what level of technical detail and in what order? Should you give features, benefits, specifications, data, test results, testimonials, or all of them?

A key issue is the information density of the copy. For most software products, you can literally write a book about the product (proof of this is the thousands of computer books published each year). But in emails, landing pages, or direct mail, you don't have that space, so you have to be selective. If telling everything about the product would sell it, we'd simply mail prospects the book.

A useful exercise in planning the content and organization of your mailing is to divide a sheet of paper or Word file into two columns. Label the left column "features" and write down your product's features. In the right column, write down the corresponding benefits, and label this column "benefits."

Now put the list of features and benefits in order of importance. The first feature/benefit should be the one that corresponds with the big promise. This becomes the lead of the promotion.

The next three to six feature/benefit combinations are the most important after the big promise, and are highlighted in the body copy.

The rest of the features/benefits are secondary and can be covered in a table. Specifications can be put in a separate box or sidebar.

A useful rule of thumb when determining content and information density is to include only what it takes to get the prospect to take the next step in the buying process. If it's to go to a website and download a free demo, that probably requires a lot less information than getting the prospect to order a $299 PC application sight unseen.

Software can command premium prices

It's often difficult for us writers to swallow, but people will often pay more for computer code than they will for the written word. Why? For a couple of reasons. First, software has more utility. In our how-to writing, we tell our readers how to do things. The software can actually do it for them! Therefore, it appeals to the highest level of how-to (recall the three levels: telling readers what to do, how to do it, and doing it for them).

Second, software has a higher perceived value than books. A paperback book in a bookstore may sell new for around $15; software sells for price points ranging from $100 to $500 or more. The higher perceived value makes software easier to sell at higher prices than other forms of content.

Turn your knowledge into high-priced software

To create your own software products or tools, go back and reread your books and other writings. Is there a step-by-step task you teach? Does it involve calculations of any kind or the storing and manipulation of data? Could it be done faster and more efficiently using a piece of software? If so, there may be an application buried in your content that you can turn into a piece of software.

To take a simple example, one of the marketing topics I teach is direct mail. One of the tasks I show the reader how to do is calculate the "break-even point"—the number of orders your direct mail promotion must generate to pay back its cost. My book goes through this step-by-step. But many people have math phobia and have difficulty following the steps. I wanted to create a tool that would calculate the break-even point automatically.

For less than a hundred dollars, I found a competent programmer in the Philippines who created this little application or "widget" for me. The tool, which I call the direct mail break-even calculator, is pretty simple, so I don't charge for it. However, to use it, you have to give me your email address, so the tool is a list-building device and has added hundreds of new subscribers to my opt-in e-list.

You can find my free direct mail break-even calculator online: www .dmresponsecalculator.com.

18

Online Courses

One category of information product—big-ticket, multi-component online courses—has proliferated, especially in recent years, despite their high cost.

My Facebook friend Donna says, "If authors share their information in an online program, they can get it out faster and make a lot more money" than by writing a book on the same topic.

What makes online courses different and potentially more profitable than e-books, paperbound books, webinars, streaming audio, and the other media described earlier in this book?

To begin with, online courses have a couple of characteristics that enable you to charge premium prices for them.

The first is that they are multimedia products; they can include such elements as webinars, streaming videos, audios, e-books, paperbound books, reference manuals, infographics, special reports, white papers, and other prepackaged content.

Long experience proves that information buyers will pay more for multimedia products than single-media products such as the standalone e-books that so many info marketers write and sell.

The second characteristic of expensive online courses is that they are a blend of the "canned" elements listed above with live coaching, consulting, mentoring, meetings, training, and access to a closed Facebook group for course students only.

The combination of great course content, plus getting customized training, advice, and answers to your specific questions, can often make the best integrated online courses more powerful learning systems than just canned content alone. In his book *Teach Your Gift* (Mirasee Press), Danny Iny suggests this distinction: traditional e-books and other low-priced formats primarily convey just information, while online courses provide education to the students.

I can't say I agree 100 percent with Danny, as I have personally heard from readers that my books changed their lives, helped them make a lot more money, start a successful small business, get published, or enter a new profession. So some paperbound books can deliver both information and education. At the same time, online courses, when done right, can in many cases deliver a superior and more transformative learning experience, enabling the student to achieve his goals more rapidly and confidently.

Target your best buyers

The people who are most likely to buy an expensive online course from you are those who already know you—and from that list, you will get the most sales from those people who are your regular followers, readers, or fans of yours. The better they know and like you and your ideas, the greater your success rate in interesting them in your course and getting them to register.

"Pick the right tribe and vibe," says Buck Rizvi, founder of Ultimate Lifespan. "By this, I mean who you're selling to and, very importantly, how you'll connect with them on a deeper level."

The ideal target market source for reaching prospects most likely to buy an online course from you is people who subscribe to and regularly read your e-newsletter or are on your opt-in e-list for any other reason.

But you can also find potential students on social media networks (e.g., Facebook friends), listeners to your podcasts or internet radio show, your book readers, your YouTube channel viewers, and subscribers to your blog. Reason: The higher the price of an information product, the more likely that your primary buyers will be people who already know you and are fans of you, your personality, and your content.

Drawing potential students into your sales funnel

It is difficult, though possible, to send an email to a prospect who, in response to that email invitation, clicks the link and directly buys your high-end course.

However, most marketers of online courses build a "sales funnel"—a series of sequential presentations and actions that lead from mild interest to high engagement to desire and finally to buying the course. The sales funnel depends on persuasive copy at virtually every step to move the sale along.

Sales funnels with a "hard entry" typically go directly to a hard-selling landing page that seeks to get the order right up front.

Sales funnels with a "soft entry" start with a friendly, informative page that gently pulls the prospect forward or else presents a free content offer. The copy might talk about the benefits of learning the skill, and could hyperlink to a next page with an online video explaining the offering in more detail.

The point of a soft entry is that more people will enter the soft funnel than a hard-entry funnel, resulting in a larger prospect group that converts to more sales. People will order a $29 e-book directly from the landing page they click to, but they need to be taken step-by-step by the hand through your big-ticket course offering: what it is, what is covered, why it is better and different than other info products on similar topics, what you get for your money, payment options and plans, terms, conditions, and guarantee.

Among the elements commonly used in sales funnels for expensive online courses are:

- *Early notification page.* You send people to this page. They enter name and email address to join a list of people who will be notified first, before other prospects, when the course become available for purchase.

- *Landing pages.* Web pages that convert clicks, using a call to action (CTA), into leads, orders, subscriptions, memberships, inquiries, or registrations.

- *Squeeze pages.* Squeeze pages are landing pages that capture leads by offering the visitor a lead magnet or other freebie in exchange for the person's name and email address. Capturing this information enables you, the marketer, to follow up with prospects via email at virtually no cost, whenever and wherever it best fits into your sales funnel.

- *Lead magnet.* A special report in downloadable PDF format offered on squeeze pages as a free gift. To get the lead magnet, prospects must submit their name and email address on the squeeze page.

- *Thank you pages.* After downloading the lead magnet or completing another step in the sales funnel, prospects are taken to a page that thanks them for taking the action step and encourages them to take the next step.

- *Welcome pages.* Once a customer makes a purchase online, they are taken to a welcome page. The page welcomes them to the course or membership they paid for and summarizes what's in store, why enrolling was a good decision, and the outcome to expect after completing the course.

- *Pre-sell pages.* A pre-sell page that reads like a short introductory ad or article on the topic of your program and the learning opportunity you are offering. Clicks generated by online ads are often directed to a pre-sell page, because some social media and ad networks block ads linked directly to sales pages that they consider either too opportunistic, too deceptive, too hard sell, or that make claims they find unbelievable.

- *Sales page.* A long-copy landing page whose objective is to persuade the prospect to purchase the course. There sales pages include large and prominent "Order Now" buttons the prospect clicks when he wants to order your program. Clicking the Order Now button takes the prospect to your shopping cart.

- *Shopping cart.* A simple page connected to shopping cart software that takes the consumer's information and payment; usually the payment is made by credit card or PayPal. Two popular shopping cart software services are Keap (formerly InfusionSoft) and 1shoppingcart.com.

- *Order page.* Sometimes an intermediate page is placed in the sales funnel between the sales page that sells the product and the shopping cart the customer uses to place the order. Order pages present a final sales pitch to increase conversion rates. Some marketers use order pages while others go straight from the course sales page to the checkout shopping cart. *Conversion rate* is the percentage of people in your funnel who click on the sales page and then buy the course.

- *Pop-under.* When the customer attempts to leave your sales page without having purchased, a pop-under appears. It's a window that offers another freebie as an incentive to enter your name and email address. You are tagged in the software's database as a visitor who did not buy. As such, you first get an email sent via autoresponder software with a link for downloading the freebie. A series of additional follow-up emails contain sales messages attempting to persuade you to click on the sales page again and this time buy the course.

- *Email autoresponder series.* An autoresponder is software that delivers the above-mentioned series of prewritten emails automatically to the prospect.

- *Online videos.* The squeeze page, welcome page, sales page, and other pages in the sales funnel may have online videos. The objective is to keep prospects engaged and help convince them to continue along the sales funnel and buy.

- *Order confirmation.* Either a page or an email, or both, that confirms the order, thanks the customer for buying, tells him what to expect next, and reinforces his buying decision.

There are many different sales funnel arrangements that sell courses online, using all or some of these elements in various configurations. You may be able to increase conversion to sales by experimenting with both the funnel elements as well as the funnel configuration—the sales path through the funnel.

Topics: broad versus narrow

Obviously a course or any other information product must be about a specific subject matter that people want to learn about.

If there is minimal competition, you can succeed by promoting the broad topic; e.g. search engine marketing. If the web is flooded with courses on that topic, you may want to narrow your course subject; e.g. marketing with Snapchat.

Remember, in a high-end course, students want to go beyond just learning. They want to master a skill or area of knowledge. And most important, you must design your course to help the student achieve the specific goal you promised on your sales page. For a course on improving your marriage, the goal might be to have a happier and more harmonious marriage and also to avoid divorce. In a course on financial planning, the goal might be to build a million-dollar IRA so you can be financially secure in retirement.

It's the combination of the "canned" or prepackaged course content with the live human component of coaching, mentoring, closed Facebook groups, and other personalized instruction and advice that has the greatest chance of helping the student not only learn the subject matter but to achieve his desired goal. The mix of course materials and personalized instruction increases the chances of the student succeeding while enabling you to charge $5,000 to $10,000 for your course.

Course modules and schedule

Just as books have chapters, online courses have modules. Each module covers one important skill, task, or other elements needed to attain a deeper understanding of the subject matter as well as achieve the ultimate goal.

High-end online courses typically have 6 to 10 modules. The material is delivered to your first students live online, and to subsequent students as a prerecorded video lecture. The screen may show the instructor speaking to the student, a PowerPoint, or a combination. Typically modules are 60 to 90 minutes each.

The first module can give an overview of the process you are teaching and include some student success stories.

The next several modules present a solid education in the fundamentals, including techniques and tricks you have learned from observation, experience, and testing.

Then, present a few modules with instruction on advanced topics and skills, especially important ones that other courses may be missing or presenting inaccurately.

Finally, the last few modules explain how to monetize your new skills and process knowledge; e.g., use the ideas to sell your own products or become an independent consultant providing services in this subject to clients. If the latter, you also should have a module showing students how to start and run a successful consulting business in the area they learned, including how to get clients, which is often a major concern.

For a 10-module course, you might choose to schedule two sessions a week. In the first session, perhaps Monday or Tuesday, the student views that week's module. In the second session, held a couple of days later, students and the instructor meet via Zoom or GoToWebinar for live instruction, discussion, and to ask questions.

As the course marketer, your best move is to create a source on a topic in which you are a recognized expert, if not nationally at least to your internet followers. And you are the lead instructor. You can either teach the entire course yourself, which is typical, or you can bring in one or two guest speakers for the live online meetings.

There are two reasons to bring in at least one other teacher. First, for variety—to give the class a break from you. Second, to have a guest expert teach a subtopic of the main course topic which that expert knows better than you do.

Instructor credentials and credibility

At minimum, your students must see you as a recognized expert in your subject. The stronger your credibility, the greater your course sales and the more money you make.

Even better is if you have a regional, nationwide, or industry-wide reputation as a guru in your field. The more famous you are, the more students who will register for your course.

There are multiple methodologies for becoming a known "guru," but most revolve around one core tactic: *prolific dissemination of content on your topic to people in your target market who are ideal prospects for your course.*

Being an internet information marketer in itself is helpful in establishing your expert reputation, especially if your products are of high quality, are popular, and well regarded.

Some of the other ways to build your status as an expert through content dissemination include: podcasting . . . YouTube videos . . . articles . . . books . . . publicity . . . websites . . . e-newsletters . . . public speaking . . . webinars . . . radio interviews . . . TV appearances . . . and many others.

"Stunts" can also work, provided you are able to pull them off. For instance, Fran Capo garnered a huge amount of publicity by repeatedly doing stunts that helped her get into the *Guinness Books of World Records* more than half a dozen times, many based on her fame as the fastest talking woman in the world. For instance, she did a 20-minute TEDx talk at a normal speaking pace. At the end, she set a new speed-talking world record by repeating the talk, in its entirety and right on the TEDx stage, in under a minute.

Less is more

Creators of online courses worry that their course is not comprehensive or complete, especially if they have written a book on the same topic.

They see their book covers so many more subtopics than the course modules. So their response is to cram many additional subtopics into the course.

On the surface, this makes sense. My book is $15, and my course is $5,000. Why would anyone pay $5,000 for my course when they can get everything covered in the modules and so much more by simply buying the book?

But rather than fill your course with a huge stack of subject matter content, Danny Iny advises course creators to do the opposite: "You should prune your curriculum mercilessly," Iny writes in *Teach Your Gift*.

"In the context of learning, there's no such thing as content that is nice to have. Everything is either critical to the understanding and success of your students or an opportunity for them to become distracted, confused, or overwhelmed."

In other words, 100 percent of the course content should be laser-focused on enabling students to gain mastery of the subject you promised to teach them and achieve the goals you said your methods and strategies could help them achieve. And that's all—no filler, no flub, no wandering tangents.

More tips for creating and selling big-ticket online courses

1. *When potential students sign up for your Early Notification list, send them to a thank you screen.* On the thank you screen, the copy at top should create excitement and sell the benefits of the course. Below

that, put a section with the heading "Fast Pass," with copy telling them if they don't want to wait, they can click a button and be taken directly to the sales page for the course.

2. *The first time you run the course, call it a "Pilot Program."* That tells students that they are the first group to get access to the training. By calling it a Pilot Program, the students will be forgiving of small glitches and problems.

3. *Limit the Pilot Program class size to 10 people.* The small group size makes it easier to quickly sell all seats to your course. More important, it increases the amount of time you can personally spend coaching and working with students both in group meetings (for which Zoom is a good platform) and individual coaching. Also, in your marketing, you can create a sense of urgency by noting there are only 10 seats available for the Pilot Program, and they will sell out quickly.

4. *Work with a partner.* Courses take a lot of work to create, market, and deliver. I do my big-ticket course on "Start and Run a Successful Copywriting Business" with my partner Fred Gleeck. For our copywriting course, I am the expert in the subject matter (copywriting) and Fred is the expert in the marketing, production, and technical aspects.

5. *For a course of $5,000 or higher, give the buyer the option of one single payment and at least one installment payment option, which could be 2 payments, 4 payments, or whatever makes sense to you.* As for the course price, use "supermarket" pricing, with the last number being seven; e.g. $4,977. The reader knows what you are doing—he sees supermarket pricing on almost everything he buys—but a price in the 4 grand range, even at the top of the range, seems less costly than something that is 5 grand.

6. *After completion of the Pilot Program, get testimonials from satisfied students and add them to your sales page, grouped together under a subhead, such as "Our Students Say It Best!"*

7. *Consider having two versions of your course, gold and silver.* Gold gives buyers access to all the content and course elements, e.g. the closed Facebook Group, interactive participation in the lesson modules, features, and bonus materials. The silver version gives the buyer access

to watch and listen to the video modules only—no other course features and no interaction participation. The silver students can only listen and watch; Fred Gleeck calls this the "fly on the wall" option. You can offer both the gold and silver on the sales page. Or, you can offer the option to prospective students who did not act in time; all gold seats were sold but they can still get a lot of the core content as a "fly on the wall" with the silver option. The silver is typically one-tenth the tuition of the gold.

8. *GotoWebinar is a good platform for giving your live PowerPoint presentations during the Pilot Program.* Use the GotoWebinar features that allows you to run a webcam and display video of you talking in a small secondary window on the screen; this personalizes your presentation and helps your students feel more connected to you.

9. *Have and state your cancellation policy up front.* Fred Gleeck suggests that the student be given a refund on the condition that you, the course provider, can find another student to take his slot. The justification is that by enrolling in the first place, the student took a seat that you had to deny others who wanted it. By the way, your Early Notification list is a good place to find a replacement, as is your e-newsletter subscriber list.

10. *Many students ask what they can do to be better prepared for the course.* I send all students a paperbound copy of *The Copywriter's Handbook* well before the course start date, and I suggest a good way to prepare for the class is to read the first five chapters of my book.

11. *Give students who go through your course a hard copy Certificate of Completion, suitable for framing.*

19

Managing Your How-To Information Empire

Writing and selling how-to information is both a craft and a business. It's been my craft and business for four decades. Others may consider it mundane or unliterary, but I love being a how-to writer and information marketer.

Teaching is a basic human need. We are teaching others all the time. Supervisors teach workers. Parents teach their children. Experts teach laypeople. The experienced pass on their knowledge to the less experienced. If you enjoy teaching and writing, why not get paid to do both as a how-to writer or information packager?

I am not a novelist,* but I imagine, aside from self-expression, one of the great rewards of novel writing is entertaining readers. As how-to writers, we may entertain our readers, but we can do much more than that: We can help change their lives for the better, often in dramatic ways.

I write and publish how-to information in areas related to making money at home on the internet, freelancing, entrepreneurship, and business success. I have heard from numerous readers over the years that they bought my book, followed my advice, and it changed their lives for the better; they

---

* But I have written a book of short stories, *Freak Show of the Gods*, also published by Quill Driver Books, the publisher of the book you are now reading.

enjoy their career more, make more money, and have more freedom and financial independence.

Those are major, life-changing benefits. Nothing thrills me more than to hear from readers that they have accomplished their major goals by reading and following the advice in my books. Readers have told me that, because of something I've written, they either achieved their lifelong dream or finally got off their butt to pursue that dream. They tell me my books and articles have helped them escape dull jobs and abusive bosses.

With my how-to writings to guide them, my readers have attained work they love and doubled or tripled their income. Results like these are what I live for as a how-to writer. Trust me—being told by readers that they enjoyed your book is nice, but finding out your advice changed someone's life in a significant and positive way is a high you cannot imagine unless you've been there.

In addition, success as a how-to writer and information packager has a cumulative effect: As the years roll by, you produce and own more and more content—material which you can sell and resell in many different ways. As a result, once someone buys and likes your book, you have many other materials to offer him. Lifetime customer value soars and your income skyrockets. When I started as a freelance writer in 1982, during my first year I earned $39,000. Now I routinely earn well over half a million dollars a year from my freelance writing.

Expand your output into multiple media

It's essential, if you want to build an information empire, to do more than write only books and magazine articles, as so many writers do. In Chapter 1, I listed over a dozen different outlets and formats for your how-to writings. These include books, e-books, audio albums, DVDs, speeches, seminars, and more, as shown in the mind map in Figure 19.1.

The figure shows a generic mind map of how you can expand your knowledge of a core topic into an information empire. We start with your core topic in the center. Above that, we map out other areas related to your core topic you can expand into. As we've already discussed, you can tighten your focus to cover even more specialized topics, or broaden it to appeal to a wider readership. You can target your market by nationality, age, income, knowledge, and experience.

Fig. 19.1. Expanding Your Information Empire

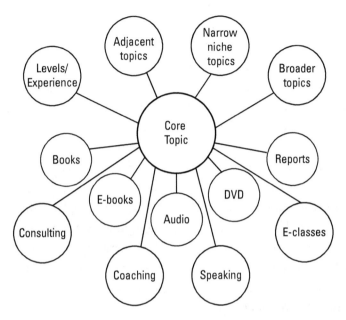

Below the core topic we expand from just writing books and articles into many other media. The first level of circles shows passive media—information products we can sell to earn us money independent of our time and labor, such as e-books, audios, reports, and other information products. The level of circles at the bottom shows ways to package our information with personal service components: consulting, coaching, speaking, online classes. The personal service makes these information products more labor intensive, but it also allows us to charge 10 to 100 times more than for a book or e-book on the same topic. And to the customer, that is money well spent because they receive your customized expert advice.

Once you have been writing for a number of years and have produced dozens of information products, from short articles to daylong workshops, you can start to bundle related products together and sell the bundles.

For instance, in the 1980s, I published, with Dodd Mead, a book on how to earn six figures as a freelance writer doing brochures, annual reports, and other assignments for corporate clients. Dodd Mead went out of business, and I bought the remainders—many hundreds of trade paperbacks—which I stored in my basement. The cover price was around $15 and I paid about

$3 per book. I began selling the remainder copies for $15 each through tiny classified ads in writer's magazines.

During that time, I also gave a daylong seminar for the Learning Annex in New York City on "How to Make $100,000 or More as a Freelance Writer." I hired a professional to audio tape the seminar with me, which we duplicated on six C60 (hour-long) audio cassettes and placed into a vinyl album.

Instead of selling the book by itself, we bundled the book with the audios and sold a multimedia program called "How to Make $100,000+ as a Freelance Writer" for $79 each. This gave me significantly higher profit per sale than selling the book alone. The advantage of bundling is that it enables you to sell your material at higher price points for greater profit margins. It also gives your reader a better value since it is a more complete education than just your book alone, and the different components can appeal to readers' varying preferred learning modalities. This bundling program allowed me to sell all my remainder copies at a profit. After I sold out my remainder copies, I took the out-of-print book to another publisher, who promptly gave me a contract to produce a new edition.

Here are some tips for bundling your information products into larger kits or home study programs with higher price points than any of the individual components:

1. Make sure you go through all the content and update the text. Review for statistics, dates, and other time sensitive content.

2. If you're creating a kit, consider adding three additional pieces that are easy to create, useful to the reader, and convey added value but involve little-to-no overhead costs (especially when downloadable). These additional pieces could be mini-reports or even tip sheets made from reprints of your published articles. Promote these as "Comes with 3 free bonuses—if you order now!"

3. Include with the bundle a welcome letter specific to the kit, congratulating the buyer for making the purchase. The welcome letter reiterates their decision, briefly explains the goal of the kit, and reinforces your credentials and the value of the content.

4. You can also add a short starter manual—a "walk-you-through" system, or blueprint for success—that explains the overall goal of the kit, as well as the objective of each element. It can also give step-by-step

pointers to get the most out of each book and the complete system. You might also add an interactive section for notes and self-evaluation, with milestones and checklists.

5. Create additional kit components or bonus materials. These could be related articles from your e-newsletter repurposed, a glossary, or a list of resources.

6. Use scarcity as a selling tactic. When I build a bundle around the remainder copies of one of my out-of-print books, I can honestly tell the buyer that only so many copies remain, and once they're gone, no more will be printed. I tell them that the only way to ensure getting a free book is to order now.

7. Do not advertise the individual elements for sale. The marketing strategy is to sell the bundle as a complete kit or system. Each element takes you to the next level and ties into the overall theme, giving the reader a "blueprint for success" . . . which you currently have and are going to teach them in your bundled home study program.

8. Make sure in the promotional flier or web page advertising for the bundle that you mention everything the subscriber is getting, including the welcome letter, starter manual, books, e-books, audios, DVDs, reports, and bonus materials.

9. Visuals are very important. The sales flier or web page promoting the bundle should show a photo or illustration with all pieces of the kit fanned out, so that it looks like the buyer is getting a lot of material for the money.

10. The title for the bundled kit should convey (when applicable) ideas such as simplicity and ease of use, profitability, convenience, work from home, best in class, community, incredible value, complete, comprehensive, A–Z, nothing is left out. Consider words like: ultimate, club, system, kit, society, program, home study course, and program. The bundle's product title should be short and pithy, powerful and sexy—something that packs a punch and is easy to remember. The subtitle should explain the product's objective; e.g., "The Internet Cash Generator: How to Make a Thousand Dollars a Day Online in Your Spare Time."

The ascending levels of how-to writing income

When you write and publish how-to information, there are five levels or stages you ascend as you move up in success, sales, and income:

- *Stage one: a few hundred dollars a month.* When you are just starting out, you may have only a single book or other information product. Unless your first book is a runaway best seller, your income in stage one is likely to be modest: a few hundred extra dollars a month, and is likely coming in sporadically. This won't make you rich. But now, your love for writing is generating a nice amount of extra cash to have in your pocket every month.

- *Stage two: a thousand dollars a month.* Your sales are still modest but steadier. The extra thousand a month can cover, in full or in part, expense burdens such as the property tax on your home or your health insurance premiums. You can breathe easier and be more relaxed thanks to the steady flow of extra cash coming in from your nonfiction writing.

- *Stage three: a thousand dollars a week.* You've ramped up your writing income substantially. It might be from building an online information marketing business, writing a regular book series, or maybe ad revenue from your YouTube channel. Whatever the source, you are generating over $50,000 a year in spare-time writing income. If your income is modest, or you have a pension or large IRA, or your spouse also works, you may be able to quit your nine-to-five job and just do the writing you love.

- *Stage four: a thousand dollars a day.* That comes to around $365,000 a year: almost equal to the annual salary of the president of the United States. And the president is working a lot harder to earn his pay than you as freelance writer and information marketer probably are.

- *Stage five: a seven-figure annual income.* A number of how-to and instructional writers and information marketers are in this bracket. I'm not, though some years I've come close. But writing and selling simple information for fun and profit has generated a steady six-figure income for me resulting in a seven-figure net worth.

5 ways to double your writing income

1. *Outsource:* You make more money when you concentrate on what you do best, what you like most, and what earns you the most money. Everything else—things others do better than you, things you don't like to do, and things that don't pay as well as your how-to writing and information marketing—can and should be outsourced. For instance, I haven't mowed the lawn, raked leaves, or shoveled snow in my driveway for decades. I outsource those activities to other people, because, as my friend Fred Gleeck puts it, "they are not the highest and best use of your time."

2. *Expanding into new media.* As an author, for decades I wrote only traditional paperbound books for mainstream publishers. Then Fred Gleeck convinced me to write and publish e-books, online courses, and other products, and sell them online. I started in 2004, and immediately added a new six-figure source of income that I continue to generate today.

3. *Expand into adjacent topics.* For decades, I have kept tropical fish. Say I had made that my writing niche. Possible adjacent niches to "keeping tropical fish" could include: keeping saltwater fish; pet turtles; design your own terrarium; and so on.

4. *Recycle, repurpose, and resell.* As a nonfiction writer, I am careful to maintain all rights to my published work, and also to keep as much of it as I can well-organized into easy-to-find subdirectories on my hard drive as well as backed to the cloud. For the how-to and instructional writer, these electronic files are your "content goldmine."

   For instance, a writer's magazine paid me $7,500 to write 10 articles on freelance writing. I negotiated with them, and they agreed that I was selling them "first rights only." First rights only means once they publish the articles, all rights revert to me. And I can do whatever I want with the content.

   As soon as the magazine published the articles, I emailed the Word files of the articles to a graphic designer. I paid him $100 to put the content into a simple black-and-white e-book format. The best part: because these were published in a magazine, I had already written all the content for my e-book. My time spent in producing this e-book was therefore virtually zero.

Then I began selling the e-book online. As I write this paragraph, we have sold 1,674 copies for gross revenue for gross revenues of $51,836. Add to that the $7,500 the magazine had already paid me, and my total learnings from writing these 10 articles comes to $59,336, or almost 6 grand per article. Average writing time per article: 2 hours—or $2,967 an hour.

Best of all, I'm not done collecting my checks. The e-book continues to sell, bringing in more money with each passing year!

If you want to reinvent the wheel every time you sit down to write, fine. But you can make more money in less time by continually going back into the gold mine and recycling, repurposing, and reselling some of the gold. For instance, you can update existing content; create new editions; combine smaller pieces into one big information product; or break up a big book into special reports and other smaller information products. The possibilities are endless.

And if you get bored with all this profitable repurposing, write something new to keep yourself fresh and entertained. For instance, after writing four business books in a row, I needed a change of pace, and so wrote and published a science biography.†

5. *Hire employees.* Having employees isn't for everybody. But when I hired a full-time assistant, both my productivity and my gross income soared.

Tailoring your how-to writing empire to deliver your ideal lifestyle

Much more so than the majority of other careers and professions, being a freelance writer or information marketer can give you a lifestyle your friends and neighbors will envy.

While they scurry off to long commutes in nine-to-five jobs at ungodly hours in the morning, you stay snug at home all day. There's no commute. You can work in your sweat pants and a T-shirt, as I often do, with the dog curled contentedly at your feet under your desk.

---

† *Charles Proteus Steinmetz: The Electrical Wizard of Schenectady* by Robert W. Bly, Quill Driver Books, 2018.

During the day, your friends and neighbors at traditional jobs will attend endless meetings, handle deadly dull and repetitive tasks, and fill out reams of paperwork. You, on the other hand, get to stay home, sitting at your computer, reading, thinking, and writing.

If you got a taste of working at home during the Covid pandemic and are now missing it, how-to writing might be just what you're looking for.

Is one lifestyle better than the other? It's not a question of better or worse—the question is, Which lifestyle appeals to you? When you follow the advice in this book, you can write, stay home, and make money as a free-lance how-to writer. You'll have no boss, no job, no commute, no meetings, no suit and tie, and no office politics.

Speaking of making money, the average American age 45 to 65 today earns approximately $50,000 a year. As a beginning how-to writer or infor-mation marketer, you can easily earn two to three times that amount or more. I earn significantly more than $45,000 a month, not a year. Even if your neighbors and friends have good white-collar or professional jobs as executives, small business owners, dentists, lawyers, or doctors, you can earn as much or more than they do while not having a "job" at all when you're a freelance how-to writer.

Cashing out: can you sell your how-to writing empire?

Traditionally, freelance writers have no equity in their freelance writing practices. When you retire, your income from writing stops, except for roy-alties from books that are still in print.

With the rise of the internet, writers are making the transition from tra-ditional freelance writer to information marketer in growing numbers. They control the publication, distribution, and marketing of most of their writ-ings, and they consequently reap greater financial rewards.

What's more, assuming you own the rights to all or most of your writ-ings, and are generating a six-figure income selling these writings, your little information publishing empire may have cash value. You'll have an easier time selling the sum of your intellectual property (IP) if your infor-mation business has its own name separate from yours, and if it runs as a legitimate business entity, incorporated with its own bank account and set of books.

How much can you sell your information empire for? The rule of thumb is that a micro publishing business will sell for between 1 and 1.5 times annual gross sales. So if your info business grosses a million dollars a year, you might be able to sell it for $1 million or even $1.5 million. That price buys the purchaser all the major assets, including the information products, your customer list, and your websites.

The information writers 80/20 path to fun and profit

Anyone can potentially make money creating and marketing information products. But not everyone should. If you do it purely because of the money, you may make money—possibly quite a bit of money—and you may come to love the business.

But for me, being a freelance how-to writer combines the best of all possible worlds.

To begin with, you're a freelancer, and you get all the benefits that come with being your own boss: freedom, comfort, and the ability to live your life on your own terms.

Next, you're in the how-to business. You have one of the most important jobs on the planet: to teach others what they need and want to know to attain all their important goals in life.

Third, you're a writer. You get to spend your day thinking and putting those thoughts on paper or the screen.

Fourth, the money is really, really good. Not great—you aren't making Richard Branson or Bill Gates money—but a six-figure income and a seven-figure net worth are well within your grasp.

I said at the beginning of the book that successful how-to writers specialize in a narrow niche or topic. The upside is that specialization is very profitable. The downside is that you may find yourself growing tired of writing about the same thing over and over.

You could choose to be a generalist. Generalists are never bored, because each assignment is on a different topic, making it new and fresh. But their learning curve for each new project is so large that their income is modest at best.

The solution is to use the 80/20 rule in allocating your time among writing projects. Spend 80 percent of your time writing content in your niche. That way, you produce a steady stream of profitable information products.

But spend 20 percent of your time writing materials in completely different areas. It most likely won't be nearly as profitable. But it will keep you fresh, prevent monotony, and keep you from ever being bored and stale.

With the 80/20 rule, you can profitably and happily work as a how-to writer until you retire—or forever. It's your choice. And it's a very nice choice to have.

Appendix A: For Further Reading

Google AdSense for Dummies, by Jerri Ledford (Wiley Publishing, 2008)

How to Make Money Blogging, by Bob Lotich (Bob Lotich, 2016)

Inbound Marketing Book, by Tom Poland (Leadsology®, 2020)

Make Money with Facebook Groups, by Abbie Unger (Bay Creek Press, 2015)

Marketing App & Selling Apps, by Albert Luton (Zoodoo Publishing, 2018)

Millionaire Success Habits, by Dean Graziosi (Growth Publishing, 2018)

Sales 101, by Wendy Connick (Adams Media, 2019)

Start Your Own Freelance Writing Business, by Laura Pennington Briggs (Entrepreneur Press, 2019)

Teach Your Gift, by Danny Iny (Mirasee, 2020)

The Sales Winner's Handbook, by Wendy Weiss (DFD Publications, 2013)

The 22 Immutable Laws of Marketing, by Al Reis and Jack Trout (Harper-Business, 1993)

Writer for Hire, by Kelly James-Enger (Writer's Digest Books, 2012)

Appendix B: Sample Documents

Sample Email Marketing Message Selling an E-Book

Subject: Read this only if you are 50 or older

Dear Direct Response Letter Subscriber:

Here is a special offer for men and women age 50 or older who want to start a home-based internet marketing business:

www.internetmarketingover50.com

Sincerely,

Bob Bly

Sample E-Newsletter

From: Bob Bly

Subject: Stop COVID-19 from derailing your business

Bob Bly's Direct Response Letter:

Resources, ideas, and tips for improving response to business-to-business, high-tech, internet, and direct marketing.   April 2, 2020

You are getting this email because you subscribed to it on www.bly.com or because you are one of Bob's clients, prospects, seminar attendees, or book buyers. If you would prefer not to receive further emails of this type, go to www.bly.com, enter your email address, and hit unsubscribe.

Your subscription brings you one regular monthly issue, usually at the beginning of the month, plus supplementary messages each week. These are typically either free tips or personal recommendations for information products on marketing or related topics. I review products before recommending them and in many cases know the authors.

We do not rent or share your name with anybody. Feel free to forward this issue to any peers, friends and associates you think would benefit from its contents. They will thank you. So will I.

Can your business weather the COVID-19 storm?

My brilliant colleague, Perry Marshall, has created a simple diagnostic to quickly determine how vulnerable your business is to disruption by the COVID-19 pandemic.

His quick and easy online tool, the COVID-19 Impact Factor, gives you a quick handle on whether COVID-19 is going to kill your business . . . force you to pivot to survive . . . set you back temporarily . . . or, conversely, cause prosperity to rain down upon you.

The tool is free, simple, and takes just 60 seconds to use. To get a better handle on where your business stands in today's corona-centric world, click here now —you will be glad you did:

www.perrymarshall.com/impact

Why online information marketing is still a terrific business

>>Fits your personal preferences. If you're an introvert, you could focus on products you create on your own. If you love the interaction with others, you can create coaching groups instead.

>>Low overhead. You only need a website, an autoresponder, and a way to process orders. Keeping expenses low means greater profits for you.

>>Handsome margins. Physical info products can sell for 5x to 10x cost. Digital products have miniscule costs (perhaps a few cents of bandwidth).

>>High perceived value. This is especially true if you include some personal support into the mix to create a coaching program.

>>Impressive repeat sales. Info seekers don't just buy one product on a subject they're interested in. They buy multiple products from different sources.

>>It's load of fun. You can spend your time on a topic where you're continually learning and sharing more with your customers.

Source: Terry Dean, 4/9/10.

Just released: 4th Edition: The Copywriter's Handbook

Last month, St. Martin's Griffin has just published the new Fourth Edition of my book The Copywriter's Handbook:

www.bly.com/copyhandbook

Originally published in 1985, The Copywriter's Handbook, with more than 100,000 copies in print, has now been thoroughly updated to ensure your continued copywriting success in today's multichannel marketplace.

In its pages, you will discover:

>> 10 tips for increasing landing page conversion rates. Page 284.

>> How to write and design a winning LinkedIn profile. Page 348.

>> A battle-tested formula for writing credible and convincing case studies. Page 392.

>> The 3 keys to writing copy that works like gangbusters in the digital age. Page 9.

>> 15 ways to improve email open and click-through rates. Page 292.

>> Secrets of writing successful ClickFunnelsTM websites. Page 275.

>> And so much more.

The Personal MBA calls The Copywriter's Handbook "the copywriter's Bible" and "an essential resources for everyone responsible for creating marketing materials that sell."

For a free sample chapter of The Copywriter's Handbook: Fourth Edition . . . or to order your copy today . . . click the link below now—you'll be glad you did:

www.bly.com/copyhandbook

Quotation of the month

"Now more than ever, writing is the one skill you need to succeed in life—and in your career. Words can move mountains. Make strong human connections. Spread a powerful idea. Change minds. Create hope. Leave a legacy. And if you don't know how to use them well, you risk being disconnected and misunderstood."

—Donald Miller

60-second commercial from Fern Dickey, Project Manager

Bob is available on a limited basis for copywriting of direct mail packages, sales letters, brochures, white papers, ads, email marketing campaigns, PR materials, and web pages. We recommend you call for a FREE copy of our updated Copywriting Information Kit. Just let us know your industry and the type of copy you're interested in seeing (ads, mailings, etc.), and if Bob is available to take your assignment, we'll tailor a package of recent samples to fit your requirements. Call Fern Dickey at 201-797-8105 or email fern1128@optonline.net.

Bob Bly   22 E. Quackenbush Ave.
Copywriter/consultant   Dumont, NJ 07628
rwbly@bly.com   phone 201-385-1220
www.bly.com   fax 201-385-1138

Sample Press Release

New Report Offers Powerful Recession-Proof
Strategies for Growing Profits During A Soft Economy

Dumont, NJ—April 12, 2020—During a time when the nation is struggling—businesses are shutting down, jobs are getting cut, houses are getting foreclosed—a new report from best-selling author and marketing strategist, Bob Bly titled, Recession Proof Business Strategies: 15 Winning Methods to Sell Any Product or Service in a Down Economy, offers proven and powerful solutions to increasing bottom line sales and leveraging existing customers.

According to Bly, "It doesn't take a recession to create problems for a business . . . the current situation is just magnifying the problem . . . business owners need to develop core income-generating solutions that succeed when times are tough."

He added, "What follows are some powerful strategies that will help business owners large and small as well as entrepreneurs and marketers increase sales while their competition is fighting to stay afloat."

Here are Bly's top 3 tips to generate cash during a soft economy:

1. **Use Low Cost "Add-On's" To Generate Additional Revenue.** In other words, bundle your products or services. According to Bly, "If one of my clients has hired me to write a sales letter for a new product, chances are, they'll want a press release to promote that product. Adding on this service provides value to the client and the additional cost is incremental."

2. **Repackage Your Services to Accommodate Smaller Customers or Reduced Budgets.** As an example, "In my consulting business," Bly said, "If a client cannot pay, let's say $5,000, for me to write him a direct mail package, I may critique a package the client actually wrote for $500." This method can be applied across the board. For manufacturers, it could be a no-frills offer or compact version of an existing product. It could also be smaller order requirements, extended payment plans or special discount incentives.

3. **Add Value to Your Existing Products or Services.** Businesses can win new customers by offering faster delivery, a larger product selection than the competition, easier payment terms, or a more attractive guarantee/refund policy. According to Bly, "These little extras always pay big dividends and provide good will to current and new customers."

Bly concludes, "Recessions do not last forever. Historically, they have lasted anywhere from 12–17 months. Don't despair. If you follow all my strategies, it is possible for your business to become busy, and more importantly, profitable again."

For the full list of winning recession-proof strategies, please visit: www.bly.com or www.bly.com/recessionsurvey.

Copyright Form

Copyright Office fees are subject to change. For current fees, check the Copyright Office website at www.copyright.gov, write the Copyright Office, or call (202) 707-3000.

For best results, fill in the form on-screen and then print it.

Form TX
For a Nondramatic Literary Work
UNITED STATES COPYRIGHT OFFICE

REGISTRATION NUMBER

_____ TX _____ TXU _____
EFFECTIVE DATE OF REGISTRATION

_____ _____ _____
Month   Day   Year

DO NOT WRITE ABOVE THIS LINE. IF YOU NEED MORE SPACE, USE A SEPARATE CONTINUATION SHEET.

1 TITLE OF THIS WORK ▼

PREVIOUS OR ALTERNATIVE TITLES ▼

PUBLICATION AS A CONTRIBUTION If this work was published as a contribution to a periodical, serial, or collection, give information about the collective work in which the contribution appeared.   Title of Collective Work ▼

If published in a periodical or serial give: Volume ▼   Number ▼   Issue Date ▼   On Pages ▼

2 a NAME OF AUTHOR ▼

DATES OF BIRTH AND DEATH
Year Born ▼   Year Died ▼

Was this contribution to the work a "work made for hire"? ☐ Yes ☐ No
AUTHOR'S NATIONALITY OR DOMICILE Name of Country
OR ⎰ Citizen of ▶_____ ⎱ Domiciled in▶_____
WAS THIS AUTHOR'S CONTRIBUTION TO THE WORK
Anonymous? ☐ Yes ☐ No
Pseudonymous? ☐ Yes ☐ No
If the answer to either of these questions is "Yes," see detailed instructions.

NATURE OF AUTHORSHIP Briefly describe nature of material created by this author in which copyright is claimed. ▼

NOTE
Under the law, the "author" of a "work made for hire" is generally the employer, not the employee (see instructions). For any part of this work that was "made for hire" check "Yes" in the space provided, give the employer (or other person for whom the work was prepared) as "Author" of that part, and leave the space for dates of birth and death blank.

b NAME OF AUTHOR ▼

DATES OF BIRTH AND DEATH
Year Born ▼   Year Died ▼

Was this contribution to the work a "work made for hire"? ☐ Yes ☐ No
AUTHOR'S NATIONALITY OR DOMICILE Name of Country
OR ⎰ Citizen of ▶_____ ⎱ Domiciled in▶_____
WAS THIS AUTHOR'S CONTRIBUTION TO THE WORK
Anonymous? ☐ Yes ☐ No
Pseudonymous? ☐ Yes ☐ No
If the answer to either of these questions is "Yes," see detailed instructions.

NATURE OF AUTHORSHIP Briefly describe nature of material created by this author in which copyright is claimed. ▼

c NAME OF AUTHOR ▼

DATES OF BIRTH AND DEATH
Year Born ▼   Year Died ▼

Was this contribution to the work a "work made for hire"? ☐ Yes ☐ No
AUTHOR'S NATIONALITY OR DOMICILE Name of Country
OR ⎰ Citizen of ▶_____ ⎱ Domiciled in▶_____
WAS THIS AUTHOR'S CONTRIBUTION TO THE WORK
Anonymous? ☐ Yes ☐ No
Pseudonymous? ☐ Yes ☐ No
If the answer to either of these questions is "Yes," see detailed instructions.

NATURE OF AUTHORSHIP Briefly describe nature of material created by this author in which copyright is claimed. ▼

3 a YEAR IN WHICH CREATION OF THIS WORK WAS COMPLETED This information must be given ◀Year In all cases.
b DATE AND NATION OF FIRST PUBLICATION OF THIS PARTICULAR WORK Complete this information ONLY if this work has been published. Month▶_____ Day▶_____ Year▶_____ ◀Nation

4 COPYRIGHT CLAIMANT(S) Name and address must be given even if the claimant is the same as the author given in space 2. ▼

See instructions before completing this space.

TRANSFER If the claimant(s) named here in space 4 is (are) different from the author(s) named in space 2, give a brief statement of how the claimant(s) obtained ownership of the copyright. ▼

APPLICATION RECEIVED
ONE DEPOSIT RECEIVED
TWO DEPOSITS RECEIVED
FUNDS RECEIVED

DO NOT WRITE HERE OFFICE USE ONLY

MORE ON BACK ▶ • Complete all applicable spaces (numbers 5-9) on the reverse side of this page.
• See detailed instructions.   • Sign the form at line 8.

DO NOT WRITE HERE
Page 1 of _____ pages

EXAMINED BY	FORM TX
CHECKED BY	

| ☐ CORRESPONDENCE Yes | FOR COPYRIGHT OFFICE USE ONLY |

DO NOT WRITE ABOVE THIS LINE. IF YOU NEED MORE SPACE, USE A SEPARATE CONTINUATION SHEET.

PREVIOUS REGISTRATION Has registration for this work, or for an earlier version of this work, already been made in the Copyright Office?
☐ Yes   ☐ No   If your answer is "Yes," why is another registration being sought? (Check appropriate box.) ▼
a. ☐ This is the first published edition of a work previously registered in unpublished form.
b. ☐ This is the first application submitted by this author as copyright claimant.
c. ☐ This is a changed version of the work, as shown by space 6 on this application.
If your answer is "Yes," give: **Previous Registration Number** ▶   **Year of Registration** ▶

5

DERIVATIVE WORK OR COMPILATION
Preexisting Material Identify any preexisting work or works that this work is based on or incorporates. ▼

a   **6**

See instructions before completing this space.

Material Added to This Work Give a brief, general statement of the material that has been added to this work and in which copyright is claimed. ▼

b

DEPOSIT ACCOUNT If the registration fee is to be charged to a Deposit Account established in the Copyright Office, give name and number of Account.
Name ▼   **Account Number** ▼

a   **7**

CORRESPONDENCE Give name and address to which correspondence about this application should be sent.   Name/Address/Apt/City/State/Zip ▼

b

Area code and daytime telephone number ▶   Fax number ▶
Email ▶

CERTIFICATION* I, the undersigned, hereby certify that I am the
Check only one ▶ { ☐ author
                    ☐ other copyright claimant
                    ☐ owner of exclusive right(s)
of the work identified in this application and that the statements made   ☐ authorized agent of _____
by me in this application are correct to the best of my knowledge.   Name of author or other copyright claimant, or owner of exclusive right(s) ▲

8

Typed or printed name and date ▼ If this application gives a date of publication in space 3, do not sign and submit it before that date.
_____   Date ▶ _____

Handwritten signature ▼

Certificate will be mailed in window envelope to this address:	Name ▼	YOU MUST: • Complete all necessary spaces • Sign your application in space 8
	Number/Street/Apt ▼	SEND ALL 3 ELEMENTS IN THE SAME PACKAGE: 1. Application form 2. Nonrefundable filing fee in check or money order payable to *Register of Copyrights* 3. Deposit material
	City/State/Zip ▼	MAIL TO: Library of Congress Copyright Office 101 Independence Avenue SE Washington, DC 20559-6222

9

*17 USC §506(e): Any person who knowingly makes a false representation of a material fact in the application for copyright registration provided for by section 409, or in any written statement filed in connection with the application, shall be fined not more than $2,500.

Form TX – Full   Rev: 11/2006   Print: 11/2006 – 30,000   Printed on recycled paper   U.S. Government Printing Office: 2006-xx-xxx/60,xxx

Sample Article Query Letter

Dear Mr. Koten:

My small company, Center for Technical Communication (CTC), has a marketing director, sales manager, office manager, controller, bookkeeper, shipping manager, and administrative assistant. Yet we don't have a single employee on the payroll.

How is this possible? Outsourcing. All of these functions are performed by independent contractors. Once a strategy embraced mainly by a down-sized corporate America, outsourcing is now being used by small businesses of all types—from accounting firms to petting zoos.

I'd like to write an article for your magazine titled, "7 Smart Secrets of Savvy Small Business Outsourcing," on how small businesses can use out-sourcing to increase their ability to serve customers without adding staff or overhead. Topics include:

- types of services that can be outsourced (and what should not be)
- how to determine whether to outsource a particular function or task
- where to find—and how to select—reputable third-party service firms for outsourcing
- negotiating contracts, fees, and payment arrangements
- how outsourcing can improve business results while reducing capital investment and operating costs
- equipment and technology that can make outsourcing more efficient
- examples of small businesses that have successfully outsourced functions previously handled in-house
- moving toward the concept of a "virtual business"—90% outsourcing, with all business partners connected via the internet
- a sidebar of major national outsourcing firms, with contact information and services offered.

By way of introduction, I am the author of more than 100 magazine articles and 50 books including *101 Ways to Make Every Second Count* (Career Press). My articles have appeared in *Cosmopolitan, Amtrak Express,* and *New Jersey Monthly.*

I can have this article on your desk in 3 to 4 weeks. Shall I proceed as outlined?

Sincerely,
Bob Bly

Sample Permission Letter

You need permission from the authors whose work you want to quote in your book. Use this form to request it:

The Center for Technical Communication
22 E. Quackenbush Ave., Dumont, NJ 07628
phone 201-385-1220 | fax 201-385-1138
Date:
To:
I am preparing a manuscript to be published by _____
Author/Tentative title _____
Estimated publication date _____ Approximate number of pages _____

I request your permission to include the following material in this and all subsequent editions of my book including versions made by nonprofit organizations for use of blind or physically handicapped persons, and in all foreign-language translations and other derivative works published or prepared by the publisher or its licensees, for distribution throughout the world.

Author(s) and/or editor(s) _____
Title of book or periodical _____
Title of selection _____ Copyright date _____
from page _____ , line _____ , beginning with the words _____
from page _____ , line _____ , ending with the words _____
Figure # _____on , on page _____ Table # _____on page____
(if necessary, attach continuation sheets)

Please indicate agreement by signing and returning the enclosed copy of this letter. In signing, you warrant that you are the sole owner of the rights granted and that your material does not infringe upon the copyright or other rights of anyone. If you do not control these rights, I would appreciate your letting me know to whom I should apply.

Thank you,

Bob Bly   22 E. Quackenbush Ave., Dumont, NJ, 07628
Name   *Requestor's return address*
Agreed to and accepted:
By _____
Signature   *Title*   *Date*
Credit and/or copyright notice: _____

_____

_____

Sample Tip Sheet

A free bonus report doesn't have to be massive; here's a bonus mini-report that fits on two sides of an 8½ x 11-inch sheet of paper or PDF file.

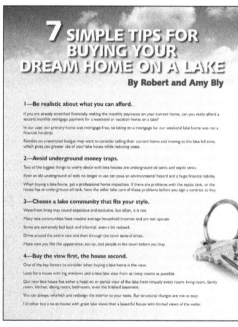

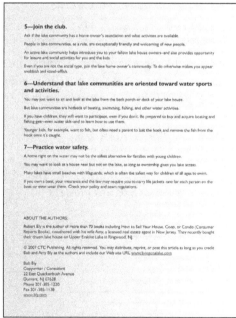

Special Report Cover

Special Report $29.00

COPYWRITING:
THE MASTER TOUCH

by Robert W. Bly
22 East Quackenbush Avenue, 3rd Floor, Dumont, NJ 07628
(201) 385-1220, Fax (201) 385-1138
e-mail: rwbly@bly.com, web: www.bly.com

Sample Book Proposal

The Science in Science Fiction

Overview

Many of the most fascinating ideas in science originated not in the laboratory but from the minds of imaginative science fiction writers. Arthur C. Clarke, author of 2001: A Space Odyssey, invented communications satellites in an article in 1945. Isaac Asimov did the same with faster-than-light travel. A large number of the scientists responsible for sending rockets to Mars say their inspiration came from Ray Bradbury's The Martian Chronicles. Aldous Huxley and many other writers predicted cloning, decades before Dolly the sheep.

[There is no other book on this topic, so the overview merely had to state the idea—a book about science facts that originated in science fiction—in a clear, engaging, and compelling way.]

The Science In Science Fiction is the ultimate reference guide to science ideas that appeared in science fiction before they were eventually embraced or conceived by the scientific community—from bionics and black holes, to warp factors and worm holes.

[This one sentence summarizes what the book is about.]

The Science in Science Fiction taps into America's love affair with science fiction and the fantastic. It appeals to the legions of science fiction fans who watch the TV shows, go to the movies, buy the books, attend the conventions, and subscribe to the science fiction magazines and fan newsletters. Yet it also appeals to both professional scientists and popular science enthusiasts, two groups that have long been a major part of science fiction readership.

[Here I touched on why science fiction and science geeks like me would want to read such a book.]

Format

The book will contain approximately six to seven dozen short essays on the most important science ideas found in science fiction, organized alphabetically for easy reference. Essays range in length from 500 to 2,000 words each. Approximate total book length: 200 to 225 book pages.

[How would I cover so many scientific developments in a meaningful way within a single book? The format section answers that question for the publisher.]

The Science in Science Fiction appeals to both fans and casual readers. Science concepts are explained in plain English; no knowledge of special terms in science fiction or science is required. Anyone can understand the ideas presented.

Each essay presents a science idea that originated in science fiction. The essay tells you:

- The author who came up with the idea.

- The book, story, or movie in which the idea was introduced.

- How the idea evolved from an SF story into a plausible scientific fact or theory.

- The science behind the idea (what it is, how it works).

- The research that has been done to support or prove the idea.

- Future developments (e.g., will matter transport, as conceived in the transporter of *Star Trek* and the "jaunt" of Alfred Bester, ever be a reality?).

Market

The markets for this book include science fiction fans, fans of specific science fiction series (*Star Trek*, *Star Wars*), professional scientists, and buyers of popular Science book.

[I said in the overview that science and science fiction enthusiasts would buy the book. In the Market section I give the publisher an idea of how many of them there are and how much money they spend on their interest in science fiction.]

Proof of science fiction and fantasy's continuing popularity is as follows:

- The sequel to *Jurassic Park*, *The Lost World*, set a record grossing $100 million within its first five days. *Independence Day* grossed $161 million in its first 13 days, and over $300 million total.

- *E.T.* had box office sales of more than $400 million. Within a month of its rerelease in 2002, *E.T.* grossed an additional $30.5 million.

- In a recent 10-week period, the *New York Times* bestseller lists (hardcover and paperback) featured more than a dozen titles in science fiction, fantasy, and horror.

- The two top science fiction short story magazines, *Asimov's* and *Analog*, have a combined circulation of nearly 200,000.

- The seven *Star Trek* movies have grossed more than half a billion dollars in box office revenues.

- *Star Trek: The Next Generation* has, at times, been the highest rated weekly syndicated TV series in America.

- Sales of *Star Trek* merchandise are approximately one half billion dollars.

- The science fiction genre is so popular it has its own book club—The Science Fiction Book Club (Garden City, NY).

- The five *Star Wars* movies have grossed nearly $3 billion worldwide, with the latest, *Attack of the Clones*, taking in $116 million in its first four days at the office box.

Competition

The only directly competing books in print I could find are as follows:

- *The Science of the X-Men* by Link Yaco and Karen Haber (New York: BP Books, 2000), hardcover, 274 pages, $22.95. Explores the science behind the superpowers of the X-Men, a group of mutant superheroes created by Marvel Comics.

- *The Physics of Star Trek* by Lawrence Krauss (New York: Harper Perennial, 1996), trade paperback, 208 pages, $13. Explores the science behind the technology of the various Star Trek TV series and movies.

- *The Real Science Behind the X Files* by Anne Simon (New York: Simon & Schuster, 1999), trade paperback, 318 pages. Gives scientifically plausible explanations for the incidents and phenomena that take place in the TV series The X Files.

About the Author

Bob Bly is the author of 50 books including *The Ultimate Unauthorized Star Trek Quiz Book* (HarperCollins), *Why You Should Never Beam Down in a Red Shirt* (HarperCollins), *The Ultimate Unauthorized Stephen King Trivial Challenge* (Kensington), and *Comic Book Heroes: 1,001 Trivia Questions About America's Favorite Superheroes* (Carol Publishing Group). A science fiction fan since age 12, he has read more than 500 science fiction novels and stories and seen dozens of science fiction films. Bob has sold short fiction to Galaxy science fiction magazine.

Bob's science credentials include a B.S. in chemical engineering and articles in such publications as *Chemical Engineering, Chemical Engineering Progress,* and *Science Books & Films.* He is a member of the American Institute of Chemical Engineers. He recently launched a website for science enthusiasts, www.mychemset.com.

Table of Contents
INTRODUCTION
THE 77 GREATEST SCIENCE IDEAS IN SCIENCE FICTION
Androids
Antigravity
Antimatter
Artificial intelligence
Artificial life
Asteroids colliding with the Earth
Atomic bombs
Big Bang, The
Big Brother
Black holes
Biological computers
Bionics
Cloning
Colonies on other planets
Communicators
Computers
Computer networks
Cryogenic preservation
Cyborgs
Deep space exploration
Dimensions, other
Electric cars
Electricity from wind, solar, hydro, and geothermal
End of Disease, the
Entropy

ESP
Faster than light travel
First contact with other intelligent beings in the galaxy
Flying cars
Food pills
Force fields
Genetic engineering
Giants
Global warming (the greenhouse effect)
Holograms
Immortality
Interplanetary and interstellar travel
Internet, the
Laser ray guns
Life on other planets
Men on the moon
Mind control
Monsters
Mutations
Neutron stars
Nuclear fusion
Nuclear war
Nuclear winter
Parallel universes
Perpetual motion
Predicting the future
Pulsars
Quarks
Quasars
Recreation of extinct species
Robots
Rocket packs, personal
Satellites
Shrinking and miniaturization
Supernova
Suspended animation

Telekinesis
Telepathy
Teleportation
Time travel
Transmutation of metals
Undersea civilizations
Utopian societies
Virtual reality
Weather control
White dwarfs
Worm holes
X-ray vision

Appendix C: Resources

Periodicals

Advertising Age 1st HQ
685 Third Avenue
New York, NY
(212) 210-0100
adage.com/

Advertising Age 2nd HQ
150 N Michigan Avenue
Chicago, IL 60611
(312) 649-5200
adage.com/

Adweek
 261 Madison Ave, 8th Floor
New York, NY 10016
(212) 493-4262
www.adweek.com/

Creative Business Inc.
20 Jay St. Suite 1016
Brooklyn, NY 11201
(718) 797-2673
www.creativebusinessinc.com/

DM News
114 W 26th Street
New York, NY 10001
(646) 638-6000
www.dmnews.com/

New Writers Magazine
Sarasota Bay Publishing
1308 Pomelo Avenue
Sarasota, FL 34239
(941) 953-7903

Public Relations Journal
By Public Relations society of America
120 Wall Street, 21st Fl.
New York, NY 10005
(212) 460-1400
prjournal.instituteforpr.org/

Sales and Marketing Management
P.O. Box 247
27020 Noble Road
Excelsior, MN 55331
(952) 401-1283
salesandmarketing.com/

Target Marketing
North American Publishing Co.
1500 Spring Garden, St. #1200
Philadelphia, PA 19130
(215) 238-5300
www.targetmarketingmag.com/

Writer's Digest
Cincinnati, OH
(715) 445-4612 or (888) 590-0020
www.writersdigest.com/

Organizations

American Medical Writers Association
30 West Gude Drive, Suite 525
Rockville, MD 20850-4347
(240) 238-0940
www.amwa.org/

American Writer's Institute
101 SE 6th Avenue, Suite A
Delray Beach, FL 33483
(561) 278-5789 or (866) 879-2924
www.awaionline.com

Direct Marketing Association, Inc.
1333 Broadway, Suite 301
New York, NY 10018
(212) 768-7277
thedma.org/

Direct Marketing Club of New York
274 Madison Avenue, Suite 1202
New York, NY 10016
(646) 741-4771
www.dmcny.org

Education Writers Association
1825 K St. NW #200
Washington, DC 20006
(202) 452-9830
www.ewa.org

Florida Freelance Writers Association
CNW Publishing, Editing & Promotion, Inc.
PO Box A
North Stratford, NH 03590
(603) 922-8338

International Association of Business Communicators (IABC)
649 Mission Street, 5th Floor
San Francisco, CA 94105
(415) 544-4700 or (800) 776-4222
www.iabc.com

National Association of Science Writers
P.O. Box 7905
Berkeley, CA 94707
(510) 647-9500
nasw.org

National Mail Order Association
2807 Polk St. NE
Minneapolis MN 55418-2954
(612) 788-1673
www.nmoa.org

National Writers Union
256 West 38th Street, Suite 703
New York, NY 10018
(212) 254-0279
www.nwu.org

Outdoor Writers Association of America, Inc.
2814 Brooks St. Box 442
Missoula, MT 59801
(406) 728-7434
owaa.org/

Society for Technical Communication
3251 Old Lee Hwy, Suite 406
Fairfax, VA 22030
(703) 522-4114
www.stc.org

E-Newsletters

Gary Bencivenga's Marketing Bullets
www.bencivengabullets.com
Master copywriter Gary Bencivenga's can't-miss e-newsletter based on his decades of tested results.

Marketing Minute
www.yudkin.com/markmin.htm
Weekly marketing tip from consultant Marcia Yudkin.

Paul Hartunian's Million-Dollar Publicity Strategies
www.prprofits.com
Great marketing e-newsletter focusing on publicity.

The Copywriter's Roundtable
copywritersroundtable.com/
John Forde's superb e-newsletter on copywriting.

The Direct Response Letter
www.bly.com
My twice-weekly e-newsletter on copywriting and direct marketing.

The Success Margin
Ted Nicholas's must-read marketing e-zine.
www.tednicholas.com

The Well-Fed Writer
Peter Bowerman's e-zine on succeeding as a freelance commercial writer.
www.wellfedwriter.com

Vendors

Printers, mailing list brokers, fulfillment houses, video production, proof-readers, transcriptionists, graphic artists, illustrators, and other vendors you may need for your writing and publishing business may be found online at:

www.bly.com/newsite/Pages/vendors.php

Index

About the Author

Bob Bly has been a professional writer for more than four decades.

He is the author of 100 books, including *Careers for Writers* (McGraw-Hill/VGM), *Secrets of a Freelance Writer* (Henry Holt), *The Copywriter's Handbook* (Henry Holt), *The Elements of Technical Writing* (Alyn & Bacon), and *The Elements of Business Writing* (Alyn & Bacon).

McGraw-Hill calls Bob Bly "America's top copywriter," and he was the AWAI Copywriter of the Year. His copywriting clients include such publishers as Kiplinger, Boardroom, Phillips, Agora, KCI, Nightingale-Conant, and Medical Economics. He has published more than 100 articles in *Cosmopolitan*, *Writer's Digest*, *DM News*, *New Jersey Monthly*, *City Paper*, and many other publications.

Bob has given lectures on marketing, writing, and freelancing to numerous groups, including the American Writers and Artists Inc., National Speakers Association, Learning Annex, American Seminar Leaders Association, and the American Society of Journalists and Authors. He is a member of the American Institute of Chemical Engineers.

He holds a B.S. in chemical engineering from the University of Rochester and has taught technical writing at New York University. Prior to becoming a full-time freelance writer in 1982, Bob was a technical writer for Westinghouse and advertising manager for Koch Engineering.

He may be reached at:

Bob Bly
Copywriter
31 Cheyenne Drive
Montville, NJ 07045
Phone: 973-263-0562
Fax: 973-263-0613
Email: rwbly@bly.com
Web: www.bly.com